P9-BIN-810

MODERN/POSTMODERN

PENN STUDIES IN CONTEMPORARY AMERICAN FICTION

A Series Edited by Emory Elliott, Princeton University

Alan Wilde, *Middle Grounds: Studies in Contemporary American Fiction*
Brian Stonehill, *The Self-Conscious Novel: Artifice in Fiction from Joyce to Pynchon*
Silvio Gaggi, *Modern/Postmodern: A Study in Twentieth-Century Arts and Ideas*

MODERN/POSTMODERN

A Study in
Twentieth-Century Arts
and Ideas

SILVIO GAGGI

upp

UNIVERSITY OF PENNSYLVANIA PRESS
Philadelphia

Copyright © 1989 by the University of Pennsylvania Press
All rights reserved
Printed in the United States of America

Library of Congress Cataloging-in-Publication Data
Gaggi, Silvio.
   Modern/postmodern.

   (Penn studies in contemporary American fiction)
   Bibliography: p.
   Includes index.
   1. Postmodernism.   2. Arts, Modern—20th century.
I. Title.   II. Series.
NX456.5.P66G34   1989   700'.9'04   88-33786
ISBN 0-8122-8154-3

for Patricia and Marisa

CONTENTS

LIST OF PLATES

ACKNOWLEDGMENTS

I would like to thank the University of South Florida for the partial release time granted me through a President's Council Award (summer 1984) and a Research and Creative Scholarship Award (summer 1985) and for a one semester sabbatical (fall 1986), during which I was able to complete most of this study. I am also grateful to the National Endowment for the Humanities for the several NEH seminars in which I participated. It was during these seminars that I became aware of ideas and issues central to this study. I would also like to thank the students and faculty of the Humanities and English Departments at USF, with whom I discussed and debated many issues related to this study, both formally in classrooms and informally in offices and hallways. Finally, I want to thank the staff of the University of Pennsylvania Press, which has been extremely considerate and professional, especially Zachary W. Simpson, who has been especially helpful and supportive.

Portions of this study have previously appeared, in somewhat different form, in various journals. Parts of chapter two appeared as "Pirandello and Antilogic," in *South Atlantic Bulletin*, 41, 2 (May 1976), 112–116, reprinted by permission, and "Brecht, Pirandello, and Two Traditions of Self-Critical Art," in *Theatre Quarterly*, 8, 32 (winter 1979), 42–46, reprinted with permission of the editors of *Theatre Quarterly* and *New Theatre Quarterly*; part of chapter three appeared as "Sculpture, Theater and Art Performance: Notes on the Convergence of the Arts," in *Leonardo, Journal of the International Society for the Arts, Sciences, and Technology*, 19, 1 (1986), 45–52, © ISAST, 1986, reprinted by permission; and part of chapter five appeared as "Brechtian and Pirandellian Aspects of the Fiction of John Fowles," in *Comparative Literature Studies*, 23, 4 (winter 1986), 324–334, reprinted with permission of Pennsylvania State University Press.

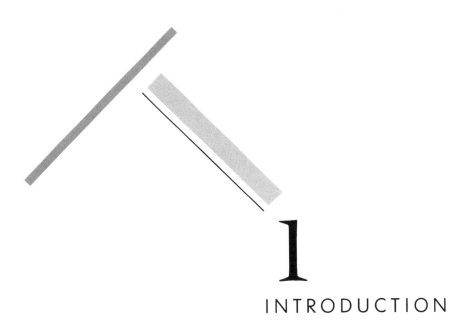

1

INTRODUCTION

Las Meninas and Other Reflections

One can study an age through its art; and one can study an age by studying the art that it studies, the art it chooses as its models, and what it discovers in those models. Early in the twentieth century Wassily Kandinsky explained the interest in "primitive" art as a necessary antidote to the repression of the spiritual in a materialistic culture.[1] The tendency he identified manifested itself throughout the first half of the century in the Cubists, Fauves, and Expressionists, and later in the Abstract Expressionists, who viewed art-making as an existential affirmation of self against a world seen as dehumanized. On the other hand, this late romantic aspect of modernism was balanced by an equally powerful classicistic trend. Corbusier, for example, looked to the ancients for an architecture that perfectly synthesized form and function in a rational style of pure geometry, and his views on the transcendental nature of mathematics—like those of Piet Mondrian—are related to Pythagorean and Platonic views of musical ratios that reflect a greater harmony in the universe.[2]

In recent decades it has become a commonplace assumption that a fundamental cultural shift has occurred and that we are now in a phase that has come to be called—perhaps unfortunately—"postmodern." As if in confirmation of this belief, the works and styles to which recent artists, critics, and theorists have looked have been quite different from those looked to by orthodox modernists; they have been characterized neither by classicist order and clarity nor by romantic assertion of the self, but by what architect Robert Venturi calls "complexity and contradiction." Venturi himself is partial to mannerist, baroque, and rococo styles,[3] complex, contradictory, and sometimes whimsical styles that fly in the face of the high seriousness and passion of orthodox modernism. Significantly, new attention has been given to a painting from the Spanish Baroque—Diego Velazquez's *Las Meninas* (*The Maids of Honor,* 1656)—a painting that, like many contemporary works, cannot be made neatly to fit into a classic-romantic duality. It has been quoted and parodied[4] by visual artists, including Picasso who, in 1956, painted over forty variations of it, and at least one video tape has been made based on it.[5] There has been at least one scholarly symposium devoted to it[6] and it has been written about not only by art historians but also by philosophers and theorists of art and culture; the French analyst of culture, Michel Foucault, begins *The Order of Things*[7] with a major essay on *Las Meninas,* and the American speech act theorist John Searle has written a close analysis of its visual paradoxes.[8] This painting by an artist who was barely known outside of Spain until two hundred years after his death has found resonances in the contemporary world that have made it a major visual antecedent to postmodernism—just as works like *Don Quixote, Tristram Shandy,* and *Hamlet* have become major literary and dramatic antecedents.

Velazquez's painting is of interest to contemporary artists and theorists because it can be viewed as an examination and problematizing of the conventions of Renaissance and "classical" perspective. Implied in this examination of painting conventions is a larger epistemological and ontological questioning of classical ways of knowing and of the traditional notion of the self. At first glance *Las Meninas* seems to conform to the rules of Renaissance perspective, but upon close examination aspects of its structure must be viewed as contradictory within the context of those rules. In this respect the painting, although historically baroque and unquestionably baroque in style, has a manneristic quality, referring to a classical style but, at the same time, subverting or at least sowing the seeds of subversion of that style.[9]

The room in which the painting's drama takes place is a simple box that could be divided into a perspective grid with a single vanishing point, like a room or piazza in a quattrocento painting. Inside that box are the Infanta of the Spanish throne, surrounded by her maids of honor, court entertainers, and guardians. Perhaps the most obvious contradictory aspect of the work is the presence on the left of the artist himself; he faces the viewer and is working on a large canvas, the front of which is invisible to

Plate 1. Diego Velazquez. *Las Meninas* (*The Maids of Honor*). 1656. Oil on canvas, 125 ¼ × 108 ¾". Museo del Prado, Madrid.

the viewer. The presence of an artist inside his own work is not, in itself, so unusual, of course. In the Renaissance artists often inserted themselves, as well as their important contemporaries, into religious scenes, and self-portraits were done long before Velazquez painted *Las Meninas*. However, there is something more disturbing about the artist's presence in this work than is the case in previous works. Here the artist presents himself in the process of painting and, though a mirror is present, it is not the means by which he paints himself: his image is not one of those reflected in it. He gazes at his subject, who appears to be in the position of the viewer of *Las Meninas*. Thus, the artist inscribes himself into his work, and this figure inside the painting appears to be painting the real individual who stands in front of it.

The contradictory aspect of the painting is further complicated by the mirror at the back of the room, which appears to reflect two individuals who seem to occupy the viewer's space in front of the painting, the same position at which the artist gazes. Searle does not agree with the common view that this image in the mirror simultaneously indicates what is being painted on the canvas we cannot see. He believes, rather, that the painting being worked on in *Las Meninas* is *Las Meninas* itself. In support of this view he argues that the painting in the painting is approximately the same size as *Las Meninas*, that it is too large for a portrait, and that *Las Meninas* is probably the only portrait of the royal couple Velazquez painted. Although these arguments are not quite conclusive, regarding the painting in *Las Meninas* as *Las Meninas* itself certainly adds to the ironies of the work. In any case, the central paradox of the painting resides in the mirror, as Searle notes, and is dependent upon the fact that the mirror reflects the apparent occupiers of the space in front of *Las Meninas* (p. 256).[10]

Logically, the space in front of *Las Meninas* can be occupied by only two possible individuals (or groups): the artist, who actually stood in front of the canvas when he painted it and could therefore be reflected in a mirror represented on the canvas, or, more literally, the viewer who, in effect, displaces the artist when he or she steps up to the painting to view it after it is complete. Velazquez's mirror, however, suggests that that space is occupied neither by Velazquez, who is somehow contained in the painting without the mediation of a mirror, nor by the viewer of the work; Velazquez's mirror reflects two individuals, Philip IV, King of Spain (Velazquez's lifelong friend and patron) and Philip's second wife, Mariana, both of whom appropriate a position hitherto reserved for the artist and his audience.

Within the conventions of Renaissance perspective, which assumes that the space represented in a work is represented coherently—as it was seen by the artist and as it might have been seen by a viewer—*Las Meninas* incorporates an irreconcilable contradiction. Both artist and viewer have been displaced by the royal couple. The artist has been moved out of the real space in front of the painting and given a spot in the illusory or virtual space inside it. The real viewer of the work has no place at all—at least none that the painting is willing to acknowledge; the mirror casts back not the image of the viewer but the image of individuals that the viewer knows himself or herself not to be. We may be flattered to find ourselves occupying the same space as the royal couple, to be able to see what only the king and queen could have seen. Or we may be threatened by the fact that our position—along with our "selves," perhaps—has been appropriated by the monarch. Our presence has been literally erased; we have been made invisible and non-existent as far as the painting is concerned. It is significant that it is the monarch, the figure of highest political and social authority, who appropriates the viewer's space, visibility, materiality, and ego.

The painting's examination of representation and reflection is reinforced by the arrangement of elements that appear on the wall at the back of the room. The greater portion of that wall is covered with paintings; in the center of it is the mirror reflecting the royal couple; just to the right of the mirror is an open doorway with an individual—the queen's marshall—visible behind it, gazing through the room at the point we occupy outside the work, a point that is also recognized by the glances of artist, the reflected monarch, and numerous other individuals in the painting. These three elements on the back wall—paintings, the mirror, and the "real" figure in the doorway—can be seen as constituting an itinerary of forms of reflection and representation.

The concern of *Las Meninas* with the nature of reflection and representation is, of course, what explains its interest to contemporary artists and writers, who are also obsessed with the various systems by which humans create representations of the world, the sign systems that enable humans to *reflect* on the world. Paintings are—or traditionally have been taken as—visual signs that reflect the visual world. In this sense they have been likened to mirrors. And Alberti described the surface of a painting as a window through which a scene is viewed.[11] His description is, of course, the formula for illusionistic painting. A painting is a two-dimensional rectangle covered by colored pigments; but the two-dimensional surface "pretends" to be, creates an "illusion" of being, an opening onto a three-dimensional world, and the pigments are applied in such a way as to create the illusion of being any variety of substances except (generally) what they really are. In the background of *Las Meninas* paintings are represented, a mirror is represented, and, if we do not have a literal window, we do have an open door with a figure behind it, suggesting Alberti's famous metaphor as well as, perhaps, the fact that perception itself is a reflection of a presumed reality.

The painting deals with problems of representation and symbolization and does so in a way that bears repercussions on our understanding of the individual and of the individual's relationship to forms of authority that exist outside the self. *Las Meninas* is what might today be called a *deconstruction* of Renaissance conventions; it "explicates" classical space in such a way as to lay bare its contradictions and limitations. For Foucault the painting is "the representation . . . of Classical representation" (p. 16). What *Las Meninas* reveals about classical systems of representation— and classical epistemology, for that matter—is that it is incapable of including in its system the individual who is doing the representing, at least not at the moment that the act of representation takes place. In their book on Foucault, Hubert L. Dreyfus and Paul Rabinow note that "the central paradox of the painting turns on *the impossibility of representing the act of representing.*"[12] Thus, the painting reveals the limits of the classical system in understanding and representing reality. *Las Meninas* is a revealing painting in that visually it grapples with the problem of representing representation and is successful, within the limits of classical representation; being successful in this qualified way, it also clarifies those limits. This grappling with metalinguistic—or metapictorial—dilemmas is a concern *Las Meninas* shares with many contemporary works of art, literature, criticism, and theory.

Because *Las Meninas* cannot represent the act of representing, according to Foucault, it instead separates and presents individually the three essential components of that act: the individual creating the representation (the artist, on the left, presented as pausing between strokes, but not actually in the act of applying paint); the viewer or audience (the figure in the doorway); and the subject of the work (the royal couple, presented indirectly by means of the mirror). Moreover, the complexity and ambiguity of the problem is revealed through the interplay of glances within the work, where the roles of the figures inside the painting and that of the work's real audience are involved in a set of complex and shifting relationships of observer and observed, subject and object, artist and audience.

This slender line of reciprocal visibility embraces a whole complex network of uncertainties, exchanges, and feints. The painter is turning his eyes towards us only in so far as we happen to occupy the same position as his subject. We, the spectators, are an additional factor. Though greeted by that gaze, we are also dismissed by it, replaced by that which was always there before we were: the model itself. But, inversely, the painter's gaze, addressed to the void confronting him outside the picture, accepts as many models as there are spectators; in this precise and neutral place, the observer and the observed take part in a ceaseless exchange. No gaze is stable, or rather, in the neutral furrow of the gaze piercing at a right angle through the canvas, subject and object, the spectator and the model, reverse their roles to infinity. (pp. 4–5)

The presence of the painter inside his own painting, gazing at a subject that occupies the position normally occupied by the artist, is only one aspect of these "uncertainties, exchanges, and feints." As a corollary to this situation, we, the viewers of *Las Meninas*, seem to be placed under the scrutiny of a figure in the work we are scrutinizing. And the invisibility of the artist's subject, which is equivalent to our own invisibility to ourselves and to the fact that we have no place in the system of representation that we create, is underlined by the fact that the painting in the painting is turned away from us. "Because we can see only that reverse side, we do not know who we are, or what we are doing. Seen or seeing?" The spectator "sees his invisibility made visible to the painter and transposed into an image forever invisible to himself" (p. 5).

Only when the spectator notices the mirror on the back wall is this denial of a self-image somewhat compensated; at least the mirror presents an image of individuals occupying the viewer-subject position. This position is the one toward which most figures in the painting are turned and, ironically, it is the position toward which the figures in the mirror itself are turned. Furthermore, it is a place "prescribed by all the lines of [the painting's] composition," yet a place "completely inaccessible because it is exterior to the picture" (p. 13). It is appropriate that this highly privileged but absolutely inaccessible position be occupied by the sovereign.

In so far as they stand outside the picture and are therefore withdrawn from it in an essential invisibility, they provide the centre around which the entire representation is ordered: it is they who are being faced, it is towards them that everyone is turned, it is to their eyes that the princess is being presented in her holiday clothes; from the canvas with its back to us to the Infanta, and from the Infanta to the dwarf playing on the extreme right, there runs a curve (or again, the lower fork of the X opens) that orders the whole arrangement of the picture to their gaze and thus makes apparent the true centre of the composition, to which the Infanta's gaze and the image of the mirror are both finally subject. (p. 14)

It is this "ideal" point outside the painting that conflates the three aspects of representation that have been separated and arrayed visibly across its surface: the artist, the subject, and the spectator. But this point is inaccessible, not part of the picture, and its contents are only indirectly indicated by the mirror. Thus it is suggestive of a gap in the system of classical representation—and, by extension, a gap in classical episte-mology.

In spite of its examination of the nature of classical space, however, *Las Meninas* conforms to classical space to the extent that it does present us with a possible visual reality, as Searle notes (p. 256). If one happened to be Phillip IV or his wife, it is quite conceivable that, while being painted by Diego Velazquez, court painter and close friend, one might request that one's daughter, her courtly attendants, guardians, and entertainers, be brought in to visit during what might otherwise be a tedious sitting. At such a time, one might have a visual experience such as that represented in *Las Meninas*, mirror and all. The problem, of course, is that this is a visual experience that neither Velazquez nor most viewers of his painting could possibly have had. Significantly, an important member of the audience of the work was the sovereign himself, who would view the painting with a coherence denied the artist and the rest of us; it is his image in the mirror and that, after all, makes perfect sense from where he is sitting. All except Phillip and Mariana, however, must view the painting with some sense of incoherence, some sense that they are out of place or have been displaced.

Thus, the painting is complex and double-edged; it makes problem-atical the classical space it establishes, and that can be understood as implying a critical examination of the classical system of viewing, repre-senting, and knowing. But the painting can also be seen to manipulate classical conventions in a way that confirms the power of the sovereign and that disrupts subtly the power of other viewers. It is really impossible to determine an unambiguous politics in the work, to decide whether we are witnessing an instance of filial piety or Oedipal subversion. The entire drama of the painting seems to exist for the pleasure of the absent sovereign; but are the king and queen, indicated only by the small and distant images in the mirror, in fact being honored or are they themselves being subjected to critical scrutiny, are they "put in perspective"? This ambivalence of tone is another aspect of the work that makes it attractive to contemporary artists, critics, and theorists, corresponding as it does to the double-edged and ambivalent tone of postmodern works.

In its handling of point of view, *Las Meninas* is "fictional" in a way we do not usually think of in terms of painting—at least portrait, still-life, or landscape painting. A writer can assume the voice of a character and tell a story from that character's first person point of view. It is not our aesthetic habit to assume that a first person narrator is the author of the work. Moreover, a rigorous avoidance of the intentional fallacy would also caution us against equating third-person narrators with the author. In certain genres of painting, however, we do expect the picture to be connected to the painter's personal visual experience of the subject, even if we acknowledge that for aesthetic reasons certain modifications of the subject may have been made in transferring it from reality to the canvas surface. In painting the tendency is to identify point of view with that of the artist; in narrative art we assume the narrator is part of the fiction. *Las Meninas* pretends to be "told" from a point of view that is not Velazquez's own. Thus it is truly a fictional painting.

This is not to say that fiction cannot, in somewhat different ways, create complex, ambiguous, and contradictory points of view. When it does the result is an art-and-life inquiry similar to that evident in *Las Meninas*. Significantly, another great work from seventeenth-century Spain—Cervantes's *Don Quixote*—provides one of the major antecedents of literary postmodernism, just as *Las Meninas* provides a major visual antecedent. Foucault regards *Don Quixote* as a work representing a transition between two periods of Western culture, the Renaissance—during which signs were understood as operating on the basis of resemblance—and the classical age—during which signs were understood as arbitrary.

Don Quixote is the first modern work of literature, because in it we see the cruel reason of identities and differences make endless sport of sign and similitudes; because in it language breaks off its old kinship with things and enters into that lonely sovereignty from which it will reappear, in its separated state, only as literature. (pp. 48–49)

Cervantes presents the narrator of his novel as an author who is not the original creator of the characters of the novel but who is relaying stories he has gathered from other sources, primarily two. The first chronicle upon which the novel's narrator has relied, unfortunately, ended abruptly at the end of chapter eight. The narrator regrets this very much, especially because at that point Don Quixote was in the midst of battle. The narrator has searched for documents that would reveal the continuation of the story, and finally, in the market place of Toledo, he comes upon an Arab manuscript that coincidentally picks up the story of Don Quixote exactly where the original manuscript left off. Thus, the novel *Don Quixote* is structured as a frame-tale—a favorite device of postmodern writers. The first part is simplest—the narrator tells a story originally told by another narrator. The second part is more complex—the Arab whom the narrator hires to translate the manuscript adds an intermediary "framing" level between the narrator of *Don Quixote* and Cid Hamete Benengeli, the author of the Arabic manuscript. Within this structure, comments on the events of the story can occur on any of the narrative levels: the narrator of the novel *Don Quixote* can comment on the action; Cid Hamete can as well; and even the Arab translator occasionally interjects his views. When one adds to these structural aspects of the novel the fact that the character Don Quixote is one who attempts to live his life emulating the knights from the chivalric romances he has read, and that, in spite of the "realities" of the Spain that is his time and place, he chooses to live his life as a character in a fictional medieval world that no longer exists (if it ever existed), it becomes clear that there is a thematic relationship between the novel's frame-tale construction and its themes as they emerge from the novel's character and action. Additional complexities are added when stories, puppet shows, or other kinds of representations are described as part of the action of *Don Quixote.*

Robert Alter regards *Don Quixote* as the "first model of the novel as self-conscious genre."[13] For Alter, the self-conscious novel is a different tradition that exists alongside the dominant tradition of the novel as a mimetic, "realistic," bourgeois genre. Alter describes in the following passage a picture of Don Quixote fighting that is shown in the Arabic manuscript.

The poised ambiguity with which Cervantes conceives the representation of reality here suggests why he stands at the beginning of a Copernican revolution in the practice and theory of mimesis. The whole passage, of course, is a representation within a representation within a representation of what one finally hesitates to call reality—a picture within a book within a narration by "the second author of this work." Its effect is like that of a mirror within a painting reflecting the subject of the painting, or the deployment of still photographs within a film: through a sudden glimpse of multiple possibilities of representation we are brought up short and thus moved to ponder the nature of representation and the presence of the artful representer. (p. 8)

Alter's comparison of the visual illustration within the narrative with paintings that include representations of mirrors calls to mind *Las Meninas.* The mirror in Alter's imaginary painting reflects, presumably, a subject already contained within the painting (in contrast to the mirror of *Las Meninas,* which reflects a subject not otherwise represented in the work). Nevertheless, Alter's interest in representations contained within representations—drawings in narratives, mirrors in paintings—does point to the kind of semiotic interplay common in postmodern works of various media, along with the epistemological skepticism that is implied by such structures, whether they come out of the seventeenth or the twentieth centuries.

Alter points out other "self-conscious" aspects of the novel: not only does Don Quixote model his life after a character from a fictional world and aspire to become himself immortalized in literature, but "the world into which he sallies is flooded with manuscripts and printed matter" (p. 5). In addition, just as Velazquez introduces himself into his painting, Cervantes introduces himself into his fictional world, both directly through a description of his real imprisonment in North Africa and indirectly through the mentioning of another of his novels (pp. 16–17). Finally, in Part II of *Don Quixote* the character Don Quixote *has* been written about and has achieved literary status; in fact, characters in Part II of *Don Quixote* have read Part I. Thus, Don Quixote's status as a literary figure affects his life outside of literature (though, of course, the existence of Part II makes it clear that this part of Don Quixote's life will also become literary).

Don Quixote has been written about not only by critics such as Alter, who are interested in postmodernism and its connection with self-reflexive traditions in art and literature, but also by creative artists, such as Jorge Luis Borges. Borges has written poetic essays about *Don Quixote*, as well as a well-known short story, "Pierre Menard, Author of the *Quixote*,"[14] in which Borges delights in playing a "quixotic" game with the *Quixote* itself. Borges's story is a parody of a scholarly essay. That essay has as its primary purpose setting the record straight regarding the scholarly and creative output of one Pierre Menard. The work of Menard that is of greatest interest to the writer of this essay is an unfinished manuscript that represents Menard's attempt to rewrite Cervantes's *Don Quixote*. Although the two chapters Menard completed are identical to the corresponding chapters of Cervantes's novel, Menard's work is by no means a slavish copying of the "original." Rather, it represents Menard's rewriting of the Quixote exactly as Cervantes created it, but from *the perspective of Menard,* a task much more difficult than merely educating and imagining himself back to 1602 and writing the *Quixote* as Cervantes himself, our scholar assures us. Given this sophistic conceit, Borges is able to compare passages of Cervantes with corresponding passages of Menard and—with a certain logical validity—arrive at vastly different interpretations and evaluations, generally favoring Menard's work above that of Cervantes.

Though exaggerated, Borges's scholar operates from an insight that would be accepted by most contemporary critics and theorists: that texts do not exist isolated from contexts and that to change context will alter the meaning of a text as much as to change the text itself. Thus, in a rare instance of negative criticism of Menard, the writer is able to find a great contrast in style between two identical passages. Menard's archaic style "suffers from a certain affectation," whereas Cervantes, he acknowledges, "handles with ease the current Spanish of his time" (p. 43). That Cervantes's Don Quixote, in a debate on arms and letters, should decide in favor of arms is only natural, given the fact that Cervantes was a former soldier; but for Menard's to do so must be explained, at least in part, by the influence of Nietzsche. Other passages of Menard are similarly enriched by their apparently fuller context—the three centuries of cultural history that occurred between the production of the two texts. So immersed in Menard's style and perspective is the essay's writer that he is able to read other sections of the *Quixote,* those not completed by Menard, as if Menard had actually written them, and discover new meaning and beauty in them. He uses his experience with Menard's *Quixote* as a basis for advocating a new kind of reading, one based on "deliberate anachronism and . . . erroneous attribution" (p. 44), a technique that will offer up new and hitherto unavailable reading experiences, one that will enliven even mediocre works.

Other works contemporary writers and critics look back to include Lawrence Sterne's *Tristram Shandy* and, in the theatre, Shakespeare's *Hamlet* and *The Tempest* and Calderón de la Barca's *Life Is a Dream.* In her study of "narcissistic narrative" Linda Hutcheon writes that *"Tristram Shandy* will indeed sit alongside *Don Quixote* as the major forerunner of modern metafiction,"[15] and Alter calls it "the first novel about the crisis of the novel" (p. 39). In a passage that might as well be describing some of the most experimental works of John Barth, Alter writes of *Tristram,*

The narrator of *Tristram Shandy* draws us so intimately and inventively into the present tense of his writing that all the other elaborately indicated times of narrated events ultimately dissolve into it, and the stumbling chase of a self trying to catch its own or any experience through an act of written communication becomes the true plot of the novel. (p. 40)

Hamlet, with its play-within-a-play and its imagery of life as theatre, is perhaps most frequently mentioned in the theatre, as well as *The Tempest,* in which Prospero rules his island like a magnificent theatrical director, a true master-of-the-spectacle. And Calderón's *Life Is a Dream (La vida es sueño,* 1636), utilizes theatrical reversals to bring out the theme of reality and illusion in a way that would only be matched by Luigi Pirandello nearly three centuries later. Lionel Abel, who says that metatheatre is theatre about "life seen as already theatricalized,"[16] states that metatheatre rests "on two basic postulates: (1) the world is a stage and (2) life is a dream" (p. 105). Clearly the first of these "postulates" echoes Shakespeare and the second Calderón, both of whom Abel takes as major precursors of modern metatheatre.

Self-referentiality is central to postmodernism in all the arts and thus the interest in great works from the past that turn in on themselves or otherwise make art itself the subject of art. Equally significant is the fact that such works can be read to echo the epistemological skepticism that is central to postmodernism and much modernism as well. *Las Meninas* is not only the representation of classical representation, it is the representation of classical epistemology, along with the limits of both; when it is read as indicating the inability of the classical system to represent the act of representation, it calls to mind for the modernist various problems and questions relating to observation and semiosis. The second part of *Don Quixote*, in which Don Quixote has already achieved literary status, one that affects his "real" life (which is also a work of literature), is seen as the Heisenberg principle in action: where the observer is always implicated in the event observed and where what we see is partly a function of the models—some would say the "fictions"—that we choose. And while Hamlet watches a play about his life, we are reminded that we are experiencing his life as a play, and we are opened to the possibility that our own lives may be similarly watched: Vladimir, watching Estragon sleep, wonders if he is also dreaming and if someone is watching him. Such works provide contemporary artists with formal and stylistic ideas in addition to some commiseration from history for their twentieth-century doubt.

The Pirandellian and Brechtian Modes

The term *self-referentiality* is used broadly in current criticism, and is applied to works that foreground style so as to make their own artifice part of their subject, as well as to works that include others: frame-tales, plays-in-plays, and so forth. Only a few attempts have been made to describe systematically the various types or modes of self-referentiality. One of those attempts is that offered by Hutcheon in *Narcissistic Narrative, The Metafictional Paradox*. Finding problems with a similar attempt at typology by Jean Ricardou, Hutcheon posits two modes of metafiction—the diegetic and the linguistic—each of which has two forms, the overt and the covert. Thus four specific types exist: the overtly diegetic, overtly linguistic, covertly diegetic, and covertly linguistic.

Overtly diegetic narcissism, according to Hutcheon, in some explicit way makes narration the subject matter of the text. She mentions the presence of Cid Hamete Benengeli in *Don Quixote* as well as John Fowles's freedom-granting narrator in *The French Lieutenant's Woman* as illustrations of this form. In overtly linguistic narcissism the self-consciousness resides on the level of the language itself rather than on the broader narrative. The author utilizes techniques that draw attention to the more atomic level of the narrative—the language upon which it is built. *French Lieutenant* is again mentioned, because of Fowles's "parodic play" with a certain style of writing, as well as stories by Barth and "pseudo-essays" by Borges, which display an "intense awareness of the text as text" (p. 100).

Covertly diegetic texts are not explicitly self-referential; their self-referentiality results from the fact that they parody certain fictional genres. For Hutcheon "parody" does not necessarily involve satire or ridicule but simply "repetition with critical distance."[17] She notes four genres most commonly used as background texts for covertly diegetic self-referential narrations: the detective story, fantasy, game structures, and erotic structures. Borges and Robbe-Grillet tend to utilize the mystery or detective story convention in order to create covertly diegetic narcissistic texts. Covertly linguistic narcissistic texts involve a highly manipulative use of language which results in language calling attention to itself; significantly, it is not explicitly referred to in such texts but stands as a concern of such texts because of the way it is used rather than what it is about denotatively. Riddles, jokes, puns, and anagrams are model devices for foregrounding language, and the language games of Joyce and Nabokov provide examples of covert linguistic narcissism. For Hutcheon, overt forms of narrative narcissism "thematize" writing—that is, they deal explicitly with problems of writing and reading or of language itself; covert forms "actualize" problems of language, writing, and reading—the narrative and its language are structured in such a way as to bring such problems to the reader's attention in encountering the text, without having to explicitly mention them as problems.[18]

The present study will take its typological cue from theatre—from the contrasting self-referential modes of Luigi Pirandello and Bertolt Brecht[19]—and will, like Hutcheon's system, identify two different, though not mutually exclusive, modes of self-reference in the arts. These modes approximately correspond to Hutcheon's overt and covert modes, but will be used in such a way as to apply to the various arts. (Hutcheon's *Narcissistic Narrative* deals primarily with literature; her *Theory of Parody* is fully interdisciplinary but does not deal with non-parodic forms of self-reference.)

Self-referential art works structured around the inclusion of one work inside another—plays-in-plays, narrations inside narrations, paintings inside paintings—will be called "Pirandellian." This category will be interpreted broadly so that a novel with a sufficiently self-conscious narrator, such as that of Fowles's *French Lieutenant's Woman*, will be regarded as a frame-tale: the interior story set in Victorian England is contained within an exterior story dealing with an author's struggle to write the interior story. Additionally, Pirandellian or frame-tale structures can be extended to multiple levels beyond the typical two levels of narrative, dramatic, or visual representation, so that narratives can be contained inside narratives that are also inside narratives. Such structures can be either "neat" or "messy." That is, the logical levels of the various narrations, dramatizations, or pictorializations can be either honored or confused. The play-inside-the-play in *Hamlet* is neat: it is clearly articulated and contained within the play *Hamlet*. Although what happens in the play-within-the-play can, indeed, affect what happens in the world outside it, it remains nevertheless clearly separate from that world. On the other hand, in some Pirandellian plays the levels become confused: a murder that occurs on the interior level results illogically in the death of someone on the exterior level. Magritte's paintings-of-paintings are generally neat; a momentary confusion of the two pictorial levels is followed by an identification of the line separating illusion and reality and the ambiguity between the two realms is resolved. On the other hand, works of Escher are often messy: they confuse the two levels so that they cannot be logically kept separate. A painting may twist back on itself so that it seems to be contained within a painting that it contains.

Parodic texts will be regarded here as forms of Pirandellianism; generally that Pirandellianism is implied though some texts do declare explicitly their parodic nature (as in *French Lieutenant*). An awareness of the background text or genre is assumed and the parodic text comments on that background text or genre; Lichtenstein's comic-strip paintings are really paintings of paintings, paintings inside paintings in which the interior painting has been moved forward so that its frame corresponds to the actual frame of the exterior painting. One surmises the duality of levels because one is aware of the conventions of the popular art form which Lichtenstein's work incorporates but clearly is not.

Works in the Brechtian mode do not necessarily make works of art or other representational systems their explicit content. Instead, they employ a variety of devices designed to foreground style and otherwise remind the audience that what it is experiencing is artifice. Style is "opaque"; it calls attention to itself and blatantly obtrudes itself between the viewer and the work's denotative content. The Brechtian mode corresponds to Hutcheon's covert or "actualized" mode, but applies to actualized self-referentiality of whatever elements or aspects are appropriate to the medium of the work in question—image, application of paint, performance, dramatic structure, camera style, editing, as well as language and diegesis in the case of narrative art. Any handling of the elements of a work that results in obtrusive stylization is Brechtian. Brecht advocated a number of ways of achieving this effect in the theatre, ways that would insure that the theatrical illusion would always be qualified and that aesthetic distance would be maximized—that the audience would never lose critical distance because of an excessively emotional involvement with character or action. All aspects of the production were to be overtly stylized, characters were to be types that did not encourage strong audience identification, and the various representational systems employed were to work against each other formally and thematically in order to produce a semiotic dissonance. This intentional stylistic abrasiveness is very different from a theatrical or operatic style in which character, action, setting, music, and lyrics are coordinated to create a unified emotional flow that "sweeps away" the viewer, minimizing his or her critical distance. In the visual arts the tradition of collage, begun by Picasso and Braque early in the century, carried further with the combines of Robert Rauschenberg in the nineteen-fifties, and culminating in happenings and art performances, generally involve an analogous semiotic dissonance. The films of Godard, with their abrasive editing, jump cuts, complex and confusing sound-image relationships, and disjointed plot structures, are the most obvious examples of Brechtian principles applied to film.

Significantly, much recent theory and criticism of literature, film, and the arts is itself written in a Brechtian style; that is, it is "difficult," more difficult, it often seems, than it needs to be, thus calling attention to itself; by the standards most of us were taught in composition classes—where the best style was that which went unnoticed, that which seemed invisible or transparent, as if one gazed through it directly at an unadorned content—it is bad writing. On the other hand, much contemporary criticism and theory operates out of structuralist and poststructuralist insights and concerns. One of those insights is an awareness of the role of the process of semiosis in constituting "reality." When contemporary criticism and theory is opaque or Brechtian it is (or at least can be justified by the claim that it is) engaged in a kind of ethical semiosis in a way that is exactly analogous to the ethical principles that lay beneath Brecht's theatrical theory. Stylistic opacity is a continual reminder to the reader or viewer that he or she is not gazing clearly at the unadorned truth but is experiencing a representation of reality conditioned by the language that represents reality.

This study, which is more a study of arts and ideas than one of theory, will apply this simplified and generalized typology—the contrast between overt stylization and the frame-tale, between art that openly declares its artifice and art that confuses the realms of art and life, between works of art that implicitly deal with their own style and processes and works of art that explicitly deal with works of art—in order to shed light on various modern and postmodern works. Where contemporary theory is dealt with it will be treated as a manifestation of modern obsessions and presuppositions that parallels the art and literature itself. That is, structuralist and poststructuralist ideas will be seen as resting on similar insights and doubts as those that inform postmodern fiction; structuralism can also, of course, be used as a method of analyzing contemporary literature and art. This study will deal with it more in the former sense and only secondarily and incidentally attempt to apply it as a critical tool. Again, although theory will be dealt with (primarily in the last chapter) and the discussions of works of art and literature will be partly conditioned by contemporary theory, this work is primarily a study in twentieth-century arts and ideas.

Modern and Postmodern

It may be that the term *postmodern* is unfortunate, for the obvious reason: if *modern* is used to describe that which relates to the present or the most recent, how can anything (except the future) be postmodern? Modern is as new or recent as anything gets, and to declare anything in the present—up-to-date though it may be—postmodern is to embrace a term that is self-contradictory and, some would say, pretentious. These objections, however, logical though they may be, do not seem to have stopped the term from being used and today one hears it applied freely to recent developments in all the arts, as well as to art and literary theory, and even to science; furthermore, one encounters it not only in professional journals devoted to contemporary art and culture but in the arts sections of city newspapers and weekly newsmagazines. It seems that postmodernism is a word that postmodernists are stuck with, at least for the moment. The historians of the twenty-first century will have to decide what they want to call us, whether they wish to accept our self-designation or create a new one with which they may be more comfortable. At any rate, the New Criticism in literary theory has survived as the New Criticism even now that it is old hat, and the film movement known as the New Wave is still used by film historians to indicate a certain body of French films, even after our students have stopped mistaking our use of the term for a recent movement in rock music, because even that is now old hat. "Postmodern" is only one degree more illogical than these designations.

The problem does not really originate in the use of the term *postmodern* but in the term *modern* itself. *Modern*, for critics and scholars of art, architecture, music, drama, and literature, has been used—in the second half of the twentieth century—to apply to those major movements and techniques in the various arts that developed early in the century: Cubism, Fauvism, Futurism, Expressionism, Surrealism, Functionalism, atonality, serialization, and stream-of-consciousness; that is, it has been used without compunction to refer to things that occurred in the past. The great modernists were (and remain) individuals whose most dramatic contribution to twentieth-century culture was made early in the century: Picasso, Kandinsky, Schoenberg, Stravinsky, Gropius, Corbusier, Eliot, Joyce, and so on. Robert Martin Adams, taking his cue from Virginia Woolf's famous remark that human nature changed "on or about December 1910," offers the following catalogue of modernist pioneers:

Picasso began working on the "Demoiselles d'Avignon" . . . in 1906–07; Stravinksy's "Sacre du Printemps" had its riotous premiere in 1913. The first book by Ezra Pound to bear the title *Personae* came out in 1909; J. Alfred Prufrock made his debut . . . in 1915. In 1914, Joyce had finished the *Portrait* and was turning his full attention to *Ulysses*. In 1914 Wyndham Lewis published *Tarr*. Roger Fry's Post-Impressionist show . . . was followed in 1913 by the New York Armory show, which introduced Post-impressionist art to America. D. H. Lawrence took his first steps as a poet and novelist in the years around 1910. From 1910 onwards, F. T. Marinetti was lecturing explosively around Europe on an ill-defined but violent esthetic program that he called "Futurism."[20]

If *modern* indicates "early twentieth century," it is then *not* so illogical that developments later in the century be dubbed *postmodern*. Two scholarly essays have dramatized this situation by their common title, "What Was Modernism?"[21] When *modernism* can thus be spoken of in the past tense, *postmodernism* can naturally be spoken of in the present.

The situation is even more complicated. Often the "Modern Period" is used to refer to the entire epoch of Western civilization since the Renaissance. *Postmodern*, in this context, suggests not simply that which follows early twentieth-century culture, but that which follows the entire Humanist tradition, a central component of the culture of the Modern Period. The creation of a new designation suggests that in some way the postmodern world is different from the modern one. Not surprisingly, therefore, the term *posthumanism* is another of the numerous "post-" prefixed words bandied about in the postmodern period. When *postmodern* is used this way, the suggestion is that certain fundamental premises of the humanist tradition—the confidence in reason as a faculty enabling humans to come to an understanding of the universe, the belief in the existence of the self and the acceptance of the individual as the primary existential entity—have been transcended or rejected as no longer tenable.

Postmodernism can be understood as differing from modernism either because it extends modernist principles further than modernists themselves did or because it rejects them. Gerald Graff, for example, sees postmodernism as a continuation of romanticism and modernism and as simply a more rigorous, consistent, and honest acceptance of the implications of modern skepticism.[22] Christopher Butler, on the other hand, identifies postmodernism with the post–World War II era and believes it is involved with the creation of new artistic languages that are quite distinct from those of modern art and literature.[23]

Wendy Steiner sees postmodernism as a continuation of modernist themes such as solipsism and interpretative failure. She chooses T. S. Eliot's *The Waste Land* and Thomas Pynchon's *The Crying of Lot 49* as exemplary works demonstrating the different handling of these themes in their respective "periods." Though *The Waste Land* contains within it no representation of a solution to the problem of historical understanding, it functions as a kind of hermeneutic exercise. Hints and allusions contained within the poem along with the reader's struggle to interpret it suggest a way in which the reader can come to correct understandings of history. The reader is not represented inside the poem, but his or her real relationship to the poem provides the basis for hope that understanding is possible. In *The Crying of Lot 49*, however, Oedipa Maas does function as an embodiment of the reader, and her solipsism and interpretative failure suggest those of the reader. The strange, complex, worldwide conspiracy onto which Oedipa, as if by chance, stumbles, hovers ambiguously, for her as well as for the reader, between existing as an objective alternative to the suburban America that she has recently inhabited, and as a paranoid delusion projected by her solipsistic ego. Oedipa finally contents herself with accepting her world as one that is always in process, always expanding, though always solipsistically limited. Though there is no possibility of arriving at a final, determinate understanding of the world outside of her solipsism, Oedipa's own world is characterized by a perpetual struggle toward that other world.[24]

This study will adopt simultaneously a historical distinction between modernism and postmodernism (rooted in the recognition of a cultural shift that has occurred in the latter part of the twentieth century) and a critical distinction between the two (rooted in formal, stylistic, and thematic aspects of art works that may exist independent of the historical moment). As with any other period or style in cultural history, one can describe modernism or postmodernism by listing a number of their characteristic features. Yet history is only partly cooperative in this regard and every specific instance in a given period will not conform, wholly or even in part, to the period style described. Moreover, works embodying the characteristics of one period may occur anachronistically in a different period. From the standpoint of this study one can speak of a postmodern period or phase that begins sometime around the nineteen-sixties and note that that phase is characterized by the ascendance of certain formal and stylistic devices and certain thematic concerns in the various arts as well as certain predominant critical concerns. This does not mean, however, that similar devices or concerns did not occur earlier in the century (in Pirandello, Brecht, or Magritte, for example) or earlier in the humanist epoch (in Velazquez, Cervantes, or Sterne, for example).

It does seem that by the nineteen-sixties some kind of *general* shift was occurring in the arts and a reconsideration of modernist premises was also occurring. Modernism involved, among other things, a rejection of mimesis as the major informing principle of art and an elevation of formalist or expressionist ideals to primary aesthetic principles. Artists tried to utilize their medium non-mimetically in order to express powerfully a response to twentieth-century life or to create harmonious objects, clearly separated from the world, that were satisfying to contemplate in themselves or because they reflected some ideal harmony otherwise inaccessible.

Art after the sixties often reasserted representationality, but what was represented were things that were already images; that is, art images began to be used as a means of examining the nature of images themselves. And stories and novels began to be concerned with the processes and problems of writing. In art, literature, and criticism, as well, the problem of representation has become a central concern. By the late twentieth century the formal-expressive concerns of modernism were no longer of primary interest to avant-garde artists, who were using art to examine art. No doubt writers like Graff and Steiner are right (in spite of their rather different evaluations of modernism and postmodernism as a whole) in viewing the continuity between modern and postmodern skepticism and doubt. Significantly, the skepticism that modernism applied to mimesis, postmodernists applied to formalism and expressionism in addition to mimesis and any other notion of art one might posit.

Even the more purely abstract art media—architecture and music—

are involved in a postmodern reevaluation of modernist principles. Generally this involves, in both media, a new eclectism, a tendency to quote, paraphrase, or rework previous styles or works. Moreover, works and styles referred to are not limited to the fine art traditions but include vernacular traditions as well: folk, popular, and commercial traditions. This tendency flies in the face of orthodox modernism, characterized by serial and aleatory systems (in music) and functional purity and disavowal of historical vocabulary (in architecture). Modernism is not entirely rejected, but is found to fall short of its ambitious and sometimes utopian aims. Certainly architects and composers feel no philosophical committment to modern principles or systems. Thus, musical compositions may freely mix tonal and atonal sections, and seemingly frivolous and incongruous references to pediments, colonnades, and keystones may embellish a dwelling that is otherwise modern and international in style, structure, and materials. As with Pop styles in other media, the tone is ambivalent. A degree of wit, whimsy, and irony may be involved, as a past work is recycled, but the new work is never a lampoon of the old; the old work is viewed as a source for creative reworking, but it is not held sacred and the new work is never simply neo-classical, neo-romantic, or "revivalist" in nature.[25]

Although one can describe postmodern concerns as different from modern concerns, one can also find roots for postmodernism in the early part of the century and even in the earlier part of the humanist epoch. Cubism, especially in its collage phase, involved a laying bare of processes and materials, materials that in themselves challenged the audience to reconsider its notions of art; Dada, of course, used "art" as a way of carrying out a frontal assault on art itself, as well as on every other sacred institution of Western culture. Joyce utilized collage structures, freely juxtaposing diverse narrative modes and creating wittily self-referential language in order to make writing the subject of his writing. And in theatre Brecht and Pirandello devised contrasting self-referential modes that would, after undergoing the transformations necessitated by different media, become central to postmodernism in the various arts.

Notes

1. Wassily Kandinsky, *Concerning the Spiritual in Art,* Documents of Modern Art, Vol. 5, trans. Michael Sadleir, Francis Golffing, Michael Harrison, and Ferdinand Ostertag (New York: Wittenborn, 1972), 23–24.

2. See, for example, Corbusier, *Towards a New Architecture,* trans. Frederick

Etchells (New York: Praeger, 1972), pp. 23, 187 (first published London: Architectural Press, 1927).

3. Robert Venturi, *Complexity and Contradiction in Architecture* (New York: Museum of Modern Art, 1966), 19–23.

4. I am using the word *parody* in the broad sense described by Linda Hutcheon in her book, *A Theory of Parody* (New York: Methuen, 1985). Hutcheon regards parody as "repetition with critical distance" (e.g., p. 6). As such it does not necessarily ridicule or satirize the text to which it alludes.

5. Juan Downey, *Las Meninas (The Maidens of Honor),* 1975. "Juan Downey's videotape is organized to interpret the Velazquez painting rather than to show portions of it for its own sake. Dancers perform with gestures appropriate to the painted figures; the actors and the Velazquez subjects are skillfully combined so that the nobles in the painting seem to perform with the dancers." Jean Lipman and Richard Marshall, *Art About Art* (New York: Dutton in association with the Whitney Museum of American Art, 1978), p. 71.

6. "Interpreting *Las Meninas*," symposium held at the Institute of Fine Arts, New York University, April 14, 1984.

7. Michel Foucault, "Las Meninas," *The Order of Things, An Archaeology of the Human Sciences,* (New York: Random House, 1973), 3–16. Translation of *Les Mots et les choses* (Paris: Editions Gallimard, 1966).

8. John R. Searle, *"Las Meninas* and the Paradoxes of Pictorial Representation," *The Language of Images,* ed. W. J. T. Mitchell (Chicago: University of Chicago Press, 1980), 247–258. The essay was first published in *Critical Inquiry,* 6 (Spring 1980), 477–488.

9. Wylie Sypher calls *Las Meninas* a "belated mannerist composition." *Four Stages of Renaissance Style, Transformations in Art and Literature, 1400–1700* (Garden City, New York: Doubleday, 1955), p. 171.

10. George Kubler goes even further in doubting the conventional interpretation and argues that the object in back containing the image of the royal couple is not in fact a mirror but is a painting of the royal couple *as reflected in a mirror* (the queen stands on the king's right rather than left, contrary to protocol). Kubler cites the laws of optics as evidence; the figures are much larger than they would be if they were mirror reflections and if correct perspective were used. Kubler's position is certainly strained. Why would Velazquez include in *Las Meninas* a portrait of the royal couple as viewed in a mirror? At any rate, the lighting of the image on the central rectangle of the back wall is so different from that of the others on that wall that one simply "reads" it as a different order of object—as a *mirror* reflecting light in the room in contrast to the surfaces of the *paintings* that surround it, which reflect less light and therefore are much darker. The simplest interpretation is to accept the object as a mirror and regard the perspectival inconsistency as poetic license. The painting maintains an impression of perspectival verisimilitude even if it is not correct mathematically. George Kubler, "The 'Mirror' in *Las Meninas*," *Art Bulletin,* 67, no. 2 (June 1985), p. 316. Kubler's *Art Bulletin* note was from a paper read at the symposium, "Interpreting *Las Meninas*." (See n. 6 above.)

11. Leon Battista Alberti, *On Painting,* trans. John R. Spencer (New Haven and London: Yale University Press, 1966), p. 56.

12. Hubert L. Dreyfus and Paul Rabinow, *Michel Foucault: Beyond Structuralism and Hermeneutics,* second edition (Chicago: University of Chicago Press, 1983), p. 25.

13. Robert Alter, *Partial Magic, The Novel as a Self-Conscious Genre* (Berkeley and Los Angeles: University of California Press, 1975), p. 23.

14. Jorge Luis Borges, "Pierre Menard, Author of the *Quixote*," trans. James E. Irby, *Labyrinths, Selected Stories & Other Writings,* eds. Donald A. Yates and James E. Irby (New York: New Directions, 1964), 36–44.

15. Linda Hutcheon, *Narcissistic Narrative: The Metafictional Paradox* (New York: Methuen, 1984), p. 8.

16. Lionel Abel, *Metatheatre, A New View of Dramatic Form* (New York: Hill and Wang, 1963), p. 60.

17. This understanding of parody is fully developed in Hutcheon's *A Theory of Parody* (see note 4).

18. Hutcheon's typology informs the entire structure of *Narcissistic Narrative*. It is summarized on pp. 17–35 and in a chart on p. 154.

19. I first discussed this distinction in "Brecht, Pirandello and Two Traditions of Self-Critical Art," *Theatre Quarterly,* 8, no. 32 (winter 1979), 42–46.

20. Robert Martin Adams, "What Was Modernism'" *Hudson Review,* 31, no. 1 (spring 1978), 19–33.

21. *Ibid.,* and Harry Levin, "What Was Modernism," *Refractions: Essays in Comparative Literature* (New York: Oxford, 1966), 271–295. First published in *The Massachusetts Review* (August 1960). Adams is fully aware of the fact that he is recycling a title already used and acknowledges this in his article.

22. Gerald Graff, *Literature Against Itself, Literary Ideas in Modern Society* (Chicago: University of Chicago Press, 1979), pp. 55, 62, 192, 208.

23. Christopher Butler, *After the Wake, An Essay on the Contemporary Avant-Garde* (Oxford: Clarendon Press, 1980), p. 160.

24. Wendy Steiner, "Collage or Miracle: Historicism in a Deconstructed World," *Reconstructing American Literary History,* ed. Sacvan Bercovitch (Cambridge: Harvard University Press, 1986), 323–351.

25. See, for example, Venturi's *Complexity and Contradiction in Architecture* and Charles A. Jencks's *The Language of Post-Modern Architecture* (New York: Rizzoli, 1977) and (for music) Garry E. Clarke's *Essays on American Music* (Westport, Connecticut: Greenwood Press, 1977), 179–210, and his essay on music in *The Postmodern Moment,* ed. Stanley Trachtenberg (Westport, Connecticut: Greenwood Press, 1985), 157–176.

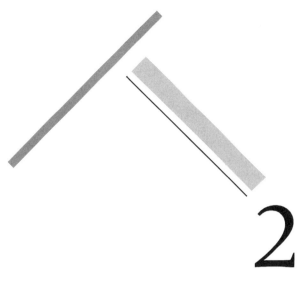

2
SELF-CONSCIOUS THEATRE

Pirandellian Metatheatre

One of the most elegant expressions of modern epistemological skepticism is Pirandello's 1917 play, *It Is So! (If You Think So) (Cosi e, se vi pare!).* The play is rooted in the assumption that contradictions can exist—that something or, in this case, someone can simultaneously be who she is and who she is not—and accepting this anti-logical premise works out the consequences (ironically) with complete logic.

In this play Pirandello creates an ideally ambiguous situation. Two different, mutually exclusive views of reality exist. Each is internally consistent and each accounts for all the facts that are known. Surprisingly, the two individuals who hold the opposing views and whose lives are most affected by the "truth" of the situation—Signor Ponza and Signora Frola—are not enemies but have a loving and considerate relationship. They have learned to live with a contradiction that, though illogical, is central to their lives. In fact, their relationship and their emotional well-being is entirely dependent upon their being able to hold that contradiction in place. Unfortunately, however, its existence is intolerable to the people of the town to which they have recently moved. The townspeople—like most authoritarian personalities—have no tolerance for ambiguity. Its presence threatens some fundamental tenet upon which they have built their lives. They are willing to take whatever action is necessary to resolve that ambiguity, even though its resolution would have no significant effect on them personally and would, instead, cause immense suffering for two quite harmless individuals.

Ponza believes that his first wife, the daughter of Signora Frola, is dead. Signora Frola, according to his story, could not accept her daughter's death and has convinced herself that Ponza's second wife is her still living daughter. Signora Frola, on the other hand, believes that Ponza is the one suffering from a delusion, one that began, according to her, when her daughter, his wife, had a short stay in a sanitarium. The jealous and evidently unstable Ponza believed that his wife must have died. When she returned he convinced himself that she was a new woman and, subsequently, his second wife. Now he is even more protective and demanding than he previously was. Frola, of course, understands Ponza's fantasy and believes that he is a good man in spite of it. She therefore humors him and this accounts for some of the odd behavior that originally aroused the townspeople's curiosity. From Ponza's point of view, of course, it is he who is humoring her.

The procedure followed by the townspeople in attempting to get at the truth is one completely proper to a scientific investigation. Their first step is to examine individually each story, each reality model, in order to determine if either is flawed internally or does not jibe with the facts. In doing so they discover that each is internally consistent and accounts for all the facts that are known. The next step is to seek additional evidence, which might be consistent with one story and inconsistent with the other. But such evidence is unavailable. The town Ponza and Frola come from has been destroyed, along with nearly all records. The evidence the townspeople are able to come up with is merely rumor and, in addition, is subject to dual interpretation. Again, nothing is resolved. Next they bring the two individuals together, believing that in a direct confrontation the truth will certainly reveal itself. If the two are placed together, in the presence of witnesses, their behavior should reveal which is the unstable one clinging to an illusion. The townspeople do not recognize the fact that Ponza and Frola have learned to live with their contradiction and have developed a relationship which is able to accommodate it. Brought together they simply humor each other; they even humor each other in humoring each other. At one point Frola, believing Ponza is crazy, humors him, and he, knowing what she is doing, humors her by acting crazy. The play takes on a beautifully perfect point-counterpoint development, like a print by Escher in which figure-ground relationships are completely reversible so that the world represented is seen to be comprised of two mutually exclusive, yet co-existing, realms. Every bit of evidence that seems to support Ponza's story can be reinterpreted to support Frola's and vice-versa.

The townspeople are, simultaneously, petty small town gossips, Aristotilean logicians who believe that contradictions cannot exist, and empirical scientists who believe in the power of evidence. They have reason on their side and reason asserts that there can be only one truth. Moreover, they regard it as their civic duty to see that the truth is revealed in unambiguous clarity. In spite of their rationalizations, however, rooted in the duty of the philosopher and the duty of the citizen, their real motivation is the excitement of scandal and the need to dominate. Clearly the play dramatizes the use of reason as a weapon of domination. If reason succeeds in this instance, the happiness of Frola and Ponza will be destroyed, as will be the possibility for love between them. Under such circumstances the quest for truth seems not so noble after all, and the truth of Frola's and Ponza's situation—could it be determined—comes to seem quite insignificant.

Since all attempts to determine the relative validity of the two reality models have failed, the final step of the townspeople is to directly confront the truth itself, and in this play the truth is symbolized by Signora Ponza, who is either Ponza's first wife and the daughter of Frola or Ponza's second wife and not the daughter of Frola. In spite of their failure to resolve the ambiguity through deductive analysis and through an empirical quest for additional data, the townspeople continue to operate under the common sense assumption that the truth can, if necessary, be *directly* apprehended. Signora Ponza, a fit symbol for a view opposed to such a naive empiricism, is veiled and dressed in black, and she does *not* resolve the townspeople's question. Ultimately unknowable as a being-in-herself, she is what you would have her be. Like the modern attitude toward the nature of light, her definition varies according to the situation. She is a wave: "I . . . am the daughter of Signora Frola." She is a particle: "I am the second wife of Signor Ponza." They insist that she *must* be one or the other but she replies, "I am she whom you believe me to be," and leaves the room.[1] Laudisi, the skeptical character who functions as Pirandello's spokesman in the play, has the last laugh.

Escher's woodcut *Day and Night* (*Dag en nacht*, 1938) is a perfect visual analogue for Pirandello's theatrical logic of contradiction. *Day and Night* presents two contradictory, mutually exclusive, yet co-existing realms and does so in a manner as elegant and flawless as the two versions of truth expressed by Ponza and Frola. The left side of the picture is the reverse of

Plate 2. M. C. Escher. *Dag en Nacht* (*Day and Night*). 1938. Woodcut printed from two blocks, 39 × 68 cm. © 1988 M. C. Escher c/o Cordon Art, Baarn, Holland.

the right side in two ways: it mirrors it, thus creating a composition that is nearly perfectly symmetrical, and it reverses the light-dark relationships so that each black area on the right corresponds exactly to a mirrored white area on the left. These reversals, in conjunction with a careful manipulation of figure-ground relations, produces an image that can be read either as dark birds flying toward the left over a village in daylight or as light birds flying toward the right over a village at night. The two realms are entirely contradictory and yet they co-exist; moreover, the existence of each is itself dependent upon the other, opposed, realm: figure cannot, after all, exist without ground. Yet an observer *inside* either realm would be oblivious to the existence of the contradictory realm upon which that observer's existence depended.[2]

Both *It Is So!* and *Day and Night* are representations of reality as relative. Still, it is a relativity that is ordered and rule-bound, not arbitrary. As in modern physics there are "laws" of relativity. The two versions of the truth, the two images, are complements that reverse one another precisely and make possible their interdependent opposed existences. Yet those who are most involved (birds or individuals) may be unaware of the paradox in which they participate.

It Is So! is not a fully metatheatrical play; its themes emerge from the plot and characters of the play but are not incorporated into a metatheatrical structure. It does hint, however, at the kind of metatheatrical structures that would inform other of Pirandello's plays. Frola and Ponza make their entrances and exits, presenting their differing stories, almost as if they were actors and the townspeople were their audience. Additionally, the notion of the self as relative, of personality as a mask that is worn and that can be changed in different contexts is a theme supporting that life is, after all, a kind of improvisatory theatre.

Each in His Own Way (*Ciascuno a suo modo,* 1924) deals with the same issues but incorporates them into a structure that itself echoes the themes implied by the play's action and characters. Delia Morello, in *Each in His Own Way,* fulfills a function similar to that of Signora Ponza in *It Is So!* She is a woman about whom individuals disagree, and it is this disagreement that provides the impetus for the major action of the play. Unlike Signora Ponza, however, she is herself involved in the struggle to discover who she is. Furthermore, the disagreement here is more subtle and complex; it is not a question of finding out the facts of her identity (whether she is the first or second wife, whether she is the daughter or not the daughter) but a question of what *kind* of person she is and what motivates her, matters about which she herself is uncertain.

Delia is, appropriately, an actress, but her personality off-stage seems no more permanently or authentically hers than that of a character she might perform on-stage. Because she herself does not know who she is—if she "is" anyone at all—she tends to assume, for herself as well as others, whatever identity is assigned to her by whomever is defining her or interpreting her behavior. Francesco Savio believes that Delia's behavior toward her artist-lover Giorgio Salvi, who committed suicide, was a case of premeditated treachery, a calculated attempt to destroy Salvi. Doro Palegari, on the other hand, has taken the position that Delia's apparently devious behavior was quite understandable and even, in a strange way, considerate of Salvi's own best interests. Delia herself, according to Doro, is the one who has suffered; she is a beautiful woman who has been dehumanized by men who are unable to see anything but her beauty. When Doro explains to Delia his understanding of her she is amazed by his insights and grateful for his understanding. "That's just the way I am! . . . And you can't imagine with what joy and with what anguish I recognized myself, saw myself . . . in all the things you found to say of me!"[3] The communication between the two of them—between he who defines and she who embraces his definition—become so nearly perfect that their dialogue merges into one continuous line of thought; they are literally "of one mind." However, Delia's sudden shift of self-definition when Doro pauses and mentions Francesco's less generous interpretation of her motives suggests that what she and Doro have been involved in was not a discovery of *the* truth but the creation of *a* truth. One moment she enthusiastically embraces Doro's view of her, and in the next she shows herself capable of accommodating a completely opposite view.

Diego, Doro's friend, is like Laudisi in *It Is So!*, the spokesman for a point of view more than a character who affects the action of the play, and it is he who best expresses the anti-logical sensibility. Speaking to Francesco Savio, Diego reveals his own attraction to Delia; it is her ability to elude the definitions she only temporarily accepts that ironically accounts for her attractiveness to the men who fall in love with her and need to define her.

I was trying to make you understand my great admiration for her; or rather I was trying to make you feel what a joy it is, what a wonderful—though terrible—joy it is, when, caught by the tide of life in one of its moments of tempest, we are able actually to witness the collapse of all those fictitious forms around which our stupid daily life has solidified; and under the dikes, beyond the seawalls, which we had thrown up to isolate, to create, a definite consciousness for ourselves at all hazards, to build a personality of some kind, we are able to see that bit of tide . . . suddenly break forth in a magnificent, overwhelming flood and turns everything topsy-turvy! Ah, at last!—A whirlwind! A volcanic eruption! An earthquake! A cataclysm! (pp. 333–334)

Here is a clear statement of the anti-logical sensibility. If logic is dependent upon the establishment of definitions and classes, then a view of reality that did not lend itself to defining and classifying would not be susceptible to logical analysis. If reality is in a state of flux in which all things merge spatially and temporally into one another, then all statements about reality are approximate, only roughly describing the temporary forms manifested at a particular moment, but invalid the next moment—invalid, in fact, by the time those statements are articulated. Any definition of the personality, one of the most mercurial of all "things," becomes to Diego the greatest fiction. A person defines his or her self and is defined by others as a certain combination of qualities forming a certain "kind" of person, but this is a process of creating rather than discovering truth. Viewed this way, truth comes to be remarkably like fiction and life becomes remarkably like theatre. And beneath all definitions, beneath all fictions and all "truths" an indefinable tide exists that can break forth and destroy all such human constructs. Diego here articulates notions of the relativity of truth and self and of human understanding as a form of creative epistemology that lie behind much of what would later be called *postmodernism.*

The same content is manifested on the level of the metatheatrical structure of *Each in His Own Way.* This work is an expanded play-within-a-play; conflict and dramatic interest exist not only within the "interior" play—where various disagreements revolve around the character and reputation of Delia Morello—but also between it and an "exterior" play—a second dramatic level that surrounds it, observes it, and struggles to contain it. The "exterior" play includes an audience, critics, performers playing the roles of the characters in the interior play, and even a playwright named "Pirandello," who exists as an offstage character. "Pirandello" has used the lives of certain real individuals as models for his play: it is a play with a "key." Delia Moreno, a real actress, has been barely fictionalized as Delia Morello. Her one-time lover Baron Nuti has provided the basis for Michele Rocca, an ex-lover of Delia Morello. Both these "real" individuals are in the audience watching the most intimate and emotionally charged aspects of their lives being placed on public display. "Pirandello" is also in the audience.

Thus, there are two levels of conflict in *Each in His Own Way.* The first involves the various conflicts and questions within the interior play, especially those revolving around the character and motivation of Delia Morello. But a higher level conflict exists between this interior play and the "play" audience that watches it. On both levels questions regarding the relationship between reality (elusive, changing, ineffable) and conceptions or representations of reality (fixed, static, and defined) are involved.

Pirandello's problem as a playwright is evident. If reality is so utterly changeable that all fixed notions about it must necessarily be more false than true, then making a play that purports to represent reality is impossible. The struggle to do so is especially ironic when the playwright is *aware* that reality cannot be represented and places himself in the self-contradictory position of trying to represent the fact that it can't be represented. Pirandello's position is literally absurd—he must make a statement regarding the futility of making statements.

Pirandello makes this very problem the content of his "theatre-in-the-theatre" trilogy (*Six Characters in Search of an Author, Each in His Own way,* and *Tonight We Improvise*). The conflict between "life" and "form," reality and representation, is dramatized as the conflict between reality and theatre, and is formally structured into the plays through the play-within-a-play device. The conflict is never resolved—individuals live by means of a language that fixes what cannot be fixed—but its inevitably destructive end is shown: feeling love and hatred simultaneously, Rocca abducts Delia Morello at the end of the second act of the interior play; during the intermission following that act, in the lobby of the theatre, this scene is repeated when Nuti sees Delia Moreno and carries her off; the play was modeled after their lives but now their lives imitate the play. Shortly afterward, the conflict between the play and its key erupts in violence between performers and the "real" people and the play cannot continue. The gap between representation and represented, signifier and signified, is unbridgeable; the *differance* that differs from and defers cannot be escaped. The attempt to use a sign—in this case a play—as a means of pinning down reality fails as it must. Pirandello's dramatization presents the impossibility of "Pirandello" 's attempt to dramatize. The representation that must be a misrepresentation is halted through a dramatic explosion.

It might be argued, of course, that the whole thing *is* a play, entirely scripted, disallowing any real incursions from the world outside of it, and therefore does present a fixed, closed statement, in spite of Pirandello's clever formal experimentation. Pirandello's plays never do include authentic improvisation or real audience participation—techniques that would disrupt the closed structure and that later experimenters would use to open up the play and make it receptive to forces originating outside of itself. But Pirandello's plays do suggest such techniques as logical next steps. In *Tonight We Improvise (Questa sera si recita a soggetto,* 1930) he goes so far as to create a situation in which there could be real confusion on the part of the audience regarding the reality of events that occur on and off the stage. *Tonight We Improvise* reaches out from the stage and fills the theatre, approaching but not achieving a synthesis with the world outside the play. In a prefatory note Pirandello states that all advertisements for the play should avoid mentioning an author. Given the play's title, such advertisements might indeed give the impression that the public was being invited to witness an authentic improvisation. The entire play is written and staged so as to reinforce that illusion. Actors are planted in the audience; there is a confusion on-stage at the outset; members of the audience begin shouting and speculating about what is going on. The director enters from the back of the auditorium, speaking directly to the audience and apologizing for the disruption. He explains that what will occur will be an improvisation based on a short story by Pirandello. Sometimes performers seem to drop character and speak as themselves, perhaps arguing with the director; at other times they seem to become so identified with their roles they forget that they are acting. During the intermission action continues on-stage and at four places in the lobby simultaneously.

In *Tonight We Improvise* Pirandello takes us to the brink of dissolving the art-life distinction without actually doing so. It is a kind of theatrical *trompe l'oeil*, the creation of a highly deceptive illusion of spontaneity and audience interaction. Yet (except for general outbursts for which it would be senseless to designate specific lines), it is entirely scripted. For this reason it functions as a forecast of later developments—which would involve real improvisation, audience interaction, and a dissolution of the actor-character distinction—but stops short of participating itself in the techniques it illustrates.

Experimental groups of the sixties, such as the Living Theatre and Open Theatre in the United States and Jerzy Grotowski's Laboratory Theatre in Poland, would utilize various techniques illustrated by Pirandello in *Tonight We Improvise*. Improvisation, the integration of the audience into the performance, and the dissolution of the line separating character and performer would be utilized in an attempt to create a more intense and profound impact on the audience. These groups were generally more directly influenced by Antonin Artaud's "Theatre of Cruelty" than Pirandellian metatheatre, and often their central concerns were more psychological, religious, or political than epistemological. Nevertheless, Pirandello's metatheatre—culminating in *Tonight We Improvise*—does illustrate what would become stock techniques of the later experimental avant-garde.

Tonight We Improvise predicts not only the integration of audience and play, but the eclipsing of author by director and director by performer as well. The director, Dr. Hinkfuss, explains to the audience that he has had Pirandello's name eliminated from posters advertising the performance because he, not the author, is solely responsible for the production; he declares, in a remarkably prophetic statement, "In the theatre the work of the writer no longer exists!"[4] Later directors in the experimental theatre had little sense of the sanctity of the written text. Productions may have been based on pre-existent dramatic literature but, if so, the text was freely treated. In rehearsals plays, literary works, myths, or historical events were used as bases for improvisation, often translated into largely non-verbal forms of expression. The rehearsal process was an attempt to identify the essential and archetypal in the source and to express this in the purest fashion possible. In Grotowski's theatre the actor engages in a ritualistic baring of the soul which is both psychotherapeutic and religious in nature. When a writer is used in such groups, he tends to become a scribe, notating the results of exercises and improvisations carried out during rehearsals and possibly helping to impose some form on what the ensemble has created. Joseph Chaikin, director of the Open Theatre, did believe that the writer had something important to contribute to the collaborative effort but acknowledged that he never found a satisfactory way of integrating him into the ensemble.[5] For Grotowski, "signs" that resulted from the encounter between the actor and the material were simply "scored" during rehearsals. That "score" provided a basis for the performance but at the same time allowed for a significant degree of freedom so that each performance was unique.[6]

In *Tonight We Improvise* the performers finally rebel against Hinkfuss' authority, thus moving beyond "director's theatre" and into "actor's theatre." In the end, however, Hinkfuss is reinstated under the condition he give the actors written parts again, things having gotten out of hand during his absence in the final quarter of the play. The later avant-garde was firmly committed to the principle of collaboration, giving the actor a position of equal importance to the director, in theory at least. Grotowski, in his argument for a "poor" theatre—a theatre that relies only on essentials and abandons all reliance on what is extraneous—explicitly stated that, besides the spectator, the actor is the essential element in the theatre.[7]

Of course Pirandello, philosopher-playwright that he was, had none of the non-verbal emphasis of the later experimental groups, nor did he anticipate the physical and psychological regimen that became part of the training of groups like Grotowski's and Chaikin's. Artaud and, earlier, Vsevelod Meyerhold, Stanislavsky's student who reacted against his teacher's theories of theatrical naturalism, provided antecedents for these aspects of the later avant-garde. What is significant about Pirandello is the tension resulting from the fact that he does not do what he describes; his avant-gardism is itself a performance contained within a play that is fully scripted and in many respects traditional, much like a *trompe l'oeil* painting that uses conventional devices so effectively it persuades the viewer that it is *not* an illusion but a collage consisting of found materials. Pirandello turns theatrical illusionism against itself and subverts traditional theatre while still operating largely within its conventions.

Pirandello's use of the play-within-a-play structure to mix and confuse reality levels is similar to analogous visual structures used by the Belgian surrealist painter Rene Magritte. Like Pirandello, Magritte was a lover of shock, irony, and paradox. Both used ambiguity to provoke the spectator into questioning his or her habitual mode of perceiving and interpreting reality. Magritte used various kinds of ambiguity in his works, but the kind most relevant here is that which is embodied most perfectly in a series of paintings beginning with *The Human Condition I (La condition humaine, I,* 1933). A painting is placed before an open window in such a way as to merge almost imperceptibly with the "reality" outside— presumably the very landscape that is its subject. This mating of the painting-within-the-painting with the "real" landscape is so perfect that at first glance the viewer might think that Magritte's painting is simply the representation of an open window—just as a viewer of *Tonight We Improvise* might at first think he or she was watching a real improvisation instead of a representation of an improvisation. Nevertheless, the illusion and deception are revealed by the legs of an easel that are visible below the "interior" painting, a clamp at the top of that painting, and its barely discernible edges.

A later variation and elaboration of Magritte's conceit is contained in his *Euclidean Walks* (*Les promenades d'Euclide,* 1955). As in *The Human Condition,* a painting in front of a window appears to merge with the scene it apparently represents. (One assumes that the painting accurately depicts the scene beyond, but since it obscures that scene it is impossible to know that for certain.) Here, however, two nearly identical shapes, approximately triangular, appear on the surface of the contained painting. One of these triangles represents the cone-shaped tower of a medieval castle, the other a road receding toward a vanishing point on the horizon. Yet, the shapes are so similar that they might at first be viewed as representing the same thing: two roads or two towers. The painting thus adds another aspect to the subversion of representation presented in *The Human Condition.* What is a triangle on a two-dimensional surface? In one context it represents the parallel lines of a rectangular shape receding toward a vanishing point. In another context it represents a cone. In the final analysis, of course, a triangle on a two-dimensional surface is exactly that: neither a solid nor a receding shape but simply a triangle on a two-dimensional surface. As in Pirandello's *Each in His Own Way* ambiguity exists on two levels. On the level of the overall metatheatrical or metapictorial structure the problem is identifying the line separating the contained work from the containing work. On the level interior to the contained work it is a question of interpreting an aspect of the representation: Is Delia a victim or a victimizer? Is the triangle a tower or a road?

Both Magritte's and Pirandello's works involve as their primary subject other works of art. In both, the border between the interior work and the larger reality that surrounds it is obscure, creating a confusion of reality levels. And both raise questions regarding the nature of art and the relationship between reality and representations of reality. Moreover, in spite of their exploitation of the play-within-a-play or painting-within-a-

Plate 3. Rene Magritte. *Les promenades d'Euclide* (*Euclidean Walks*). 1955. Oil on canvas, 64 × 51 ¼″. The Minneapolis Institute of Arts.

painting structure, both remain dependent upon an illusionism of a traditional kind in order to achieve their effects. In this sense they are stylistically conservative. Magritte, in contrast to other modern painters, does not make a point of acknowledging the two-dimensional surface of the painting; Pirandello is not concerned that his productions reveal themselves as artifice. Nevertheless, while operating within the tradition of illusionistic art, both Pirandello and Magritte subvert that tradition. Utilizing, within their respective media, the illusionistic devices developed since the Renaissance, they turn illusionism against itself, creating illusions inside illusions, ambiguous structures that confuse the audience and threaten to break down the distinction between art and life.

Various movements of the nineteen-sixties, in the visual as well as the theatrical arts, continued the Pirandellian impulse to confuse art and life. Pop art was a form of meta-art, the common element behind its diverse manifestations being its selection as subjects images of things that were *already* symbols, generally images from the world of popular and commercial art. Visual artists' involvement with happenings and performance art created an obfuscation of the distinction between art and life and a merging of painting with theatre or, at least, theatrical kinds of activities. And as painting was becoming theatricalized, theatre was, in the work of groups like Living Theatre, fully shattering the barrier between the architectural theatre and the world outside.

Brecht's Self-Referential Theatre

The Pirandellian confusion of art and life (and the *fusion* of art and life toward which it points) is exactly the opposite of Brechtian theatre, which aims at clarifying the distinction, at clearly demarcating the limits of art. Brecht carries out his project of maximizing aesthetic distance and encouraging a critical response to his plays through production techniques, acting style, and characteristics of the plays themselves. Through his theory of Epic Theatre and the *verfremdungseffekt,* Brecht, like Pirandello, makes art a concern of art, but he does so in a manner quite different from that of Pirandello: Brecht's drama rarely deals explicitly with art itself. Rather than *depicting* the process of creation, as Pirandello does, Brecht utilizes techniques that force the viewer to observe the artificiality of the very production he or she is watching. The viewer does not psychologically lose himself or herself in the work but remains apart from it, regarding it critically and intellectually.

For Brecht the *verfremdungseffekt* was a way of creating an ethical form of propaganda. He wanted to use the theatre as an instrument of social change and to do so in an "objective," rational way. In order to do this it was necessary forthrightly to acknowledge the artifice of art, to recognize that while art might deal with reality it should not be mistaken for reality. A prefatory note to the first German edition of *Saint Joan of the Stockyards* (*Die Heilige Johanna der Schlachthoefe,* 1930, preface in 1932), a play overtly Marxist in content, states that "the intention is to exhibit not only events but the manner of their subjection to the processes of literature and theatre."[8]

All aspects of Brecht's productions were controlled so as to avoid excessive illusionism. Techniques employed were to openly reveal themselves and overtly call attention to their artificial nature. Dim, mysterious sets were avoided in favor of bright, clearly lit ones. Furthermore, light sources were not to be hidden in order to create an illusion of natural light but were to reveal themselves as the artificial stage lights they really were. Sources of music were also to be on stage and visible. Musical selections interrupted the action, often at unexpected places, and scenes were sometimes introduced by projected signs that summarized what was to happen in an entirely literary fashion that subverted dramatic illusionism. The result was a kind of semiotic dissonance that promoted aesthetic distance. The various representational systems that comprise theatre were not, for Brecht, to merge into a Wagnerian *gesamtkunstwerk* that might overwhelm the audience emotionally and sensually, but were to maintain a degree of independence and even contradiction, in order to insure that the audience would not be so overwhelmed.

Brechtian acting also had as its goal the *verfremdungseffekt.* Its style is exactly opposite that of Stanislavski. For Brecht, a successful actor is not one who identifies fully with the role but one who is able to be himself or herself and simultaneously *relate* the character. In an essay entitled "The Street Scene" Brecht attempts to explain this style by using as a model the eyewitness of an accident, who attempts to explain to a group of bystanders what has taken place. At times during the explanation he imitates the actions of someone involved in the accident. But there is never any attempt to pretend that he *is* that person; he is always himself, a witness; his "acting" is more a *quoting* of events than an illusionistic recreation of them.[9] Brecht devised a technique of "gestic language": body positions, movements, facial expressions, and intonations meant to convey aspects of the social behavior of humans. These "gestures" were not supposed to appear natural and spontaneous, as if they were unplanned, unconscious manifestations of inner feelings, but were to be blatantly artificial and stylized, like the symbolic conventions used in oriental theatre.

The plot and characters of Brecht's plays aim at a similar effect. *Mother Courage* (*Mutter Courage und Ihre Kinder*, 1939) is structured around twelve relatively independent scenes. Each deals with the struggle of Anna Fierling ("Mother Courage") to survive during the Thirty Years' War and the sacrifices she makes in order to insure that survival. Absent from the play are the characteristics of a conventional plot that tend to involve the audience emotionally—suspense, momentum resulting from the causal development of a single major action, and formal movement created by a structure organized around conflict, rising action, and climax. Instead, the plot is an episodic sequence, a structure analogous to that of a painting that lacks a focus but achieves unity through the repetition of similar formal or conceptual motifs. With such a structure one tends to become less engrossed in the overall plot. Suspense and dramatic involvement are further diminished by projected statements that precede each episode and explain what will happen. These verbal projections subvert the "dramatic" nature of the production and enhance instead the "epic": the illusion that the events depicted are actually happening in the present is avoided and, instead, those events are *related* rather than reenacted. Songs interrupt the action, further emphasizing the artificiality of the production. Finally, the moral ambiguity of the protagonist (to what extent is Mother Courage a victim of circumstances and to what extent does she herself share responsibility for those circumstances?) makes identification with her difficult—at least this was Brecht's intent.

Although audience reaction did not always accord with Brecht's intentions (Mother Courage was regarded at times as a folk heroine rather than as someone who shared the responsibility for war and suffering), it is significant that his conscious intent was to create a rational, communist theatre. He wanted to appeal to reason more than emotion and in order to do that developed techniques designed to distance the audience and keep it aware of the work itself as well as of its subject matter, of the *signifier* as well as the *signified*: "The illusion created by the theatre must be a partial one, in order that it may always be recognized as an illusion."[10]

Brecht's attitude toward the theatre corresponds to the Russian Constructivists' attitude toward the visual arts. Both Brecht and the Constructivists rejected the notion of art as an end in itself; both were committed to Marxist ideology and saw the proper role of art as a socially engaged involvement in the creation of a communist society. And yet, that socialist content, they felt, should be presented in an ethical manner; the work of art must always manifest itself as such and must appeal to the critical faculties of the audience more than to its emotions. This ethical semiosis—the "foregrounding" of the signifier in order to subvert illusionism, the use of opaque signifiers that obtrude themselves between the audience and the work's content—remains very much a part of contemporary Marxist art theory in the West.

Constructivism can be regarded as Cubism with a socialist content. The Constructivists adopted from the Cubists the anti-illusionist impulse and the technique of integrating collage elements into art constructions. But they substituted for Cubist hermeticism an emphasis on the social function of art. Although influenced by Cubism, they rejected pure formalism just as they rejected the excessively personal thrust of expressionism. In 1923 Boris Arvatov, an early Soviet art theorist, wrote:

The constructivists have declared that the creative processing of practical materials is the basic, even the sole, aim of art. They have widened the applicability of artistic craftsmanship by introducing into easel compositions many other materials (apart from paint) that hitherto have been considered "unaesthetic"; stone, tin, glass, wood, wire, etc., have begun to be used by artists—to the complete bewilderment of a society unable to comprehend the aim and meaning of such work.

However, painters once and for all have discarded the illusion of perspective because it does not correspond to the actual qualities of material, and have switched from the two-dimensional picture to the practical three-dimensional construction.[11]

This rejection of illusionism—the insistence that the materials of art objects reveal their authentic, inherent properties—corresponds closely to Brechtian staging, which similarly demands that art acknowledge itself as artifice. For the Constructivists, art should also be practical, applying itself to the construction of buildings and other functional objects. When it seems not to have such obvious utilitarian functions there is at least a metaphoric relationship between the ethical construction of an art object that is true to the nature of its materials and the construction of an architectural structure or even a new society. Aratov wrote of Cubism that the artist "began to process the picture just as a joiner processes a piece of wood."[12]

Thus, Brecht's notion of the *verfremdungseffekt* is closely allied to the constructivist notion of "realism," a "realism" that does not imply the creation of an *illusion* of reality—as in traditional Western mimetic art—but rather the creation of an art involved in social and political realities that self-referentially reveals its structure and materials. Both

Brecht and the Constructivists were often misunderstood by the Soviet Communists, who preferred to have their new message presented in a more traditional package.

Genet: Pirandellian Ritual, Brechtian Mask

Jean Genet's theatre incorporates aspects of both Pirandello and Brecht. Most obvious are the Pirandellian: Genet's plays frequently revolve around performances and theatrical kinds of activities. Usually those performances are ritualistic exorcism carried out by oppressed individuals—servants, blacks, or the powerless clients of a brothel who masquerade as the leaders who dominate them. Such individuals engage in a theatrical ritual that allows them to express their desire to emulate their masters and, simultaneously, to express their hatred for their masters. The ritual is often held in secret: it is a taboo activity concealing itself from the legitimate world outside the performance. Participants in the ritual, in spite of their hatred and even in spite of their understanding of their circumstances, nevertheless remain bound by the envy and awe they feel for their oppressors.

The ritual cannot solve the social and psychological conflicts it is intended simultaneously to contain and express. When secret, its secrecy is fragile, for the participants are perpetually in danger of discovery. "Even the game is dangerous," Claire declares in *The Maids* (*Les Bonnes,* 1947). More significantly, the ritual—because it both contains and expresses suppressed longings and hostilities—prevents those energies from being utilized in socially engaged action that might alter the structure of repressive social relationships. Ironically, therefore, society at large is dependent for its continuation upon the taboo ritual it outlaws. If the performers were not making plays they would be making war.

Because the ritual cannot solve the problem with which it grapples, the ultimate solution for the performers is often self-inflicted violence. Claire, playing Madame, chooses to drink the poisoned tea she originally prepared for the real Madame; Roger, the revolutionary, castrates himself while playing the role of the police chief in the theatrical brothel of *The Balcony* (*Le Balcon,* 1956). Such "solutions" give expression to the performers' self-hatred as well as their hatred for the characters they perform. Furthermore, through death or castration—symbolically an ultimate relegation of the individual to a condition of powerlessness—the individual is finally relieved of the conflict that motivates the ritual.

In Genet's plays, however, individuals do not merely perform when participating in the ritual; their lives themselves are performances. In the ritual the oppressed play the roles of the oppressors, but outside the ritual oppressed and oppressor alike are already performers. When, in *The Maids,* Madame finally enters, she seems more false than the Madame of Claire's performance. She glories in the romantic potential of her husband's arrest, and her words, which seem modeled after those of a sentimental romance, echo those which Claire used in her performance of Madame earlier.

I shall never desert him, never. You see, Solange, it's at times like this that you realize how much you love someone. I don't think he's guilty either, but if he were, I'd become his accomplice. I'd follow him to Devil's Island, to Siberia. . . . Of course none of this is serious, but if it were, Solange, it would be a joy for me to bear his cross. I'd follow him from place to place, from prison to prison, on foot if need be, as far as the penal colony.[13]

The lives of the two sisters—as well as that of Madame—are literally roles into which they have been cast and in that sense are no truer to their "selves" (if one can speak of an authentic "self" in Genet) than the roles they play in the ritual. In *The Blacks* (*Les Nègres,* 1958), a play intended to be performed by blacks before a white audience, Archibald, who officiates over the interior performance, says to his fellow blacks, "We are what they want us to be. We shall therefore be it to the very end, absurdly," and "On this stage, we're like guilty prisoners who play at being guilty."[14]

The result is a complex, convoluted series of performances in performances which Martin Esslin describes as a "hall of mirrors."

Genet's game of mirrors—in which each apparent reality is revealed as an appearance, an illusion, which in turn is revealed as again part of a dream or an illusion, and so on, *ad infinitum*—is a device to uncover the fundamental absurdity of being, its nothingness. The fixed point from which we can safely watch the world, made up of deceptive appearances perhaps, but always reducible to an ultimate reality, is itself shown to be a mere reflection in a mirror, and the whole structure collapses. The first *coup de theatre* in *The Maids* is a case in point . . . what had appeared to be the lady is Claire, the maid; what had appeared to be Claire now turns out to be Solange; what had appeared to be the opening scene of a conventional play is revealed to be a piece of ritual play-acting within a play.[15]

Esslin's description of Genet's theatre as a "hall of mirrors," where one comes to doubt the existence of an "ultimate reality" that exists behind the series of reflections and reflections of reflections, points out the connection between Pirandellian metatheatre (after which Genet's metatheatre is at least partly modeled) and poststructural theories such as deconstruction, which doubt the existence of any "transcendental signified," an ultimate ground of being that lies behind the infinite play of language. Jacques Derrida asks, in a way that sounds much like Esslin's reading of Genet, if "the meaning of meaning . . . is infinite implication, the unchecked referral of signifier to signifier? And that its force is a certain pure and infinite equivocality which gives signified meaning no respite, no rest, but engages it in its own *economy* so that it always signifies again and differs?"[16] In Genet performances can be of performances of performances, perhaps *ad infinitum,* just as for Derrida every signified may itself be a signifier, producing a regress that may ultimately have no firm foundation.

Although Genet's theatre-in-theatre may seem predominantly Pirandellian, there is also an important Brechtian aspect to his work. Regarding *The Maids,* Genet has written,

I tried to establish a *distantiation* which, in allowing a declamatory tone, would carry the theatre into the theatre. I thus hoped also to obtain the abolition of characters . . . and to replace them by symbols as far removed as possible, at first, from what they are to signify, and yet still attached to it in order to link by this sole means author and audience; in short, to make the characters on stage merely the metaphors of what they were to represent.[17]

Genet here describes a style of acting that clarifies the gap between performer and character, a goal similar to that articulated by Brecht in "The Street Scene." Genet desires a "declamatory tone," a self-conscious, blatant artificiality of performances that are "symbols" rather than illusionistic representations. The Brechtian aspect of Genet's theatre helps explain his motivation when, prior to the 1947 Paris production of *The Maids,* he insisted that the three women in the play be performed by men. (Louis Jouvet, the producer and director of that production, did not comply with Genet's wishes, however.) When characters of one sex are performed by actors of another the gap between character and performer is emphasized and a tension is created between the audience's perception of character and its perception of performer. This equivocation between character and performer is Brechtian; one might even argue that it is Derridean, the sexual discrepancy between character and performer itself being a sign of the *différance* inherent in all signification.

Genet utilizes a similar device with the onstage audience in *The Blacks;* that audience consists of masked blacks performing white characters. The racial crossing between character and performer has an effect similar to the sexual crossing Genet recommended for *The Maids.* In *The Blacks* both kinds of contradictory relationships—the racial and sexual—are utilized

Plate 4. M. C. Escher. *Prentententoonstelling (Print Gallery).* 1956. Lithograph, 32 × 32 cm. © 1988 M. C. Escher c/o Cordon Art, Baarn, Holland.

when Diouf, a black male character (played by a black male performer) assumes the role of a white female who is murdered as part of the blacks' ritual sacrifice.

Genet's "game of mirrors" is echoed in Escher's visual work *Print Gallery (Prentententoonstelling*, 1956). *Print Gallery* is a more convoluted working out of the painting-in-the-painting structure than Magritte's *The Human Condition* or *Euclidean Walks.* Magritte's paintings of paintings are usually "neat"; although the line separating the two levels of painting may be vague in places, it nevertheless is present, and the two levels are nowhere confused. In *Print Gallery*, however, the picture contained in the painting is the painting, *Print Gallery*, itself. Thus, it is "messy" and the confusion of logical levels results in an infinite regress. A boy stands in a gallery looking at a picture; yet, as one moves clockwise around *Print Gallery* it becomes clear that the boy himself is inside the picture he is looking at. If one continues to move around in one direction the result is an infinite series of pictures in pictures; in the other direction it is an infinite series of pictures framing other pictures—although it is really always the same painting containing or contained within itself.

The paradox of *Print Gallery* is, as Douglas R. Hofstadter has pointed out, the visual analogue of the Epimenides paradox: Epimenides, the Cretan, declares that Cretans are liars, a paradox that can be simplified to "This statement is a lie."[18] Escher's print declares the picture it contains to be an illusion, but also reveals itself to be that same illusion. Such paradoxes seem to be the result of a very literal form of self-reference in which a sign system turns in on itself and attempts to make itself its own subject. Such paradoxes can take the form of infinitely looping logical constructions. The attempt to determine the truth or falseness of Epimenides' paradox results in a line of thought something like the following: ". . . if this statement is true, then it is false; but if it is false, then it is true; and if it is true. . . ." In works of art the result can be cycles of pictures inside pictures, stories inside stories, or plays inside plays. Genet's plays perhaps do not work out this paradox as simply and as elegantly as is possible in a picture or in a short literary work; nevertheless, the complexity of roles and roles-inside-roles performed by his characters suggests the vertiginous hall of mirrors that Esslin notes.

Two Directions of Self-Critical Art

The differences between the theatre of Brecht and that of Pirandello point to two divergent modes of self-critical art. These two modes can best be understood if we first examine the *traditional* relationship between art and reality, play and audience, in Western culture.

Traditional drama achieved a very specific play-audience relationship by balancing certain opposing forces. In the naturalistic drama of the late nineteenth century the audience received certain signs clearly indicating, on the one hand, that what it was experiencing was to be understood as art and not as "reality." On the other hand, other signs attempted to give just the opposite impression and create the illusion that what was occurring was reality and not art. The traditional relationship between art work and audience in the West has been dependent on some such balance of apparently opposed forces.

Thus, the time set aside for a traditional play is clearly segregated from other life activities. Spatially, the play takes place in an architectural structure specifically designed for art performances. The stage, like the base of a sculptural work, has as one of its functions the defining of that which it supports as art. Most of the action and scenery are placed behind the proscenium arch which, like the frame of a painting, states that what it encloses is art. The audience is therefore secure in the knowledge that no matter how moved it may be by the performance, it will not be harmed in any real way. It is ironic that only by virtue of this feeling of safety, itself a result of the temporal and spatial separation of art from life, can the audience "suspend its disbelief," identify emotionally with characters on stage, and respond to the events represented as if they were *reality*.

Various aspects of the production are designed to aid the audience in doing exactly that. Illusionistic sets, a plot governed by the laws of causality, characters that are psychologically convincing, and a style of acting in which the performer identifies with his or her role all contribute to creating the illusion that what occurs—in spite of theatre, stage, and proscenium arch—is reality and not art.

This paradoxical balance between opposing forces existed in other art media, most obviously painting, where the frame defined the work as art but visual illusionism aimed at creating the impression that the work was a window onto a real world. This balance has essentially defined the art-audience relationship since the Renaissance. Discussing the novel, Alter writes that Cervantes understood the "serious tension between the recognition of fictions as fictions and the acceptance of them as reality."[19] It is significant that in the Renaissance the development of illusionist painting was synchronous with the secularization of art: the separation of art from religious and ritualistic sources. Ironically but appropriately, the creation of a clearly articulated field of art activity and art experience, distinguished from other aspects of human existence, coincided with the demand that art create an *illusion* of other aspects of human existence. This combination of *separation from* but *illusion of* informs most artistic activity between the Renaissance and the late nineteenth century.

In the twentieth century this half-millenium balance is disrupted and art shifts in both possible directions. That is, at one extreme it moves toward art as manifestly art, while at the other it moves toward art as life, toward a maximizing of aesthetic distance on the one hand and minimizing it (that is, merging art and life) on the other. It is evident that in the theatre Brecht and Pirandello both disrupt the traditional balance, but they do so in opposite ways: with Brecht the movement is toward art as manifestly art. While his plays are still representative of life as he saw it, and while they still may *inform* the audience about reality (otherwise they could not have the propagandistic function he intended), he destroys all illusion that they *are* life. Pirandello, on the other hand, struggles to merge, fuse, and confuse the work with reality. He intensifies the very ambiguity that Brecht is determined to avoid.

A similar split between art-as-art and art-as-life occurs in painting. Impressionism represents a watershed in the history of art. The impressionist concern with the "objective" documentation of visual phenomena, the attempt to see with an innocent eye divorced from knowledge and intellectualizations about the subject, can be regarded as a highly refined, scientistic version of the connection with visual reality that had dominated painting since the Renaissance. Each brush stroke was, supposedly, the documentation of a bit of visual data. On the other hand, however, that brush stroke tended to call attention to itself as paint and to the two-dimensional surface of the canvas. Thus, the illusionistic connection between painting and visual reality was subverted at the same moment that it was carried to this point of high refinement. Thereafter painting could move in one of two possible directions: toward a non-illusionistic art that was fully and clearly distinguished from life, or toward an art that merged more closely with life.

Skepticism and Self-Critical Art

A number of reasons can be offered to explain—or partly explain—the modern and postmodern breaks with traditional art. To some extent modernism can be viewed as the result of an internal dynamic operating within art history. By the end of the nineteenth century there may have developed the feeling that the ancient idea of art as imitation—with painting assigned visual appearances and theatre assigned human actions—was "played out," that little new could be done in the area of illusionistic art. Other sources of aesthetic values were embraced: the expressive, the formal, and the self-referential, for example, values that had always existed but had generally manifested themselves within limits dictated by the dominant principle of mimesis. Another cause may have been the belief that mimetic art had been co-opted by science and technology. Mimetic art, after all, was always in part scientific or, at least, scientistic: linear perspective in the Renaissance, the optical theories of the

Impressionists, causality and psychology in fiction and the theatre. Tracing the outline of an image projected onto the back of a *camera obscura* was really a kind of mechanical photography. The development, in the nineteenth century, of chemical photography and later of cinema may have created the impression that the mimetic foundation of traditional art had been taken over by a technology that was simpler, quicker, and (supposedly) more objective. Finally, the example of art of other cultures provided Western artists with alternative understandings of art and new lines of development that might be pursued.

None of these causes or influences, however, would have had much effect had not the culture been set for a change. An intense epistemological skepticism, a willingness to doubt not only traditional beliefs but also our very ability to know lies at the heart of modernism and postmodernism. The first results of this skepticism were the radical breaks with tradition that produced the major modern movements in the first few decades of this century. Expressive and formalist ideas manifested themselves in a purer form than had been possible in the past, at the expense of art's mimetic foundation. Later, even formal and expressive values were brought into question, and art engaged in an examination of its own processes and of the sign-making capacity of humans. Although the abandonment of mimesis in favor of formal/expressive values is associated with modernism and self-reference is associated with postmodernism, the line cannot be clearly drawn, and much of the self-consciousness of postmodernism has antecedents earlier in the century, in the work of Joyce, Duchamp, Brecht, and Pirandello, for example.

It also has earlier antecedents. The self-critical aspect of twentieth-century art is reminiscent of the self-conscious artificiality of Mannerism. The mannerist style of the late Renaissance occurred at a time when vast and threatening cultural changes—the fragmentation of Christendom being the most obvious—subverted High Renaissance idealism and produced a complex, artificial, self-conscious art and literature. This style was characterized by ambiguity, blatant artifice, and shifting reality levels and at times derived its imagery from previous works. Wylie Sypher describes mannerist painting of southern Europe, which he relates to Shakespeare's theatre and "metaphysical" poetry somewhat later in the north, in terms that could apply to much twentieth-century art:

Mannerism has two modes, technical and psychological. Behind the technical ingenuities of mannerist style there usually is a personal unrest, a complex psychology that agitates the form and the phrase. . . . Mannerism is experiment with many techniques of disproportion and disturbed balance; with zigzag, spiral, shuttling motion; with space like a vortex or alley; with oblique or mobile points of view and strange—even abnormal—perspectives that yield approximations rather than certainties. It deflects toward some inward focus the clear mathematical perspective renaissance art had taken upon the outside world. It "opens," dislocates, or disintegrates the harmonious closed order of the grand style. . . . Mannerist space is either flimsy and shallow, concealing volumes behind a papery facade, or narrow, curving, *coulisse*-like. . . . By means of such techniques mannerist art holds everything in a state of dissonance, dissociation, and doubt— *Zweispalt.* This is the art of *Hamlet,* where ambiguities and complexities are exploited.[20]

But it is also the art of Pirandello, Magritte, Escher, John Barth, and Robert Venturi, where complexities and contradictions are exploited and are, similarly, formal techniques reflecting uncertainty and doubt. Mannerism suggests the erosion both of High Renaissance style and of the ideational basis for that style. The twentieth century stands in a similar relation to the late nineteenth, as the sixteenth did to the late fifteenth. The nineteenth century was certainly not characterized by classical idealism, but it did have faith in a scientific, positivistic epistemology. Self-conscious art of the twentieth century suggests a crisis of confidence in such cultural assumptions.

Certainly, many developments of the early twentieth century served to disrupt previously accepted ideas about the nature of reason, the universe, and human consciousness. Quantum theory was introduced and achieved its "final shape" during the first three decades of the century.[21] It seemed not only to violate common sense (Why was it that light could be emitted and radiated from bodies only in discrete amounts? Why did atomic electrons exist only at certain specific energy levels? How could light be simultaneously a particle and a wave?), but Werner Heisenberg's famous "uncertainty" principle suggested a fundamental limit on the human ability to know: not a technical limit that might be overcome in time, but one that was built into the nature of things, one that was philosophical as well as scientific in its implications. This limit resulted from the realization that in order to observe anything (such as an electron) it must somehow be "touched" by something (such as a ray) and it therefore would be affected. The Heisenberg principle implied a literal limit for atomic scientists, but it has become a stock metaphor for those who are skeptical about the possibility for "objective" observation on any number of other levels.

In *Physics and Philosophy* Heisenberg discusses various implications that modern physics, both quantum theory and relativity theory, has for the tradition of western philosophy. Included among these implications are the following:

1. The applicability of traditional and "common sense" concepts such as space, time, causality, and substance is limited. Kant believed such concepts to be categories of mind and not aspects of reality outside the mind; modern empirical science is forced to confront this understanding when it attempts to apply such concepts to non-everyday reality, that is, to reality on the subatomic or cosmic level. In light of modern science these concepts may have to be radically revised (as understandings of time and space are in relativity theory) or even brought into question (as causality and substance are in quantum theory). Heisenberg emphasizes, however, that such concepts remain valid and useful on the normal human scale.[22]

2. There is no possibility of purely objective, non-participatory, disengaged observation of subatomic phenomena. This has radical consequences for the philosophy of science because science traditionally has been based on the principle of clearly separating the observer from the object of study. Heisenberg says this amounts to separating the object from the universe as a whole, of which the scientist is himself a part. The separation, however, is always imperfect and on the level of atomic and subatomic phenomena—the "objects" of quantum physics—the inevitable imperfection of the isolation of the object becomes significant. The object of observation must, in order to be observed, come into contact with something—a gamma ray, for example—and that something, the scientist's "measuring device," is connected to the rest of the universe. Because of this inevitable interaction between the object and the rest of the universe and because the scientist can never know all the factors operating in the universe, of which he is himself a part, there will always be an element of unpredictability in science (pp. 53–55).

3. Modern science, quantum theory in particular, involves an understanding of the world that violates the most fundamental tenets of Aristotilean logic—the laws of identity, contradiction, and the excluded middle. Heisenberg describes an imaginary experiment in which a moving atom cannot be said to be on one or the other half of a box divided by a partition with a hole in it. Common sense and Aristotilean logic demand that the atom be on one side or the other. Yet, according to quantum theory, the atom's position can be described in terms of a probability of its being observed in one place or the other. This is not a probability of its *being* "really" in one place or the other. The atom may actually be *to some extent* on both sides of the box. At any moment it has a potential for existing on one side or the other, but only when it is observed does it actually manifest itself on one of the two sides (pp. 180–186).

4. Ultimately the situation in modern physics leads to an epistemological and ontological skepticism suggesting that any attempt to create a

model of what happens on a subatomic level that will be comprehensible to common sense and common language will be problematical and will ultimately fail. The word "happens" is itself finally called into question. It is not just the fact that we cannot directly observe subatomic events, but it is a questioning of the very notion of an event occurring outside of its being observed. This is not subjectivism—although it is likely to be popularized as such—but a revision of our understandings of what knowledge and event really are.

The transition from the "possible" to the "actual" takes place during the action of observation. If we want to describe what happens in an atomic event, we have to realize that the word "happens" can apply only to the observation, not to the state of affairs between two observations. It applies to the physical, not the psychical act of observation, and we may say that the transition from the "possible" to the "actual" takes place as soon as the interaction of the object with the measuring device, and thereby with the rest of the world, has come into play; it is not connected with the act of registration of the result by the mind of the observer. (pp. 54–55)

Other twentieth-century developments reinforced the subversion of common sense most pointedly carried out in physics. Freud postulated an unconscious mind existing alongside a conscious one that had little awareness of its existence. He substituted the word "rationalization" for the word "reason," completely subverting the manner in which individuals regarded their apparent motives and decision making processes. As in physics, things were not what they appeared to be. The First World War confirmed the picture of human kind as irrational and reinforced the doubt and skepticism that arose simultaneously in other quarters.

Physicists, through their dealings with subatomic phenomena, were forced to adopt an ontologically skeptical attitude similar to that adopted by the pragmatic philosophers. C. S. Peirce, generally regarded as the founder of pragmatism, presented an instrumentalist view of meaning: propositions predicating qualities for things should be rephrased as "if . . . then" statements. The statement, "A body is heavy," can be recast as, "If I drop it, it will fall." The second statement can be tested and, equally significant, it skirts the issue of ontology. William James and John Dewey applied Peirce's operational test to religious, ethical, and aesthetic matters. "Truths" were judged by their effects and were held as tentative; ontological questions were side-stepped.

Epistemological and ontological skepticism provided the ideational underpinnings for Tristan Tzara's "Dada Manifesto" of 1918. Partly provoked by the First World War, Dada was an expression of disgust for the entire condition of western culture and everything western society traditionally held as lofty or sacred: science, philosophy, religion, and art, each of whose value Dada was willing to lampoon. Dada equated the lofty and the banal, the most sacred images with the basest bodily functions. Marcel Duchamp presented a urinal as an artwork and used a great work of art as a vehicle for an obscene joke. Tzara writes,

A work of art is never beautiful by decree, objectively and for all. Hence criticism is useless, it exists only subjectively, for each man separately, without the slightest character of universality. Does anyone think he has found a psychic base common to all mankind? . . . How can anyone expect to put order into the chaos that constitutes that infinite and shapeless variation: man?[23]

Tzara's skepticism encompasses all systems, including such modern systems as psychoanalysis and Marxism:

Psychoanalysis is a dangerous disease. It puts to sleep the antiobjective impulses of man and systematizes the bourgeoisie. There is no ultimate Truth. The dialectic is an amusing mechanism which guides us / in a banal kind of way / to the opinions we had in the first place. Does anyone think of that, by a minute refinement of logic, he has demonstrated the truth and established the correctness of these opinions? Logic imprisoned by the senses is an organic disease. To this element the philosophers like to add: the power of observation. We observe, we regard from one or more points of view, we choose them among the millions that exist. Experience is also a product of chance and individual faculties. (p. 79)

Later Thomas Kuhn, in his widely read and influential study, *The Structure of Scientific Revolutions*, would apply ontological skepticism and pragmatism to an understanding of the history of science. New scientific theories, according to Kuhn, are often accepted for reasons that have nothing to do with their conformity to the "truth" and, having won acceptance, are maintained because of the conservative posture of scientific communities, which behave essentially like other social bodies. Only to the extent that a later theory is better at solving problems—that is, only to the extent that it is pragmatic—can it be regarded as an improvement over earlier theories; nonetheless, the improved problem-solving ability of later theories is not a result of their more closely approximating the truth but rather of different environments. Kuhn attempts to articulate his anti-ontological position and at the same time defend himself against charges of relativism:

Later scientific theories are better than earlier ones for solving puzzles in the often quite different environments to which they are applied. . . . Compared with the notion of progress most prevalent among both philosophers of science and laymen, however, this position lacks an essential element. A scientific theory is usually felt to be better than its predecessors not only in the sense that it is a better instrument for discovering and solving puzzles but also because it is somehow a better representation of what nature is really like. . . . There is, I think, no theory-independent way to reconstruct phrases like "really there"; the notion of a match between the ontology of a theory and its "real" counterpart in nature now seems to me illusive in principle. . . . I do not doubt . . . that Newton's mechanics improves on Aristotle's and that Einstein's improves on Newton's as instruments for puzzle-solving. But I can see in their succession no coherent direction of ontological development.[24]

Pirandello's *It Is So! (If You Think So)* is as perfect a theatrical expression of the anti-ontological position of modern physics as is possible. This is certainly not to say that Pirandello conceived his play specifically in terms of science, but only that the situation he created in his imaginary work parallels the one experienced by modern scientists, and that both have similar philosophical implications. The tensions inherent in Pirandello's metatheatrical structures dramatize the discrepancy between reality and representation. Characters in his plays—as well as in Genet's later— shift roles according to context and are themselves uncertain about their identities and motivations. Works of visual art by Magritte and Escher imply an epistemological doubt similar to that suggested by these playwrights; they are playful inquiries into the nature of knowledge and perception, the relationship between reality and illusion, and the relationship of observer to observed.

In contrast to Pirandello, Brecht does not confuse life and art but clarifies the line separating them. The *verfremdungseffekt* attempts to ensure aesthetic distance so that the audience will not equate the representation and the reality. Brecht's semiotic honesty caused him to create plays that proclaimed their artifice, even as they attempted to represent the world and to provoke thought and action. This overt stylization and artificiality implies a recognition and declaration of the inescapable gap between the world and the representation of the world.

Pirandello and Brecht, along with Artaud, were major influences on later experimental theatre. Sixties groups such as the Living Theatre and the Performance Group fully violated the barrier between audience and stage and between the stage and life outside the stage. Thus, they ceased to be Pirandellian at the very moment they fully realized the development that Pirandello had anticipated: the Pirandellian tension between art and life is dependent upon a distinction between the two that is threatened and confused. Later groups such as the Mabou Mines have created a politically engaged, expanded Brechtian theatre. *Dead End Kids* (1982), for example, an anti-nuclear piece, was a collage structure composed of "found" texts (historical, literary, occult, scientific), found images that were projected, performance, narration, music, recorded voice over, and film—all structured as a dissonant counterpoint that resulted in a highly engaging and thoroughly Brechtian work. Squat Theatre, a group of extrapiate Hungarians, creates an elegant neo-Pirandellian theatre. Plays with political and social themes are performed in front of a large storefront window. Often the content is outrageously sexual or violent. Passersby stop and watch, likely mistaking the performance for reality, and themselves become part of the performance from the point of view of the "real" audience within. Scripted parts of the action may also originate in the street (along with the unplanned "performances" of the passersby) and film and video frequently add another aspect to the interplay of representation and reality.

Notes

1. English version by Arthur Livingston, *Naked Masks, Five Plays by Luigi Pirandello,* ed. Eric Bentley (New York: Dutton, 1952), p. 138.

2. The relationship between Escher's visual paradoxes and the paradoxes of logic has been fully explored by Douglas R. Hofstadter in *Godel, Escher, Bach, An Eternal Golden Braid* (New York: Basic Books, 1979).

3. English version by Arthur Livingston, *Naked Masks*, p. 302.

4. "In teatro l'opera dello scrittore non c'e piu," *Maschere Nude*, I (Verona: Mondadori, 1958), p. 230.

5. Theodore Shank, *American Alternative Theatre* (New York: Grove, 1982), p. 49.

6. Margaret Croyden, *Lunatics, Lovers, and Poets, The Contemporary Experimental Theatre* (New York: Delta, 1974), p. 167.

7. Jerzy Grotowski, "The Theatre's New Testament," *Towards a Poor Theatre* (New York: Simon and Schuster, 1968), p. 32.

8. English translation by Frank Jones, *Avant-Garde Drama: Major Plays and Documents Post World War I,* ed. Bernard F. Dukore and Daniel C. Gerould (New York: Bantam, 1969), p. 115.

9. Bertolt Brecht, *Brecht on Theatre, The Development of an Aesthetic,* ed. and trans. John Willet (New York: Hill and Wang, 1964), pp. 121–129.

10. *Ibid.,* p. 219.

11. From *Iskusstvo i klassy,* trans. John Bowlt, *The Tradition of Constructivism,* ed. Stephen Bann (New York: Viking, 1974), p. 44.

12. *Ibid.,* p. 45.

13. Jean Genet, *The Maids and Deathwatch, Two Plays by Jean Genet,* trans. Bernard Frechtman, intro. Jean-Paul Sartre (New York: Grove, 1978), p. 67.

14. Jean Genet, *The Blacks: A Clown Show,* trans. Bernard Frechtman (New York: Grove, 1960), pp. 126, 39.

15. Martin Esslin, *The Theatre of the Absurd* (Garden City, New York: Doubleday, 1969), p. 177.

16. Jacques Derrida, *Writing and Difference, trans. Alan Bass (Chicago: University of Chicago Press, 1978), p. 25.*

17. *Letter to Pauvert, quoted in Esslin, The Theatre of the Absurd, p. 178.*

18. Hofstadter, *Godel, Escher, Bach,* 15–17.

19. Robert Alter, *Partial Magic, The Novel as a Self-Conscious Genre* (Berkeley and Los Angeles: University of California Press, 1975), p. 15.

20. Wylie Sypher, *Four Stages of Renaissance Style, Transformations in Art and Literature, 1400–1700* (Garden City, New York: Doubleday, 1955), 116–117.

21. George Gamow, *Thirty Years that Shook Physics* (Garden City, New York: Doubleday, 1966), p. 4.

22. Werner Heisenberg, *Physics and Philosophy, The Revolution in Modern Science* (New York: Harper & Row, 1962), pp. 92, 114. Future citations in parentheses.

23. Tristan Tzara, "Dada Manifesto," trans. Ralph Manheim, *The Dada Painters and Poets: An Anthology,* ed. Robert Motherwell (Boston: G. K. Hall, 1981), p. 77. Future citations in parentheses.

24. Thomas Kuhn, *The Structure of Scientific Revolutions* (Chicago: University of Chicago Press, 1970), p. 206.

3
REPLICATIONS AND
CONVERGENCES

Pop as Postmodern

Andy Warhol's Marilyn Monroe prints have become virtual icons of the early nineteen-sixties. Through a photographic process, Warhol transferred an image from the mass media to a silkscreen from which his prints were made. The mass media image itself was derived from a photograph. Warhol's image, therefore, is a print from a silkscreen taken from a magazine image derived from a photograph created from a negative that resulted from light reflecting off a presumably "real" person—someone known to millions of people, but known to almost all of them only by means of the mass media itself. Warhol's images, when viewed with an awareness of the process that formed them and with an awareness of the processes of image replication in the popular and commercial arts, contain an implication of the same hall of mirrors that Esslin found in Genet and that was suggested by works like Escher's *Print Gallery*. The regress in Warhol's print continues when one considers the woman who supposedly lies in the distance, behind the series of "Marilyn" images that stand between her and us. The "real Marilyn" was, after all, herself an artifice, a creation, an actress, like Pirandello's two Delias, a fact most pointedly made by the difference that exists between her public name and the one she was born with. Warhol heightens the sense of persona as artifice by printing the faces in garish and artificial colors that parody the use of

Plate 5. Andy Warhol. *Marilyn Monroe.* 1962. Acrylic and silkscreen on canvas, 81 × 66 ¾". Photo courtesy of Leo Castelli Gallery, New York.

make-up as a means of transforming performer into character. The reproducibility of the image, implicit in the photo-transfer process, is made explicit in some examples from this series, in which several nearly identical images have been printed on the same canvas. The differences among these images is equivalent to and is as interesting or uninteresting as the differences among the images of various television sets tuned to the same program. The question must be asked: if one could find the Norma Jean Baker who lay behind all the images of Marilyn and behind the actress called Marilyn, would the regress end there, or would she also be a signifier pointing back toward another elusive signified? Philosophical questions about the ability to know and the reality of the self become part of the lived experience of individuals living in a society that is permeated by mass produced popular and commercial imagery.

Lawrence Alloway describes Pop as "an art about signs and sign-systems."[1] As such it is more closely associated with other paintings-of-paintings than may at first seem to be the case. Warhol's silkscreens of celebrities and Roy Lichtenstein's images of comic book stereotypes are, like Magritte's *The Human Condition,* visual art works taking as their subjects other visual art works. Unlike Magritte's work, they derive their subjects from popular and commercial sources rather than the tradition of fine art suggested by Magritte's landscape. A work like Lichtenstein's *Hopeless* (1963) is as much a painting of a painting as Magritte's painting, but its meta-pictorial structure is less explicit. In Lichtenstein's painting the interior painting has shifted position; it has come forward so that its surface and edge coincide with the surface and edge of the real painting. Because a viewer cannot see the border of the interior painting, the existence of the interior painting must be inferred. The fact that the subject of Lichtenstein's painting is an image rather than a young girl, that the painting is not a stereotypical depiction but a depiction of a stereotype, is evident from his meticulous and ironic rendering of the casual abbreviations of his popular sources. Lichtenstein carefully and clinically replicates what was spontaneous and automatic in his sources: the formulaic tear drops, the conventionalized starbursts that signify explosions, the linear streaks suggesting movement, the balloons with dialogue and thoughts, and, finally, the ben-day dots, inherent to the process of image printing in comics, that are not part of Lichtenstein's process but are an aspect of his subject. This meticulous representation of what was casual and schematic makes it clear that his subject matter is not humans and their relationships, but representations of humans and their relationships. Lichtenstein's paintings are parodic, and parody involves an implied frame-tale or

Plate 6. Roy Lichtenstein. *Hopeless.* 1963. Oil on canvas, 44 × 44″. Photo courtesy of Leo Castelli Gallery, New York.

meta-painting, in which a source work is "contained" within a framing work but the frames of the two levels correspond. The critical distance between the work and its source substitutes for the existence of a literal frame inside the frame. Without that critical distance the work would not be a parody but simply a work of art modeled after an earlier work or convention.

The exact correlation between certain fundamental properties of the painting and those of the subject depicted by the painting—as in the coincidence of surface and edge in Lichtenstein's comic strip works—was presaged by Jasper Johns's flag paintings of the middle and late nineteen-fifties. Johns chose as his subject something with formal properties nearly identical to those of the painting itself. Because the surface and edge of a flag correspond precisely to the surface and edge of a similarly proportioned rectangular painting, Johns made moot the problem of reconciling the two-dimensionality of the painting with the objects from the three-dimensional world it depicted, a formal problem that was a central concern of painters since Cezanne. It might be asked, in fact, whether Johns depicted flags or simply made flags, just as it might be asked whether Lichtenstein depicted comic strip panels or painted comic strip panels. For both questions, the answer is the same: Johns's flag paintings are not flags in spite of their closeness to their subject—they will not wave. Lichtenstein's paintings are too large to be comic book images and, more significantly, they hang on the walls of galleries, individually or in groups of two or three at most, divorced from the narrative context that is as essential to comic strip panels as waving is to flags. But the fact that the question arises, that the closeness between work and subject may make one wonder if these are, in fact, works of art at all, suggests a movement of such works toward what Robert Rauschenberg called the "gap" between art and life.[2]

Lichtenstein's comic strip paintings are always formal improvements on his sources. He refines the compositions both on the level of the detail—the repetition of the fingers of a hand, the decorative pattern created by schematized hair or ocean waves—and on the level of the overall structure, perfecting the work's unity, balance, and variety. Comic strip conventions, of course—flat, schematic, abbreviated—are ideal starting points for the kind of formal play in which Lichtenstein engages. But he refines his sources, often very subtly, so that the impact of his works is stronger than that of the originals even as he remains faithful to the style and conventionalized vocabulary of those originals. At the same time, the cool, clinical aspect of his works distances the viewer. It is precisely this combination of fidelity to and distancing from the source that is the hallmark—and the difficulty—of the Pop "attitude." Pop, at its best, involves an affectionate acceptance of popular style and imagery. At the same time it maintains a critical distance regarding that style and imagery. Pop is neither sentimental nor satirical but achieves a tone somewhere in between. It is a form of parody which, according to Hutcheon, is "repetition with critical distance" that does not necessarily involve lampooning the source.[3]

Major Pop artists do not limit the sources of their subjects to the

Plate 7. Jasper Johns. *Flag.* 1955. Encaustic, oil, and collage on canvas, 42 ¼ × 60 ⅝″. Collection, The Museum of Modern Art, New York, Gift of Philip Johnson in honor of Alfred H. Barr, Jr.

popular arts but turn their attention away from soup cans, comic books, and movie stars in order to examine works derived from the fine art tradition as well. Lichtenstein applies his refined comic book style to works by various modern masters; he has produced what is in effect a catalogue of modern movements since Impressionism. When he deals with relatively "hot" or emotionally engaged styles an ironic distance results from the strong contrast between his anonymous surface and the personal touch of the original artist. When he deals with the "cool" or more distanced styles the irony results from his exaggeration of the disengagement of the original. The scientistic aspect of Impressionism, for example, is parodied in his series of Rouen Cathedral and haystack lithographs done in 1969. Ben-day dots parody the phenomenologically "objective" brush strokes of Impressionism. Lichtenstein's works form a series of prints in different colors, paralleling Monet's systematic treatment of Rouen Cathedral under different lighting circumstances. Lichtenstein has stated that his process is "an industrial way of making Impressionism—or something like it—by a machine-like technique. . . . I think that changing the color to represent different times of the day is a mass production way of using the printing process."[4] As is often the case with Pop, however, the irony may be as much directed at the present as it is at the earlier period. Lichtenstein's cathedral prints may be read as implying either that comic strip mass production is the natural result of Impressionist objectivity, or that it is what contemporary society does with Impressionism, which, after all, retained its individuality and humanism, in spite of the attempt at pure visual documentation. But in neither case is the tone that of a lampoon or even a satire. Rather, it is a quiet wit that has a great deal of affection for its objects—comics and cathedrals. In Pop works like this the source of the parody is doubled: the painting refers to a work from the fine art tradition, from which it derives its subject, and to the popular or commercial arts, from which it derives its style. In relation to both sources parody and irony are involved and are compounded by the unlikely juxtaposition of those two sources.

Lichtenstein denies any intentional social comment in his work. When he explains his motivation in choosing certain subjects and treating them in a certain way, he does so in terms of curiosity—a desire to redo an old work in a new way—and in terms of his process of formal refinement. Any kind of social comment, to the extent that it is present, enters without his conscious intention.

I don't think I deliberately *put* it in . . . but it's pretty hard not to read social comment in it. That is, I'm commenting on something, certainly. I don't think it's direct and I don't think I'm saying that society is bad. That's not the meaning of *Cathedrals* or *Modern Heads* or *Peace Through Chemistry*. But obviously they comment on some aspects of our society. They observe society and come out of our society.[5]

Lichtenstein's paintings of brush strokes are ironic and—consistent with the double-edged character of Pop—affectionate subversions of Abstract Expressionism. They pay homage to the style in a manner that is antithetical to it. This does not make that homage less sincere; it does, however, inject a note of humor that contradicts the heroic high-seriousness of the Abstract Expressionist artist. The painterly drips, which existed as indices of the action painter's personal, emotionally charged engagement with his or her medium, are transformed into meticulous, linear, and totally impersonal renderings of painterly drips. The care with which Lichtenstein renders each drip suggests a reverence for the original that, ironically, subverts the aesthetic principles of the original. The artist's

Plate 8. Roy Lichtenstein. *Little Big Painting.* 1965. Oil on canvas, 68 × 80″. Collection of the Whitney Museum of American Art, purchase with funds from the Friends of the Whitney Museum of American Art.

unique, readily identifiable signature in paint was the *sine qua non* of Abstract Expressionism. Lichtenstein's surface is anonymous. His brush stroke paintings of the nineteen-sixties are related to Jean Tinguely's "meta-matic" machines of the late nineteen-fifties—works of kinetic sculpture that mechanically produced Abstract Expressionist style paintings. Both groups of works are witty reactions to Abstract Expression and represent a cooler style with less high-seriousness and a greater sense of humor. Still, Lichtenstein's tone is much more equivocal and less blatant a lampoon. Pop's parodic homage to its sources, its filial piety combined with Oedipal subversion, is a double-edged attitude characteristic of postmodernism in all the arts. Ihab Hassan says that "postmodernism . . . demands a double view. Sameness and difference, unity and rupture, filiation and revolt, all must be honored."[6]

Mel Ramos, like Lichtenstein, takes a style derived from the popular arts and applies it to works from the fine arts tradition. Ramos' popular sources are the slick, sexy cartoons of soft-core pornography. Such cartoons are more illusionistic and less two-dimensional than Lichtenstein's comic strip sources and are therefore less ideal starting points for the kind of formal play in which Lichtenstein engages. Similarly, Ramos's fine art referents are not, for the most part, derived from the modern period as are Lichtenstein's, where flatness predominates, but are works of the great masters of previous centuries, especially those from the tradition of female nude painting. Ramos is clearly much less concerned with formal subtlety and intricacy than Lichtenstein. He re-works nude masterpieces of the past in his style of soft-core pornography in order to produce paintings whose humor is more obvious and less deadpan than that of Lichtenstein's work.

Velazquez Version (1975), for example, is modeled after Velazquez's *The Toilet of Venus* (1648). Velazquez's sensual nude is transformed into a too perfect sex object, which seems to lack all sense of real flesh. An earlier work by Ramos, *Val Veeta* (1965), implicitly compared a pornographic stereotype to the overly processed cheese product from which the woman of the title derived her name, and commented on sex in advertising at the same time. The highly polished surface of *Velazquez Version,* which lacks nearly all trace of the quality of paint as paint, contrasts with Velazquez's own painterly touch just as the flesh of Ramos's Venus contrasts with that of Velazquez's Venus. Ramos's painting is an obvious comment on a contemporary sexual cliché, an image of a dehumanized, machined perfection. But it can also be read as suggesting that there is a voyeuristic component in Velazquez's original as well—and, perhaps, in the entire tradition of female nude painting. Ramos's Venus seems barely human next to Velazquez's; yet it can be seen as the logical extension of Velazquez's. Both are visually delightful images—illusionistic visual signifiers that stand in for the real thing. The sword cuts both ways: Velazquez is used as a vehicle for achieving critical distance regarding soft-core porn, and soft-core porn is used as a vehicle for achieving critical distance regarding Velazquez.

Still, there is no anger in these revelations. Ramos is willing to enjoy the sexual stereotype even though he is conscious of the illusion, just as Lichtenstein accepts and enjoys comic book style at the same time that he maintains critical distance. Pop is not a revolutionary or even a reformist style; it accepts the facts of life in a system of corporate capitalism where mass media images are used to condition values that will produce appropriate consumer behavior. It is willing to accept what pleasure it can from those images. But it does not do so stupidly; it maintains some

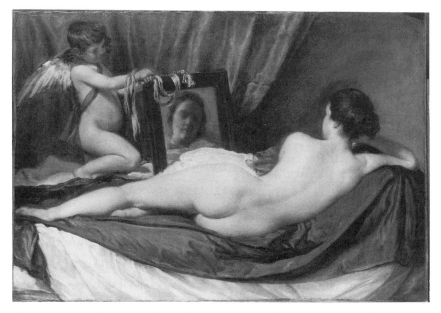

Plate 9. Diego Velazquez. *The Toilet of Venus.* 1648. Oil on canvas, 48 ¼ × 69 ¾". Reproduced by courtesy of the Trustees, The National Gallery, London.

distance even as it participates. Only with Warhol, partly because he is the most utterly deadpan of all the Pop artists and partly because of some of the subject choices he makes, does one suspect a despair beneath the apparently ingenuous surface. But he never drops character. He performs a role of artless innocence and naïveté, asserting that he really likes Campbell's Soup and that his depictions of death and disaster are the result of subjects chosen by chance or because of their formal qualities.

The public persona Warhol maintains is itself artifice and invites the same questions regarding the reality of being and the self as those suggested by his celebrity paintings. Along with the coterie that surrounded him in the "Factory" (his loft-studio and social gathering place of the early nineteen-sixties) Warhol presents a philosophically anti-essentialist face to the world. Just as he denies that his paintings have content, he denies the existence of a self behind his own surface. "If you want to know all about Andy Warhol, just look at the surface of my paintings and films and me, and there I am. There's nothing behind it."[7] In a 1974 interview Warhol was asked if he expected the viewers of one of his

Plate 10. Mel Ramos. *Velazquez Version.* 1974. Oil on canvas, 44 × 66″. Photo courtesy of Mel Ramos.

automobile accidents to imagine a real disaster. He responded that he wanted them "just to see it as a black and white design . . . like a dress fabric."[8] Warhol thus emphasizes surface rather than depth, the mask rather than the self, and the concrete rather than the abstract. The self—as a locus of personality that manifests itself through speech and action—is denied. Works of art are surfaces to be perceived and appreciated on purely formal grounds: looking for an ethical theme or social statement in them is beside the point. Stephen Koch has described Warhol as someone who

wasn't really a person in the ordinary sense of the word, certainly not a person like the rest of us, who reveals his desires and satisfactions and distastes with every move, for whom the incarnation in the world, the body and face and hands, is animated with whatever sustains one's life and makes it a life. Warhol seemed not to have a personality in this sense: Instead, he had a persona; his actions revealed not so much who he was but *what* he was. He was Andy Warhol, that phenomenon, Andy Warhol.[9]

It is difficult to accept Warhol and his work at "face" value. So many of his prints of the early nineteen-sixties focus on the grimmer aspects of contemporary American society that it is impossible not to believe that some kind of comment is involved. Images of electric chairs, automobile accidents, atomic explosions, and racial violence are loaded both because they are violent and because they relate to emotionally charged referents in American society. One cannot overlook what they signify and treat them as ethically neutral images of interest only because of their formal characteristics.

Nonetheless, because Warhol incorporates into his life the same strategy he uses in his art, it is essential for him to remain deadpan, to maintain a role of complete ingenuousness, to insist that he lacks all complexity as a human being and enjoys surfaces for their own sake, and to remain *in character*. Yet a minimal self remains, a self like Wylie Sypher's "anonymous self," a human center that lingers after the self has been all but entirely effaced.[10] Koch says that Warhol's silence and retreat is a strategy for dealing with a profound doubt about the value of life and that his career is "an attempt to redeem . . . despair without belying it."[11] It is this humanistic remnant that accounts for the ethical dimension that remains in Warhol's work. In an unusually candid statement, Warhol once said, "I still care about people but it would be so much easier not to care . . . it's too hard to care . . . I don't want to get too involved in other people's lives . . . I don't want to get too close . . . I don't like to touch things . . . that's why my work is so distant from myself."[12]

From Combine to Performance

Warhol's "Superstars," members of the Factory entourage who appeared in his films, were parodies of movie stars, exaggerating the artificial manners, the make-up, and the scandalous behaviour of their Hollywood counterparts. They were individuals whose lives became works of Pop Art—three-dimensional, animated versions of Warhol celebrity prints. As such, many of them became quite famous, became, in fact, "stars" in their own right, though they were stars twice removed, stars whose stardom arose from their performances of star stereotypes. For Warhol, painting expanded into theatre: his medium was not only paint on canvas but also his own life and the lives of those willing accomplices who surrounded him.

The movement from painting to performance had already begun as an extension of the collage tradition begun by Picasso and Braque in 1912 and carried on by Dadaists like Kurt Schwitters. Robert Rauschenberg's "combines" of the late nineteen-fifties and early nineteen-sixties differ from earlier works integrating found objects and materials into painting in some important ways. In combines the objects are often larger and fully three-dimensional—compared with the railway tickets, pieces of newspaper, and playing cards used by the Cubists. The Cubists, like Jasper Johns in his flag paintings, reconcile painting and reality by choosing to present or depict two-dimensional objects, thus avoiding the discrepancy between the qualities of the representation and those of the thing represented. Rauschenberg's combines tend in the opposite direction: he integrates *three-dimensional* objects from the world into his combines, thereby making his works literally—not illusionistically—three-dimensional. It is true, of course, that Picasso made sculpture as well as two-dimensional collage paintings out of found objects, but Rauschenberg's combines are not fully sculpture, in spite of their three-dimensional components. He maintains a dialectic between the two-dimensional ground of his combines (consisting of paint, photographs, and other relatively flat attachments) and the three-dimensional objects (stuffed birds and animals, clocks, electric lights) attached to that ground. Even in his famous *Monogram* (1959), made of a stuffed Angora goat with a tire around its middle, the goat is mounted on a painted and collaged platform that alludes to the two-dimensional field from which combines historically emerge.

Carla Gottlieb has written, "Rauschenberg's Combines marry painting to manufactured objects, like Cubist Constructions. But they differ from these works in one major aspect: they do not create a new medium by blending the component elements of the old ones."[13] The various aspects of a combine—painting and found object, for example—are only partly integrated into a whole. Rauschenberg maintains an uneasy balance of opposed aspects or elements. The incorporation of found objects into the work helps him to "act in the gap" between art and life because those objects are not fully appropriated by the work of art. They rest uneasily between being what they are—clocks, light bulbs, stuffed animals—and being parts of an art work. Earlier Cubist collages and even the "dada" collages of Kurt Schwitters were quite formal. The found components were fully appropriated by art; in a sense they ceased to be that which they originally were and became the materials of art. With combines the appropriation of found object by art is never complete, always tenuous.

Rauschenberg also operates in the gap when he structures his works. They are informal but not formless; they have an extremely casual formality. If the artist's hand were less evident, they might not be perceived as art at all; if it were more evident, it would be too obvious.

Similarly, Rauschenberg's combines, as well as the photo-transfer

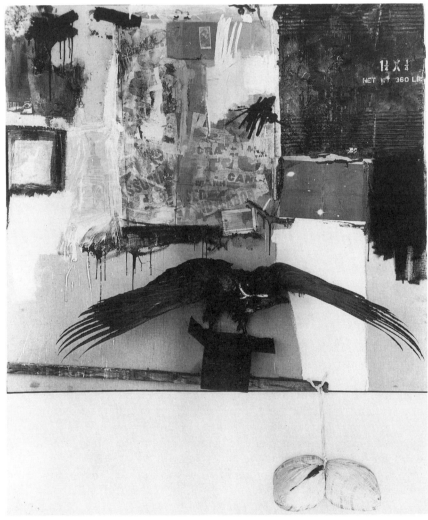

Plate 11. Robert Rauschenberg. *Canyon.* 1959. Combine painting, 86½ × 70 × 23". Collection Mr. and Mrs. Michael Sonnabend, New York. Photo courtesy of Sonnabend Gallery, New York.

Plate 12. Robert Rauschenberg. *Tracer.* 1964. Oil and silkscreen on canvas, 84 × 60″. The Nelson-Atkins Museum of Art, Kansas City, Missouri (Nelson Gallery Foundation).

collages that he began doing in 1962, equivocate between significance and insignificance. Their titles—most obviously in examples such as *Monogram* and *Rebus* (1955)—often suggest interpretability. Titles such as *Canyon* (1959) and *Tracer* (1964) hint at a conceptual unity underlying the diverse images and/or objects comprising the work. If such works are studied, some of their components will seem to relate to the titles, sometimes literally, but often through some kind of pun. In *Tracer* there are photo transfers of Rubens's *Toilet of Venus* (is traditional painting a "tracing" of reality?) and an army helicopter is printed three times (tracer bullets?); there are two schematic cubes drawn or printed in red paint, suggesting the lines of a tracing. Of course a photographic transfer is itself a chemical and mechanical tracing, a source image transferred to a silkscreen and then to a canvas. On the other hand, all the imagery of a Rauschenberg work cannot be related to the title, and interpreting even those images that can be related may seem forced. The title is a tease, enticing the viewer into seeking a conceptual unity—an attempt that will be only partly successful. Rauschenberg's works equivocate between meaning and lack of meaning just as they do between form and formlessness.

Another important tension in Rauschenberg's works is that which exists between the personal and the impersonal. The incorporation of found objects and the use of photographic transfers suggest an effaced artist in the tradition of Duchamp and his ready-mades. Yet, in both his combines and his silkscreens of the early nineteen-sixties Rauschenberg includes brush strokes and drips of paint, alluding to the highly charged, emotionally engaged personal handwriting of the Abstract Expressionists—a style with a mood quite different from that suggested by found object, combine, and transfer. These two aspects of Rauschenberg's work create a kind of dissonant counterpoint; they resonate against one another and set each other off. They do not harmonize but challenge each other, the personally applied pigments contradicting the mechanically applied transfers or the attached objects, and vice versa. The equivocal formality of the work ameliorates the dissonance but does not quite create a new unity.

The result of the incomplete assimilation of the components of Rauschenberg's works into the whole is a semiotic dissonance between various kinds of signifiers—brush strokes, photographs, photo-transfers, as well as "real" objects. Tom Wesselman's statement describing the relationship among the various aspects of his own constructions may be applied to Rauschenberg's work as well:

If there was any single aspect of my work that excited me, it was that possibility—not just the differences between what they were, but the aura each had with it. That each had such a fulfilled reality; the reverberations seemed a way of making the picture more intense. . . . Therefore throughout the picture all elements compete with each other.[14]

The bringing together of diverse elements into an incomplete synthesis is closely related to Brecht's aesthetics of theatre. Esslin describes Brechtian structure in a manner similar to Wesselman's description:

Just as isolated episodes of the play retain their individual significance even if taken out of the context of the play as a whole, the non-literary elements of the production—decor, music, and choreography-also retain their independence . . . instead of pulling in the same direction as the words, they enter into a dialectical, contrapuntal relationship with them.[15]

Rauschenberg's and Wesselman's visual constructions do not synthesize art media in order to induce a sensual and emotional experience that reduces aesthetic distance, but they utilize semiotic dissonance to ensure critical distance.

Still, Wesselman's sculptural tableaux pull toward unity in a way that Rauschenberg's combines do not. They are more rigorously formal, and the various elements are incorporated into a logically coherent whole—frequently the representation of a nude female in a domestic setting. The fact that Wesselman, like Rauschenberg, incorporates his object in their entirety helps explain why they nevertheless maintain their individuality and remain incompletely integrated. As in Rauschenberg's combines they represent different orders of signs; *trompe l'oeil* visual representations, schematic visual representations, and actual objects. Brechtian distancing is further enhanced by the conflicting responses that they invite: the blatantly erotic nudes are highly charged images, parodies of sex objects that evoke a strong emotional response of one kind or another, but Wesselman's rigorous formalism invites a cooler contemplation of the work as an aesthetic object.

The movement from combine to performance was carried out by Allan Kaprow in his development of the happening in the late nineteen-fifties. Kaprow was influenced by the Action Painters, especially Jackson Pollock, and by John Cage. He also had contact with Rauschenberg, himself influenced by Cage. Kaprow brought together aspects of the emotionally engaged Abstract Expressionist style and the cooler, more distanced style of Rauschenberg and Johns. From Pollock he inherited his interest in

Plate 13. Tom Wesselman. *Great American Nude No. 44.* 1963. Collage painting with radiator and telephone, 81 × 96 × 10″. Courtesy of Sidney Janis Gallery, New York.

spontaneity and improvisation as well as in paintings that had an environmental effect, a result of the great size of many of Pollock's paintings. Cage's "concrete" sounds translated themselves into found objects in Kaprow's art.

There is an important difference between the improvised and the aleatory, although the two are easily confused. Improvisation is properly associated with surrealistic and expressionistic movements as well as jazz; randomness is characteristic of Dada and Cage's sound events. Improvisatory art is often personal and emotional; indeterminate or aleatory art suggests, in contrast, the effacing of the artist. Kaprow, in his shift from Abstract Expressionism through collage to happenings, tends to move from the personal and the improvisatory to the impersonal and the aleatory. This development, from expressionistic spontaneity toward a scored indeterminacy (the creation of works that provide for the incursion of the unpredictable), is evident in Kaprow's description of his development of the happening:

I developed a kind of action-collage technique, following my interest in Pollock. These action collages . . . were done as rapidly as possible by grasping up great hunks of varied matter: tinfoil, straw, canvas, photos, newspaper. . . .

The action-collage then became bigger, and I introduced flashing lights and thicker hunks of matter. These parts projected farther and farther from the wall and into the room and included more and more audible elements; sounds of ringing buzzers, bells, toys. . . .

Now I just simply filled the whole gallery up . . . When you opened the door you found yourself in the midst of an entire Environment. . . .

But I complained immediately about the fact that there was a sense of mystery until your eye reached a wall. Then there was a dead end. At that point my disagreement with the gallery space began. I thought how much better it would be if you could just go out of doors and float an Environment into the rest of life so that such a caesura would not be there. . . . I immediately saw that every visitor to the Environment was part of it. . . . And so I gave him occupations like moving something, turning switches on—just a few things. Increasingly during 1957 and 1958, this suggested a more "scored" responsibility for the visitor. I offered him more and more to do until there developed the happening.[16]

Kaprow presented his first public happening, *18 Happenings in 6 Parts,* at the Reuben Gallery in 1959. Six performers and seventy-five audience participants were involved in each of the six performances of the work. Invitations informed individuals that they would become a part of the same events they were experiencing. The gallery was divided into three rooms by plastic sheets and the walls were covered with paint, collage, and painted words. Each member of the audience was given a program sheet and three cards with individual instructions. The instructions explained that the events would be divided into six parts, each consisting of three "happenings" simultaneously occurring in the three rooms. They also explained that during the performance individuals were to change their seats according to a pre-established plan. A bell would indicate when seats were to be changed; when it rang twice the entire performance would be over. Individuals would not necessarily occupy all three rooms during the evening, and chairs were arranged facing in different directions. Obviously no one would experience the work in its entirety: no participant would see each event that took place in the three rooms. Colored lights were strung throughout the gallery and slides and films were projected onto the walls. Full-length mirrors reflected a complex environment, and there were various music and sound sources throughout.

The six performers had a strict sequence of movements to perform: they all were parallel or at right angles to the walls and were carried out to definite "beats" that the performers counted mentally. Some of those movements were "everyday" (such as squeezing oranges), some were enigmatic or "surreal" (obscure actions involving toys or other common objects), and others seemed purely abstract and formal. At one point a flute, ukelele, and violin were played, and at another an orchestra of toy instruments played. Non-human performers included a dancing toy and a pair of constructions on wheels. Each evening two members of the audience painted a canvas together (during one performance these were Johns and Rauschenberg). Verbalizations included abstruse, philosophical statements about, for example, the nature of time ("It is said that time is essence . . . we have known time . . . spiritually . . . as expectation, remembrance, revelation and projection, abstracting the moment from its very self") and at other times they were poetic ("fine cock-feathered moon me friend"); sometimes commonplace statements were isolated from their appropriate context ("My toilet is shared by the man next door who is Italian"); but in the end speech degenerated into the repetition of monosyllabic words and nonverbal sounds: "eh?" "mmmmmm . . . ," "uh," "But," "Well," "oooh."[17]

In spite of the non-traditional nature of the production, happenings did have a structure, and, although there were differences between performances, they did not allow for improvisation. Michael Kirby calls them "nonmatrixed"; no illusionistic time and space were created and performers did not attempt to create an illusion of character. Performers— as themselves—performed the actions indicated. They might do it differently on different nights and such differences might be interesting but they were not significant, at least not in the sense that they might affect the success or failure of the happening. This is, of course, completely different from a jazz improvisation or even a traditional theatrical or musical performance, where all differences between performances are significant, either in terms of what is being expressed or in terms of the quality of the performance. In a happening the performer simply carriers out the action. As Kirby points out, the unpredictable aspects of happenings are better described by the word indeterminacy than by the word improvisation.

There was great variability in the nature of the happenings and artist's theatre that occurred in the wake of *18 Happenings*. Some, like *18 Happenings*, had a relatively tight script while others were looser, with greater indeterminate elements. Some involved performers and audience members while others involved performers only. Some involved moving spectators, while in others they remained in the same seat for the entire performance. And some confined themselves to a gallery space while others took place outdoors, perhaps even in different parts of a city or region.

European happenings were often more political than American happenings, whose radicalism was, after all, primarily aesthetic. Jean-Jacques Lebel, a French contemporary of Kaprow, organized happenings that were more shocking and politically radical than those of his American counterparts. Lebel was closely associated with Daniel Cohn-Bendit, a leader of the 1968 student uprising, as well as with Julian Beck of the Living Theatre, itself involved in radical attempts to effect sexual and political change. Another Frenchman, Yves Klein, was mystically inclined and engaged in a number of performance activities, one of the most extreme being his *Le Vide* (*The Void*) exhibition of 1962. Visitors entered a totally empty gallery which, in spite of its emptiness, was guarded by two Republican Guards in full uniform. The gallery had been cleansed of the "presences" of other artists and filled with Klein's own "presence" by being carefully cleaned and whitewashed. "Immaterial" paintings from the show were paid for in gold, which was then disposed of, perhaps by dropping it into the Seine.[18]

Such works must be regarded, at least in part, as a response to the appropriation of art by investors. That appropriation is well illustrated in an exchange between Robert Scull, a prominent New York collector, and Rauschenberg. In 1973 Scull and his wife sold the major part of their collection at an auction at Sotheby Park Bernet for over two million dollars, a profit of several thousand percent. A Rauschenberg combine they paid $900 for in 1958 was sold for $85,000. A filmed documentary of the auction shows Rauschenberg saying to Scull, "I've been working my ass for you to make a profit?" and Scull replying, "You're going to sell now, too. We've been working for each other."[19]

Scull's statement suggests a bankruptcy of aesthetic values and a debasement of art perhaps more shocking than Duchamp's famous *Fountain,* a urinal presented as a ready-made sculpture in 1917. When works of art enter the marketplace they are taken over by forces that have little to do with aesthetic value—whatever aesthetic value system one subscribes to. Works of painting and sculpture are unique, "precious" objects that have what Walter Benjamin called an "aura."[20] When they are used as objects of speculation they can achieve an inflated value far greater than what might reasonably be ascribed to them, in the same way that stamps, historical objects, or bottles of wine can achieve values greater than what might reasonably be derived from their beauty, historical interest, or flavor. This appropriation of art by the forces of capitalistic speculation is not as easy when there is no unique, permanent, and possessable art object involved. Mass produced art—books, recordings, tapes—are possessable but not unique. Theatre and performance, on the other hand, produce unique works but do not produce permanent objects that can be owned. The movement of visual artists into performance and conceptual modes can be seen as an attempt to avoid co-option by the marketplace. Painting and sculpting become theatricalized; they integrate with the environment, take on some of the indeterminacy of life outside of art, and achieve that fusion and confusion with life that Pirandello illustrated and predicted in his scripted plays. When the performance is finished there is little left to be owned or copyrighted. The "script" has little literary value, in contrast to a traditional play, which can be read, studied, and to a great extent appreciated outside of its performance. Obviously there is a price for this strategy. Little cultural legacy is possible; future generations are left with sketchy descriptions, a few photographs, and scripts that are sets of instructions rather than dramatic texts.

The Convergence of the Arts

One of the most interesting twists on the frame-tale structure applied to visual art is George Segal's *Portrait of Sidney Janis with Mondrian Painting* (1967). In this work Segal creates a sculptural tableau consisting of one of his characteristic white plaster figures, this one of his art dealer, a fine English display easel, and a real Mondrian painting, *Composition* (1933). The irony of this work, in the context of previous works-containing-works such as Magritte's *Human Condition,* is apparent. Rather than depict one work, illusionistically, inside another, why not actually include a real work inside another? Segal's sculpture is a representation, but inside that representation is a "real" painting. Ethical questions are certainly raised here. The Mondrian painting has been permanently appropriated by another work of art: Janis insisted that Segal agree that the painting would always remain within the tableau and a reproduction never be substituted.[21] Thus, as long as that agreement is enforced, Mondrian's work will not exist as itself again; it will be inaccessible to scholars, critics, historians, and the general public except as a part of Segal's work. The fact that the work deals with the issue of ownership of art is evident from the description in the Museum of Modern Art's catalogue of the Janis collection. The catalogue's use of the word "stable" in this context, with its connotation of pimps and prostitutes, is especially telling.

Plate 14. George Segal. *Portrait of Sidney Janis with Mondrian Painting.* 1967. Plaster figure with Mondrian's *Composition,* 1933, on an easel, 67 × 50 × 33". Collection, The Museum of Modern Art, New York. The Sidney and Harriet Janis Collection, gift to The Museum of Modern Art, New York.

Through the informal stance, the hand on the frame, the careful scrutiny of the picture, Segal has conveyed Mr. Janis's fondness for this painting, his connoisseurship, and his possessiveness as a collector, together with his showmanship. He has thus subtly delineated the complex relationship between a collector-dealer and the art and artists of his stable.[22]

A similar, though less controversial, work by Segal is his *Alice Listening to Her Poetry and Music* (1970–71). The poet Alice Notley sits at a table; a tape recorder is on the table and behind it is a window. The piece is placed against a wall so that the spectator tends to view the figure from behind and see the face only indirectly, reflected in the window. On the recorder a tape of Notley reading her poetry plays audibly. Here Segal, in a kind of expanded sculpture, has incorporated poetry into a sculptural tableau. However, because poetry can be reproduced (in texts and on tape), it lacks the "aura" of precious, one-of-a-kind objects. Notley's poetry can continue to exist in live performance, as well as through mass production, even as it exists as part of Segal's tableau; therefore there is no ethical problem here as there was in the Sidney Janis portrait.

Such works present an expanded sculpture capable of assimilating "real" objects as well as other art media. Other artists would include live performers inside their works of sculpture, thereby expanding sculpture toward theatre, just as Kaprow did with his "action-collage" painting. It is, of course, no coincidence that Segal was one of the artists who was earlier involved in the creation of the happenings.

Alice Listening, a form of expanded sculpture, is reminiscent of some of Samuel Beckett's highly reduced theatrical works. The image—an individual listening to her own voice on a tape recorder—is especially reminiscent of Beckett's one act play *Krapp's Last Tape* (1958), in which the aged Krapp sits at a table listening to a taped diary he made thirty years earlier. Most of the speech of the play comes from the machine and although Krapp does perform some actions, nothing like a conventional plot evolves. Beckett's highly reduced theatre increasingly tends toward the sculptural. Even in *Waiting for Godot* (1952), which Tom Stoppard said "redefined the minima of theatrical validity,"[23] what is most memorable is the image of waiting that it offers: the mound, the tree, and the characters Didi and Gogo, killing time.

Segal's *Alice Listening* is also reminiscent of Beckett's later *Rockaby* (1981). This play consists of a single character, an old woman in a rocking chair. Nearly all speech comes from a voice offstage (a recording of the actress's own voice). Occasionally the woman onstage speaks a single word, "More," once at the outset before the taped voice begins and on three other occasions during pauses on the tape. Also, just prior to these pauses and again at the end of the play, the woman speaks short phrases in unison with the taped voice. The physical action of the play consists simply of the rocking of the chair, which pauses occasionally along with the verbal pauses.

The extreme reductionism of *Rockaby* is even greater than is first apparent. The movements of the rocking chair, which may seem to be controlled by the actress, are actually controlled mechanically. Thus, the actress's performance is further narrowed, limited to her facial expressions and the occasional interjections of words and brief phrases.[24] In theatrical works like these Beckett creates a kind of theatre that consists of a striking image with a poetic accompaniment, *a tableau vivant* with a recorded voice-over. The mechanized movement of *Rockaby* underscores the rapprochement between reductionist theatre and an expanded sculpture that moves.

Sculpture need not incorporate living performers in order to approach theatre. Certainly one of the most theatrical works of sculpture was Jean Tinguely's *Homage to New York,* the 1960 self-destruction of an elaborate machine in the garden of the Museum of Modern Art. *Homage* was an enormous construction, consisting of literally tons of machinery that included, among other things, a weather balloon, smoke bombs, a piano rigged to play a monotonous three-note motif and go up in flames, scores of bicycle and baby carriage wheels, a child's bassinet, the drum from an old washing machine, and two complete meta-matic sections. Also incorporated into *Homage* was a contribution by Rauschenberg, a "money thrower" which, when set off by a bit of flash powder, flung out silver dollars. In spite of its mechanical nature, Tinguely's *Homage* was, like his earlier machines, quite anthropomorphic. This quality did not result from its appearance, certainly, but from its behavior. Like the earlier machines, *Homage* did not act precisely as it was supposed to. Among other things it refused to destroy itself utterly and finally had to be laid to rest by a fireman and two museum guards. Such behavior in his machines delighted Tinguely; it was as if a kind of perverse freedom entered the works and enabled them to do things their own way, regardless of their creator's intentions. Rauschenberg said of *Homage,* "There were so many different aspects of life involved in the big piece. It was as real, as interesting, as complicated, as vulnerable, and as gay as life itself."[25]

Homage seems more like theatre than kinetic sculpture. Invitations were sent to two hundred people and indicated that the "spectacle" would begin at 6:30 on the evening of March 17. The end of the spectacle would occur, of course, when the machine completed its task of self-destruction or, as things actually turned out, when it was helped toward that end by the fireman and the guards. As in theatre there was an element of uncertainty about how well the machine would perform. Thus, because of the temporal limits, because the action was developmental, struggling toward a resolved conclusion, and because of the anthropomorphic qualities of unpredictability and fallibility, one is tempted to regard *Homage to New York* as theatre, in spite of the fact that it was performed by a machine.

Similarly, *Breath* (1969), perhaps Beckett's most "reduced" play, a piece that lasts little more than half a minute, remains theatre, in spite of the fact that it includes no live performer. Two identical recorded cries frame the "action" of *Breath*. An amplified recording of a slow inhalation followed by a slow exhalation is played simultaneously with a gradual increase and decrease of light on a littered stage. Unlike *Homage, Breath* is exactly scripted; there is nothing indeterminate about it.[26] But, like *Homage*, it is a performance without a performer. For both works this absence does not, however, result in a sense of complete dehumanization. Tinguely's machine is anthropomorphic in its willfulness, and Beckett's littered stage is a metaphoric mindscape, a simple and elegant image of the dawning and dimming of consciousness. Moreover, both works satisfy certain traditional expectations of the theatre. They have beginnings and endings in time and temporal structures that result in a sense of wholeness and completion. In contrast to most works of sculpture or painting, even kinetic or optical visual works, those temporal structures require that the audience witness the work from one specific point in time—the beginning—to another specific point in time—the ending.

Sculpture does, of course, sometimes incorporate live performers and still remain sculpture. In Nam June Paik's *TV Cello* (1971) a woman plays a cello constructed of three television monitors. In spite of the live performer this work seems more like sculpture than theatre because it does not have a specific beginning and ending in time. One has more of a sense that the work is *put on display* when the woman begins performing and is *taken down* when she stops, that spectators can come and go at different times as they would with a traditional work of sculpture. Gilbert and George's *Red Sculpture* (1975) is more ambiguous. Gilbert and George are British artists who declared their bodies to be works of art. In *Red Sculpture* they walked slowly, mechanically, and precisely through various poses, seemingly in response to phrases played on a tape recorder. They wore suits and ties and their faces and hands were painted bright red. The satirical content of the piece is clear, perhaps too obvious, and the piece was not without visual interest, as the conservatively dressed but brightly painted figures moved through their paces creating a variety of configurations. The problem with the work is that it was ninety minutes long and there was some ambiguity regarding whether it should be seen from beginning to end (like a play) or as long as the spectator saw fit (like a piece of sculpture).

In recent decades there has emerged a new genre, "performance art," "artist's performance," or simply "performance," that exists ambiguously between the visual arts of painting and sculpture and the traditionally performed arts of theatre, dance, and music. The immediate parent of this genre is the happening, although contemporary performance can be related to performance activities within major modern movements earlier in the century: Italian and Russian Futurism, Constructivism, Dada, Surrealism, and the Bauhaus.[27] The genre virtually merges in some instances with experimental theatre; thus, artists like Robert Wilson and Richard Foreman are as likely to be mentioned in discussions of contemporary theatre as in discussions of contemporary art performance. There are no rules for the genre; it is, perhaps, easier to say what it is not than to say what it is. Performance tends to be non-narrative, non-dramatic, and non-mimetic. There is no distinction between actor and character; often the artist-creator is also the performer. Similarly, there is no distinction between set and setting, whether the setting is a loft or gallery, a stage, the streets or rooftops of a city, or the countryside. The voice is used, but coherent dialogue is avoided; language tends to be poetic and evocative, or the voice is used non-verbally. Kaprow said of happenings that they are "events which, put simply, happen. Though the best of them have a decided impact . . . they appear to go nowhere and do not make any particular literary point."[28] Performance artists enter a visual and auditory space where they use their bodies and voices to create an art that is not dramatic but much more closely related to the visual arts.

Life Imitates Art

Life imitates Art far more than Art imitates Life, and I feel sure that if you think seriously about it you will find that it is true. Life holds the mirror up to Art, and either reproduces some strange type imagined by painter or sculptor, or realises in fact what has been dreamed in fiction. (Oscar Wilde, "The Decay of Lying," 1889)

Wilde's statement is true today in a way that could not have been foreseen in the late nineteenth century. The capacity for mass producing art has resulted in a proliferation of popular and commercial imagery that pervades all aspects of life in Western and Westernized societies. Landscapes may have begun to look like Impressionist paintings because Impressionism taught people how to look or what to notice in what they saw, and Victorian women may have come to resemble Pre-Raphaelite types, either because women imitated paintings or because men began to notice in them qualities they saw in the paintings. But today mass production has dramatically increased the power of art to condition consciousness—to propogate value systems, life styles, understandings of reality, and understandings of the self that serve the interests of those who control the machinery of sign production—whether they are the producers of goods and services in a consumer society or the political leaders of a totalitarian society. More than ever, life imitates art.

Furthermore, if language differs from and defers reality, other sign systems may have the same effect. Whether or not Derrida is philosophically correct when he suggests that signification is an infinite regress of signifiers linked to signifieds that are themselves signifiers, the fact is that the mass production of signs places us more and more in a mediated reality, more and more in a world where the words and images we experience have been selected and processed by individuals and institutions outside our control. Reality is the creation of those who create images of reality. Plato's cave is not an allegory but a fact of modern life. Shadows, prints, and tracings—visual and auditory, mechanical, photographic, and electronic—have thrust individuals into a Genetian hall of mirrors where they are confronted with the kind of epistemological questions once reserved for professional philosophers.

Pop is a visually Pirandellian art-about-art, fine art that takes as its subject matter the style and imagery of popular and commercial art. It is parodic in that it involves critical distance in relationship to its subject matter, but it is not harsh or angry in relationship to that subject matter. At the same time it is Brechtian in that it focuses attention on the signifier by aesthetically formalizing it or otherwise foregrounding style. Rauschenberg, whose combines preceded Pop in America, utilizes semiotic dissonance to produce Brechtian distantiation and to lay bare the process of creation. In a manner analogous to the "epic" relationship of scenes in Brecht's theatre, the images Rauschenberg employs "have a rendezvous in each work but not a sequential or causal arrangement."[29]

The understanding of art as a creator rather than as a reflector of reality can be utilized as a basis for making an art that is more overtly political than Pop itself. Art can thus be used as a means of deconstruction, of subverting the ontological claims of previous works and styles, revealing that what presented itself as natural or true is in fact cultural, a product of language, art, and ideology. Or art can be used in an attempt to reconstruct reality, to create a reality more in accord with the ethical and political views of the artist. The interest in image replication associated with Pop has, in the nineteen-seventies and nineteen-eighties, been turned to much more blatantly social and political ends. Feminist painters such as Sylvia Sleigh and Alice Neel paint erotic male nudes in a manner that parodies traditional female nude painting, and reverses the conventional sexual roles of male artist and female subject, along with the relationship of power and domination implied in those roles. Sherry Levine appropriates whole famous modern works—paintings by Van Gogh and Malevich, photographs by Edward Weston (simply rephotographed by Levine), thus performing a gesture of sabotage on a system that has managed to co-opt and make into commodities the most apparently subversive of aesthetic modes. To accuse Levine of plagiarism is to call into question an entire tradition in which artists have always inevitably drawn on one another; to accept her work is to accept something that lacks what has always been most valued in Western art—the genius of the individual.

In a variety of ways Hans Haacke appropriates the visual and verbal language of economic power and turns it against itself, creating a political pastiche art that reveals the complicity of economic power, political repression, fine art, and commercial art. Some of Haacke's works involve images that echo corporate plaques or magazine advertisements, incorporating also information about the company's politics or its activities in the collecting and promoting of art. Another strategy he has tried involves the conjunction of various panels describing verbally and "objectively" the history of the ownership of a major work of art and a reproduction of the work (or the work itself, in one unrealized project). This strategy, which is a conventional "provenance" of an art work presented formally as a work itself, reveals the incredible escalation of prices of art—its role in capitalist society as an object of economic speculation—and, through the politics of its owners, its frequent complicity with reactionary forces.

The movement into performance, in its political guise, can be seen as another strategy for avoiding capitalistic co-option. American happenings themselves were not so political, however, but represented an explosion in the dialogue between two and three dimensions that had been implicit since painters began applying formal principles to the depiction of things, and that had been an explicit concern since Cezanne. Kinetic sculpture and sculpture incorporating live performance suggest another route that visual art follows toward theatre. Art moves out of the frame or off the pedestal, into the gallery, and into the street where it becomes, in some instances, indistinguishable from developments in the experimental theatre, developments predicted earlier by Pirandello. Significantly, it also becomes a mode that can be utilized politically by individuals interested in something broader than the internal dynamics of art history. Such works are no longer plays in plays or paintings in paintings; the Pirandellian tension between life and form has now shattered the real frame and the representation now denies its status as representation, claiming a reality equal to that of the thing it once represented. Such shatterings of the semiotic line, the line separating signifier and signified, art work and reality, stage and street, leave few texts and artifacts, little for collectors, speculators, and historians to claim, possess, or discuss.

Notes

1. Lawrence Alloway, *American Pop Art* (New York: Macmillan, 1974), p. 7.

2. Quoted, for example, in Calvin Tomkins, *The Bride and the Bachelors, Five Masters of the Avant Garde* (New York: Viking, 1968), p. 193.

3. Linda Hutcheon, *A Theory of Parody* (New York and London: Methuen, 1986), p. 6.

4. "Interview: Roy Lichtenstein by John Coplans," *Roy Lichtenstein: Graphics, Reliefs, & Sculpture,* catalogue for exhibition at University of California, Irvine, October 27 to December 6, 1970 (Los Angeles: Gemini G. E. L., 1970), p. 8.

5. *Ibid.,* p. 11.

6. Ihab Hassan, "The Question of Postmodernism," *The Performing Arts Journal 16,* 6, No. 1 (1981), p. 32.

7. Andy Warhol, *Andy Warhol,* published on the occasion of the Andy Warhol exhibition at Moderna Museet in Stockholm, February-March, 1968 (Boston: Boston Book and Art, 1970), unpaginated.

8. Phyllis Tuchman, "Pop! Interviews with George Segal, Andy Warhol, Roy Lichtenstein, James Rosenquist and Robert Indiana," *Art News,* 73 (May 1974), p. 26.

9. Stephen Koch, *Stargazer, Andy Warhol's Films and His Work* (New York: Praeger, 1973), p. 8.

10. Wylie Sypher, *Loss of the Self in Modern Literature and Art* (New York: Random House, 1962), 147—155.

11. Koch, 15—16.

12. Andy Warhol, *Andy Warhol,* unpaginated.

13. Carla Gottlieb, *Beyond Modern Art* (New York: Dutton), p. 204.

14. "What is Pop Art? Part II," interviews by G. R. Swensen, *Art News,* 62 (February 1964), pp. 41, 64.

15. Martin Esslin, *Brecht, The Man and His Work,* new revised edition (Garden City, New York: Doubleday, 1971), p. 135.

16. Allan Kaprow, "A Statement," Michael Kirby, *Happenings* (New York: Dutton, 1965), 43–46.

17. This discussion is based on Michael Kirby's description in *Happenings,* pp. 67–83.

18. Gottlieb, *Beyond Modern Art,* 87–88; Tomkins, *The Bride and the Bachelors,* 160–161; Adrian Henri, *Total Art: Environments, Happenings, and Performance* (New York: Praeger, 1974), p. 144.

19. Calvin Tomkins, *Off the Wall, Robert Rauschenberg and the Art World of Our Time* (New York: Penguin, 1981), p. 296. The 1974 film documenting the auction of Scull's collection is *American Pop Collector,* shot by Susan and Alan Raymond, and originated and produced by E. J. Vaughan.

20. "The Work of Art in the Age of Mechanical Reproduction," *Illuminations,* ed. and intro. Hannah Arendt, trans. Harry Zohn (New York: Harcourt, Brace, and World, 1968), 222–223.

21. Jan van der Marck, *George Segal,* (New York: Abrams, 1979), 146–147.

22. The Museum of Modern Art, *Three Generations of Twentieth-Century Art, The Sidney and Harriet Janis Collection of the Museum of Modern Art,* foreword Alfred H. Barr, intro. William Rubin (New York: Museum of Modern Art, 1972), p. 166.

23. Quoted in Ronald Hayman, *Theatre and Anti-Theatre* (London: Secher & Warburg, 1979), p. 2.

24. *Rockaby and Other Short Pieces by Samuel Beckett* (New York: Grove, 1981), 7–23.

25. Quoted in Calvin Tomkins, *The Bride and the Bachelors,* p. 175. My discussion of *Homage to New York* is based on Tomkin's description, 169–182.

26. In Samuel Beckett, *First Love and Other Shorts* (New York: Grove, 1974), p. 91.

27. RoseLee Goldberg surveys the history of performance art in *Performance, Live Art 1909 to the Present* (New York: Abrams, 1979).

28. Allan Kaprow, " 'Happenings' in the New York Scene," *Art News,* 60, No. 3 (May 1961), p. 39.

29. Alloway, *American Pop Art,* p. 55.

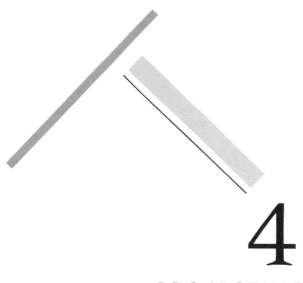

4

PROJECTING GENRES, PROJECTING SELVES

Godard's *Breathless*

In Jean-Luc Godard's classic film of the French New Wave, *Breathless* (*A bout du souffle*, 1960), Jean-Paul Belmondo plays Michel Poiccard, and Michel models himself after the heroes of American *film noir*, living out his life with a fatalism a degree removed from that of the characters he imitates. For if the fate of those characters is a function of the squalid American city they inhabit, Michel's fate is a result of his need to live out in Paris the role he learned from them. The light and shadow of the American films convey a pessimistic realism; things happen because a causality plays itself out to a bleak conclusion. In Godard's homage and subversion things happen because they are part of the script.

Michel is a petty gangster who kills a cop while traveling to Paris to collect money owed him and to persuade his girlfriend, Patricia Franchini (Jean Seberg), to run off with him. Patricia is an American studying at the Sorbonne and beginning a journalistic career; she also sells the *New York Herald Tribune* on the Champs-Elysées. Michel's love for Patricia is quixotic—he loves her for the same reason the romantic knight-errant loves Dulcinea. It is part of the chivalric tradition that knights love idealized women and dedicate their good deeds to them; and it is part of the *film noir* tradition that the protagonist loves a *femme fatale* who brings about his downfall in the end. And if Dulcinea is Don Quixote's invention, Patricia is Michel's, at least insofar as he is able to see her.

Michel—like Godard himself and all the New Wave directors—is fascinated by American films and, in a famous scene, imitates Humphrey Bogart in front of a movie poster of the star, rubbing his thumb across his lip, a Bogie mannerism he repeats throughout the film. Michel's tough guy cynicism and male chauvinism are puerile emulations of the American heroes he uses as models. When Patricia announces to him that she is pregnant he is irritated and reprimands her, telling her that she should have been more careful. This may be the epitome of male chauvinism, but it is also a result of the fact that the reality of Patricia's pregnancy is incomprehensible to Michel; it has no place in the script he lives. Her pregnancy—probably but not certainly by Michel—does, however, increase the urgency of her situation and contributes to her decision to remove herself from his script by reporting his whereabouts to the police. Of course that betrayal removes her from his script only from her perspective; it results in his death and therefore, from his perspective, consummates her role in his movie.

Michel is also a parody and caricature of the existential hero, carrying the supposed characteristics of that hero, based on a popularized and simplified understanding of those characteristics, to a nearly comic extreme. He is careless and impulsive, concerned only with the present, amoral, and alienated. He steals money from a girlfriend, sneaks out on paying a breakfast bill, steals cars when he needs them, robs a man when he is broke, and shoots a cop when he is about to be apprehended. Certain visual-verbal signs heighten the parodic aspect of this existential gangster. At one point the camera focuses on a sign that says, "To live dangerously to the end," words that echo a Nietzschean call to danger, an awareness of death, and an insistence on living in the present. At another point there is a poster for the movie *The Harder They Fall,* a title that suggests both the existentialist's awareness of death and the gangster's fated downfall.

Michel is a puerile imitation of an American movie gangster and he also echoes a kind of fashionable cafe existentialism, but both roles are overplayed. Some viewers might, indeed, take Michel's existentialism seriously and view his death as tragic or pathetic. But this would be to miss the parodic aspect of the movie. One simply cannot believe Michel Poiccard is in any sense "real." Late in the film Patricia herself says to him, "I've watched you for over ten minutes and I see nothing, nothing, nothing," and the viewer is inclined to agree. It is not that he is a bruised anti-hero who has learned to hide himself defensively, or that he suffers from an existential conflict between existence and essence. Rather, he has only as much reality as Andy Warhol claims to have—he is only a surface. It is easier to believe this of Michel than of Warhol, however, since Michel is incontrovertibly a character and not a person.

Allusions to film and art are frequent in *Breathless*. Throughout the film Patricia increasingly enters a realm of aesthetic and theatrical representations that are part of Michel's world. Indeed, her conflict is between the attraction she feels for that world and the attraction she feels for the world she is—and finally chooses to remain—a part of. At one point she and Michel hide from the police in a movie theatre. Clearly the conflict suggested is between Michel's movie world and the forces of "reality" that threaten it. Only his death can resolve the two: reality will collect its dues and his death will also provide a fully satisfactory conclusion to his own script.

The final "hide-out" of Patricia and Michel is the apartment of the girlfriend of one of Michel's associates. When they enter, the girl, a model, is in the midst of a photo session. After she and the photographer leave, Patricia, in a completely inexplicit way, hints at the possibility of her and Michel getting married. Michel asks if she would stop dating her boss—a journalist she has also been seeing who could be the father of her child, though she denies having slept with him—but the unstated subject is quickly dropped. They listen to a recording of a Mozart clarinet concerto and a fade-out/fade-in suggests the transition to the following morning. The fade-in is to the curtain of a loft that looks exactly like that of a stage. Michel, off camera, announces Patricia's name, as if she were a star. She opens the curtain revealing herself and gets up, walking by large murals that resemble the illusionistic flats of a stage set. The scenes in this apartment, in which everything is role or illusion—the role the model plays, photographic representations, the theatrical curtains and murals— highlight Patricia's entrance into a complicated world of signifiers behind which any sense of reality may get lost, just as the Michel behind the Bogie mask is either lost or non-existent. The compelling realities of her life—her pregnancy, her desire for freedom, her desire for a career, the obvious unsuitability of Michel for fatherhood, and her own romantic dreams— stand in stark contrast to this world and to Michel's *film noir* script. It is perhaps this irreconcilability that causes her to phone the police and report his whereabouts. At least one unresolved conflict of her life will be settled and things will be slightly less complicated.

When Patricia returns from an errand she tells Michel that she has reported him. A long, dizzying shot, tracks first her and then him around the apartment as they engage in a disjointed conversation in which they seem to speak as much to themselves as to each other. This shot suggests the conflict between them and their different dreams, and also suggests something of the vertiginous nature of Michel's world and the world of the apartment, in which Patricia seems temporarily caught but from which she is about to be extricated.

Shortly afterward, Michel is shot by the police on the street. His death is simply a continuation of his performance. He releases a puff of smoke after he falls—that last puff from the obligatory cigarette—makes a series of childlike faces at Patricia (echoing a game they played earlier), refers to something or someone as "disgusting" (Patricia? his situation? the role he is completing?) and dies, closing his eyes with his own fingers. The faces he makes are his parodies of Patricia's "looks," expressions she assumes in order to convey certain attitudes. Perhaps his parodies are meant to remind her of her own role playing. Patricia, regarding the dead Michel, rubs her thumb across her lip, repeating herself the Bogie mannerism that has been his habit throughout the film. The significance of this gesture is ambiguous. Perhaps it is simply a farewell gesture that carries with it some sentiment since it echoes Michel's visual "signature." Or perhaps it is a kind of "tit for tat": she mirrors his look for him after he mirrors her looks for her. Or perhaps Patricia has come to understand Michel's attitude toward self and role. Her final, visual response to him may be a recognition of their complicity, the fact that they are both playing the same game after all.

Michel is a character who imitates American movie gangsters, but that role is betrayed by his not quite comic exaggeration and schematization of the Bogart model. However, not only does Michel play a role, he is himself a character in a movie (*Breathless*) and seems aware of that fact, periodically turning to the camera and speaking directly to the audience. If Michel is a character who plays a role, *Breathless* is a film that plays a role: it parodies—through its plot, characters, and conventionalized jazz score—American *film noir* and gangster B-movies. But that parody, like Michel's role playing, is also exposed. Godard employs various devices that result in an opacity of the cinematic signifier and articulate a gap between *Breathless* and the films it emulates.

The most famous of these devices is his special use of the jump cut. Conventionally the jump cut is simply a way of eliding a portion of the narrative that the viewer can easily imagine and whose presentation would simply slow down the story. Thus, a shot of a man closing the door of an apartment on the tenth floor of a building may be followed by a simple cut to a shot of him closing the door of a taxi; it would be senseless to carry him down the elevator and out the lobby if nothing significant to the plot occurred in those places. Moreover, with this conventional kind of jump cut, some kind of continuity between the images is maintained—perhaps a formal similarity in direction of movement—so that the cut is as unobtrusive as possible, in spite of the elided material. Godard's jump cut is quite different. Godard cuts within a single action, but his cuts are not between shots that are significantly different in range or angle. It is as if the film has been damaged and frames have been removed from within a shot, producing a jerk in the movement of the image. This kind of cut is non-functional and highly obtrusive. The device, of course, has become more familiar since the release of *Breathless*—it has, in fact, become a stock device employed in experimental films and in music videos. But its effect at the time Godard employed it was—and to a great extent remains—highly Brechtian. Godard is generally recognized as the clearest example of a Brechtian filmmaker, both because of his political concerns (more overt in films made in the late nineteen-sixties and nineteen-seventies) and because of the distancing devices he employs, among which the jump cut of *Breathless* stands as a symbol for all the rest.[1]

But even Godard's other cuts are abrasive, and his editing often seems incoherent, though in less obvious ways. Continuity cutting—a set of conventionalized rules for making shot changes unobtrusive—is avoided. Angles may be changed for no apparent reason. Scenes may procede through a series of closeups without establishing shots so that the overall spatial relationships remain unclear. Leaps in time and space stand like confusing gaps in the narrative.

Furthermore, the camera is often hand-held, a simple device that reminds the viewer of the camera's presence. The sound track is similarly abrasive; traffic sounds and other environmental noises obtrude, making the dialogue difficult to understand. Volumes of various parts of the sound track may shift suddenly in ways that seem arbitrary; at least they cannot be rationalized on the basis of changes in the shot or scene. Similarly, the jazz track may shift volume suddenly, exaggerating the dramatic use of jazz in conventional gangster films and producing a Brechtian effect. At times there is a dissociation between sound and image: while a dialogue seems continuous and complete, shifts in the positions of the characters between shots suggest that something has been left out. In such instances the sound suggests that film time is equal to the time represented in the scene, but the visual aspect suggests that parts have been elided.

Scenes in *Breathless* are generally shot in one of two ways: either with the abrasive style of cutting described above or in one or a few very long takes, characterized by elaborate camera movement, the camera usually following characters as they move around or through an apartment, street, or building. Such long takes are reminiscent of some shots of Orson Welles, but are much more Brechtian in effect, a result of the generally hand-held camera. Moreover, at times frames from within such long shots are removed, producing jump cuts and creating a synthesis of Godard's dissonant editing and his long take style.

These aspects of the film's style and technique may be partly explained on the basis of pragmatic and economic exigencies. The film's low budget makes its B-movie allusion felicitous. That low budget necessitated the hand-held camera and even the use of a supermarket cart as a dolly. In addition, the film, as originally shot, was much too long—about three hours as opposed to the hour and a half to which it was finally cut. Godard chose to shorten it not by eliminating scenes or segments but by keeping all the shots, shortening each to what was absolutely essential.[2] This partly explains the staccato editing that is the film's most obvious stylistic feature. Still, the consistency of the style of *Breathless* with Godard's later films— which push the disruptive aspect of his style even further when there was less economic necessity to do so—and the appropriateness of these devices for the obviously self-referential aspects of plot and characters make it clear that they are not merely pragmatic and economic. Perhaps aspects of the style of *Breathless* were first conceived as a result of Godard's need to conserve money and time, but having been identified they were subsequently used as part of a coherent Brechtian film style.

The screenplay for *Breathless* was based on a scenario written by Francois Truffaut in 1957. Truffaut's main character in this unrealized project was named Antoine Doinel, the character finally realized in his cycle of films beginning with *The Four Hundred Blows* (*Les Quatre cents coups*, 1959). It is easy to imagine the Antoine of *Four Hundred Blows* as the central character of a film with the same general plot as *Breathless*. If this older Antoine, a young man rather than a boy, were the protagonist of a *Breathless* directed by Truffaut rather than Godard and were played by Jean-Pierre Leaud (who played Antoine Doinel in all of Truffaut's films of that cycle) rather than Jean-Paul Belmondo, it would have been an extremely different film. Truffaut's films are nearly always poignant and few moments in film history are more poignant than the famous final freeze frame of *Four Hundred Blows*, depicting the face of Antoine Doinel, abused, neglected, and misunderstood by school, family, and criminal justice system, gazing into the camera after he has escaped from a juvenile home. *Breathless* could have been filmed as a continuation of the Antoine

Doinel story, the tragic end of an individual outcast through no fault of his own, and the death of Antoine could easily have been made into an emotionally moving scene. Antoine Doinel, however, is a far cry from Michel Poiccard, in spite of their common origin. Godard, in his filming of the death of Michel Poiccard, and Belmondo, in his performance of that scene, avoid all poignance; the scene, instead, is characterized by wry wit and critical distance. One has little sense of Godard's Michel as a sympathetic criminal, someone outcast because of the abuse and neglect of social institutions. One has little sense of Michel as having any history at all, in fact. Rather, he dies because he imitates characters in movies he has seen. One does not feel sympathy but examines his death as one would examine the death of an actor performing a role in a Brechtian manner. Later Godard would, indeed, put the fate of individuals into a larger social context of power, economics, and language, but his tone would remain extremely cool. In *Breathless* such issues are barely implied.

Truffaut's freeze frame stands in significant contrast to Godard's jump cut. The frozen shot of Antoine exists as if to allow the audience a moment to contemplate a face that presumably reveals a character's soul: the face expresses a disarming directness and candor that exist in spite of its isolation and inevitable hardening. None of this suggestion of a suffering personality behind the mask exists in the character of Michel Poiccard, who is nothing more than a mask, a character in a film; the jump cut serves as one of numerous reminders that this is, in fact, really all that he is.

Of course self-reference is characteristic of Truffaut's films too. His films are filled with allusions to works of literature and film that have been important to him, and many of his movies, like Godard's *Breathless,* are examinations of certain genres of film making—the gangster film, the romance, and the science fiction film, for example. *Day for Night (La Nuit americaine,* 1973) is a full blown meta-movie, a movie about making a movie, in which Leaud plays the leading man, a character with a personality similar to the Antoine of the later films of the Antoine Doinel cycle, and Truffaut himself plays the director. Some Brechtian devices are also employed. During the credits an optically printed sound track corresponding to the actual audible sound track is projected visibly onto the screen; the visual pattern that encodes sound on cellulose can be decoded visually as well as aurally. The fact that it is decoded here in both ways simultaneously and that one of those ways—the visual projection of the sound track—is unconventional forces the audience to attend to aspects of the process of cinematic replication: the projection of light through translucent cellulose and the auditory playback of recorded sounds.

But for Truffaut, the balance between homage and critical distance shifts much more strongly toward the side of homage. His works stand more as affectionate tributes to the models they parody than as critical examinations of them. And *Day for Night* is itself a tribute to the process of film making as an activity and a work, to the intense struggle of a director, crew, and cast to make a film in spite of seemingly overwhelming factors that work against and sometimes prevent its completion—the extreme complexity of a large collaborative creative project; the director's own difficulties in grappling with creative and practical problems in realizing the project; the frivolity and unpredictability of human beings involved in the production; and, even, the disruption of death. It is significant that, in spite of important similarities, there should be such a contrast between the two most important New Wave directors as well as between their earliest features, the two films that virtually defined the movement. Both directors view film as a phenomenon of the intelligence, a vehicle for the elucidation of ideas, and both are concerned with the nature of film language and its narrative structure.[3] But when Truffaut examines the conventions of film, alludes to films and literary works, or makes a film about film making, he does so with great affection; when Godard does these things he does them with critical analysis and distance.

Later Godard's film making becomes much more radical politically as well as formally, and his style and themes become even more self-referential. Ultimately narrative is nearly entirely abandoned, and film becomes for him a mode of thinking about relations of power, money, sex, language, and signs. *Two or Three Things I Know About Her* (*2 ou 3 choses que je sais d'elle*, 1966) is really a visual-auditory essay on these issues, loosely surrounding a minimal narrative that consists of the events in a day in the life of a Parisian housewife who prostitutes herself during the day in order to improve her financial situation. There is an intense formal disjunction in the film, not only between and within images themselves but also among the various elements of the film—the images, its language, other sounds, and music. Godard's own voice-over intensifies the implication that in this film he *"thinks with* images and sounds."[4] The minimal narrative functions only as a provocation for his critical inquiry into the social, economic, and sexual structure of the region of Paris. Godard's sharing of the contemporary obsession with the role of language in shaping human consciousness is evident throughout, perhaps most blatant in his voice-over paraphrase of Wittgenstein: "The limits of language are those of the world . . . the limits of my language are those of my world."[5] Further radicalization after the strikes and demonstrations of 1968 has led not only to an increasing difficulty in Godard's style but also to a quest for alternate forms of production and distribution that have made most, though not quite all, of his later works—most of which have been the results of collaboration, first with Jean-Pierre Gorin and subsequently with Anne-Marie Mieville—unavailable to most viewers.[6]

Bergman's *Persona*

Elisabeth Vogler (Liv Ullmann), in Ingmar Bergman's *Persona* (1966), is an actress who decides not to act. She is complex, sophisticated, aware, and disenchanted. She stops speaking for over a minute during a performance of *Electra* and afterward refuses to speak and act in life as well as in the theatre. She is put under the care of Alma (Bibi Andersson), a seemingly uncomplicated, conventional, and idealistic nurse. If all roles are masks or fictions, Elisabeth's refusal to engage in speech and action suggests a refusal to participate in the inevitable lie of life, or so she would persuade herself. But she is also engaging in a form of what existentialists would call bad faith—persuading herself that it is possible not to act and not to be ethically engaged. Alma, on the other hand, is locked into, or chooses to limit her understanding of herself to, what phenomenologists call the "natural attitude"—a belief that she is nothing more than a sum of facts about herself. When she introduces herself to Elisabeth she enumerates some of those pertinent facts: her name is Sister Alma, she is twenty-five years old, she is engaged to be married, she graduated from nursing school two years ago, her parents own a farm, her mother also was a nurse. If Elisabeth, having worn many masks on as well as off stage, decides to wear no mask, Alma does not question her own single mask—her *persona*—and believes that this mask is an identity with her self. Elisabeth is too sophisticated to make the same mistake. Yet, as her perceptive doctor notes, Elisabeth's silence is itself only another role that she will eventually tire of. Moreover, reality will not allow her the luxury of silence and inaction. In spite of her efforts, it will make its way into her attempted isolation and force her to react. In *Persona* the reality that makes inevitable incursions into individual psyches is represented on the personal level by the existence of Elisabeth's husband and son and on the larger social and political level by a photograph that she carries of a boy from the Warsaw ghetto being arrested by Nazis and by a television news film she watches of a Buddhist monk immolating himself in Vietnam.

Elisabeth's doctor suggests that the two women go off together to a beach cottage she owns. Probably the doctor is aware that this therapeutic vacation is not simply a way of encouraging Elisabeth's recovery from her vague illness, but that Alma will also be affected by the relationship that will result from the women's shared seclusion. Elisabeth will function as a catalyst in transforming Alma from the simple girl she seems to be to someone more aware of her own complexity. Alma, as well as Elisabeth, is being treated. The maladies of the two women are complementary, the one attempting to reject all masks or roles, the other accepting her one mask without question. Alma's acceptance of her identity as something clear, uncomplex, straightforward, and obvious may be a result of simple naïveté; or it may be a defense against the ineffability and unpredictability that lies just below her surface. Alma names herself and makes herself into an object that can be easily described and understood in order to control herself, in order to domesticate herself and define away anything wild she may contain. The doctor plays a godgame (to use John Fowles's term from *The Magus*) and, under the guise of a doctor-nurse-patient relationship, sets up a situation designed to provoke a shattering growth for nurse as well as patient.

The fact that Alma is intimidated by Elisabeth is suggested from the outset, her statement of the facts of her identity apparently a defense of the role she wishes to keep when confronted by something that threatens it. After visiting Elisabeth again, Alma, alone in her room, reconfirms to herself her plans for the future, finding comfort in the fact that they are clear and determined. Of course Alma's role—like any mask—is not significant merely because of what it is but also because of what it is not, because of what it denies. As Alma's relationship to Elisabeth grows it becomes increasingly apparent that there is much about Alma—an erotic and violent potential—that is left out of the self-definition she consciously states. The fundamental threat to Alma's identity that Elisabeth represents is made explicit shortly afterward when Alma tells the doctor she may not be the right person to work with Mrs. Vogler because she may not be able to deal with her mentally.

Elisabeth, in the manner of other Bergman artists, has little warmth in her immediate relationships with other human beings. She is emotionally moved by the Buddhist's immolation and the boy from the ghetto—both of which she experiences only through representations—but seems incapable of love for her son and may also have difficulty expressing it towards her husband. Early in the film she laughs at a sentimental melodrama on the radio, but is moved by a Bach sonata on a different station. Emotion, for Elisabeth, must be refined, sublimated, or otherwise mediated. Significantly, the dialogue of the melodrama suggests the themes of guilt and loneliness, major Bergman obsessions. The sentimental words uttered on the radio are not really so different from the existential dialogue of a character in a Bergman film. Later, after the crisis in their relationship, Alma's words resemble those of the radio character. By the same token, those words may not be so far from expressing feelings Elisabeth herself has had, perhaps in relation to an absent God if not to a fickle lover or friend.

Though Elisabeth's rejection of the popular melodrama is apparently the result of her preference for aesthetically superior forms, it may also result from the fact that the melodrama strikes too close to home for her comfort and that the emotions expressed are too blatant and undisguised. Ethically and aesthetically, Elisabeth removes herself from what is immediate and responds to what is distanced. She responds to major human atrocities she sees in pictures, but abdicates responsibility for those with whom she is personally engaged.

The relationship between the two women can be taken as a literal relationship between two people or, metaphorically, as a relationship between two parts of a single person. Since the "reality" of the film's narrative becomes increasingly surreal as the film progresses, even if the film is viewed generally on the more literal level, numerous scenes must be understood as exteriorizations of aspects of their relationship rather than as actual occurrences. On the metaphoric level the film involves the description of a single *persona,* in the sense of *person* rather than *mask.* The development of the film is the representation of a dialogue between self and mask and finally a resolution of the conflict between them, with Elisabeth representing the self and Alma the mask. There are ironies here. Elisabeth, the actress, is *not* the mask, as one might expect. She has decided not to act, to take off her mask. Moreover, Alma's name means "soul" in Spanish as well as "nurturing" in Latin, but metaphorically she suggests the mask. She defines herself as her role. This is, of course, a simplification; both women have both parts and enact, within themselves individually, the same struggle. But also between them, metaphorically, they play out the struggle.[7]

On the island Alma, previously a listener, is locked into a situation with someone who refuses to speak. As if silence were a vacuum that must be filled, Alma begins speaking herself and soon reveals aspects of her character that are inconsistent with the personality she asserts. Elisabeth acts like a classical psychoanalyst, silent, seemingly withholding judgment, a figure upon whom the patient projects any personality that is appropriate for her psyche. Elisabeth holds the power; not only is she a famous actress Alma stands in awe of, but she learns a great deal about Alma, who learns nothing about her. In this case the speaker has less power than the silent one. Susan Sontag, comparing the situation in the film to that in Strindberg's one-act play, *The Stronger*, writes, "as in the Strindberg play, the one who talks, who spills her soul, turns out to be weaker than the one who keeps silent."[8]

In a long monologue Alma relates her experience of a spontaneous orgy that she and a friend had with two strange boys on a beach. The result was a pregnancy, the deception of her fiancé, an abortion, and continuing guilt. She is unable to reconcile these experiences with the persona she has chosen; they stand as subversive facts that lie just below the personality she defines, making it impossible for her to accept her Sister Alma role with the comfort and confidence she would like. It is because of the presence of these incongruous aspects of her character that she immediately recognizes Elisabeth as a potential threat. Yet quickly she begins to read Elisabeth as a sympathetic listener and comes to recognize the therapeutic value of a confidant. For Alma the relationship becomes affectionate and sisterly, with sexual overtones. Because Elisabeth does not speak, it is hard to say whether she reciprocates those feelings or is simply curious and non-judgmental. Certain actions and expressions of the silent Elisabeth do suggest that Alma's feelings are at least partly reciprocated, though they may also suggest simply a bemusement with the younger, unsophisticated girl.

The turning point of the film occurs when Alma opens an unsealed letter Elisabeth has written. In it Elisabeth, describing Alma, reveals her feeling of superiority to her and indicates that she enjoys studying the girl. As with other Bergman artists—such as the father in *Through a Glass Darkly* (*Sasom i en spegel,* 1961), who cooly studies the psychological degeneration of his daughter—Elisabeth enjoys clinically observing Alma, possibly in order to get ideas that might at some point prove useful to her on stage. Whether this attitude negates the possibility of her simultaneously valuing their relationship on a more personal level is not made clear, but Alma responds as if it does. Thereafter both women feel betrayed, Alma for being made into an object, something an artist studies for what she can learn, and Elisabeth for having her personal correspondence opened by someone for whom it was not intended. The primary guilt for the incident is perhaps Alma's, for opening the letter, though Elisabeth's handing it to her unsealed suggests that she planned or hoped that Alma would do what she did.

With the exception of a self-referential and surrealistic prologue the film up to this point has been realistic in that the sequence of actions represented has been generally plausible, given the premise outlined at the beginning: an actress, for obscure psychological or philosophical reasons, decides to stop speaking and to reduce as much as possible her involvement in life. After the opening of the letter the film becomes increasingly surrealistic; some scenes seem to have really happened, some seem to be dreams, some are ambiguous. In fact the film achieves a level where it is unnecessary and fruitless to attempt to rationalize what is shown as dream or reality. Improbable scenes need not be justified on the basis of possibility nor need they be interpreted as the dreams of one of the two women. They can be regarded as exteriorizations of the two women's psycho-social reality or of the relationship between two parts of a single psyche. Robin Wood says that such scenes are to be understood as *"in some sense* really happening."[9]

The more surrealistic second part of the film is characterized by overt and intense conflict and violence between the two women, as well as a power shift in their relationship. The division between the two parts is marked by a brief self-referential interlude—including an illusion of the film burning up in the projector—that occurs after Alma, in retribution for the betrayal she discovers, leaves a piece of broken glass in a place where Elisabeth will likely step on it. After Elisabeth does in fact step on it close-ups of their faces reveal an awareness of something new in their relationship. Alma has been surprised and hurt, but her violence demonstrates that there is something in her that Elisabeth did not anticipate and that Elisabeth will have to contend with. Not only does Alma have an erotic side not immediately evident from her surface, she has a potential for violence when provoked that is even less evident.

The personalities of the two women begin to merge, and Bergman employs various devices—some verbal, some visual—to create this sense of merging personalities. A struggle ensues between the impulse to merge, on the one hand, and the desire not to merge, on the other. Both women take both sides in the conflict at different points. Elisabeth, at times, is portrayed as a vampire who sucks Alma's blood (literally at one point), but at other times she draws back when Alma begins to understand her, as if clairvoyantly. Alma seeks to reestablish their friendship after the crisis, but resists when she feels herself *becoming* Elisabeth. Overall, Alma gradually achieves dominance and Elisabeth is reduced to passivity and near catatonia. The dual impulse toward and against reconciliation and merger can be understood on both the literal and metaphoric levels. On the literal level it is a struggle between the impulse to love to the point of ego dissolution and the impulse to remain separate and maintain one's integrity. On the metaphoric level it is the struggle of the psyche to integrate itself as opposed to the tendency to keep its aspects compartmentalized: the ego or *persona* that wishes to keep its darker aspects at bay and simultaneously wishes to harmonize itself by incorporating those darker aspects.

In the end this highly disturbing film, filled with emotional and physical violence, is optimistic. During several "dream" scenes the division between the two personalities becomes obscure, Alma achieves a violent domination of Elisabeth, Elisabeth becomes nearly catatonic, and language disintegrates into incoherent sequences of words and phrases. Alma wakes to discover Elisabeth packing. She finishes preparing the house to be closed up and Elisabeth seems no longer to be present. Viewing herself in a mirror, Alma brushes her hair back. An image seen twice earlier in the film is superimposed over her mirror reflection. This is a shot of the faces of both women, Elisabeth behind Alma, pulling Alma's hair back, away from her face. The presentation of Elisabeth's image here as an illusion—part of a superimposition dissolved over a shot of Alma's mirror reflection—combined with the fact that Elisabeth is suddenly and inexplicably no longer present suggests the primacy of the metaphoric level of interpretation of *Persona*. We never see a "real" Elisabeth leave the cottage and here she exists only as an image in or aspect of Alma's mind. After much violence, Alma has reconciled herself with her own Elisabeth. Perhaps Elisabeth never existed at all as a separate person and Alma always was the real—and only—patient. Alma leaves alone, seemingly at peace. Two quick shots of Elisabeth, involved in theatrical and film performances, are inserted as Alma leaves, suggesting Elisabeth's continuing presence in Alma as she begins to resume her life after her violently therapeutic retreat. On the more literal level they suggest in Elisabeth a development that complements that of Alma. Elisabeth is now willing to assume roles again, and Alma has learned that she is more than a single role. Finally, the inserted shots function as a transition to a surrealistic and self-referential epilogue that, in conjunction with the prologue, forms a frame for the film's narrative.

Persona hovers between surrealistic psychodrama and postmodern obsession with and consideration of the power of art, theatre, and language. The bewildering and disturbing prologue presents in a non-narrative fashion themes that will emerge from the story. The first image in the film is an extreme close-up of the striking of an arc of light between two glowing carbon rods of a projector bulb; this is followed by close-ups of parts of a projector in motion and then by film leader with numbers counting down seconds to the start of the film. Of course in this case the film has really already begun and the leader is itself part of the movie. There is a zoom into the front of a lens and a cartoon figure is seen upside down, as if the film is being viewed as it moves through the projector rather than as it is projected onto a screen. Thus, the film begins with images of a film beginning. According to Bruce Kawin, the earliest images of the film are a representation of its constituting itself, a process analogous to a personality's constituting itself. Kawin suggests a metaphor between the "masking" of white light by a film strip and the creation of a persona from a self.[10] A visible image can be formed only if parts of a bulb's projection are blocked out—masked—by darker, more opaque areas on sections of cellulose, just as an individual can only exist in the world if she is willing to assume roles, wear "masks," that will always "project" less of her than what she feels herself to be.

The self-referential images that initiate the film gradually give way to a sequence of shots that are of a more surrealistic or symbolic nature, relating to themes of death, disease, isolation, and suffering. Included are several shots of a sheep being slaughtered, followed by several of a nail being driven into a hand. The Christ connotations are obvious, even heavy handed. The suffering of Christ clearly is to be related to the suffering that results from the psychological cruelty between the two women as well as that represented in the photograph of the Jewish boy and the film of the Buddhist monk. A number of shots relating to death appear: a churchyard in winter, corpses of old people, a boy in a hospital room. The auditory modulation of the sound of churchbells into the sound of a ringing telephone help effect a transition to a longer sequence of the sick boy. His room, like the one the corpses are in—apparently a morgue—is white, unadorned, and antiseptic, like many of the images of *Persona*. These visually austere images have a classical, geometric simplicity and formality.

It is almost inevitable that the viewer will associate the sick boy—who reappears in the epilogue—with *Elisabeth's* son, at least in retrospect. But he also has associations with things that lie outside the film *Persona* itself. He is the same actor—and probably must be viewed as the same character—as the boy in Bergman's *The Silence* (*Tystnaden*, 1963). He is reading the same book as the character in that movie, who was the neglected son of one of two sisters whose relationship to a great extent parallels that of the women in *Persona*. More significantly, the boy suggests Bergman himself, who conceived of *Persona* while hospitalized, believed for a time he would never again make a movie, and was bothered by a persistently ringing telephone.[11]

The boy gets up and moves slowly toward the camera, as if he sees something, as if he has perhaps noticed our presence as audience to his illness. He moves his hand in front of him, as if feeling from behind the large flat surface of the movie screen. This is one of several shots in *Persona* in which characters seem to watch the audience watching them. There is a cut to a one hundred eighty degree reverse shot and we see the screen he is watching, a large, glowing surface upon which large images of Elisabeth's and Alma's faces, in extremely soft focus, slowly dissolve back and forth. This is the first of many shots in which the two faces are visually related so as to suggest that they are different aspects of the same character rather than two different people. The boy, like other Bergman characters, is unhealthy, neglected, and dependent on the mother figure from whom he is separated—here by a transparent, invisible, impenetrable screen, and in the film's narrative by Elisabeth's emotional remoteness that prevents her functioning as a "nurturing" mother, as an *"alma" mater*. The women's faces presented in this way—hazy, shifting images on something that is perhaps more like a large television screen than a movie screen—have an archetypal quality, the technological counterpart of the stone goddesses represented in prehistoric carvings. An electronic tone gets slowly louder and reaches a climax with the interruption of a percussive, electronic accompaniment to the title sequence. The credits are given simply, black letters on a white ground, and are separated by extremely quick shots (lasting no more than a fraction of a second) of various images: several of the boy's face, a few of Elisabeth's face, a few of Alma's, the Buddhist monk burning, trees, the sea, rocks on the beach, a fragment of a slapstick comedy, as well as others. There is a cut to white and a dissolve to a shot of a white wall with a white door. The door opens, Alma enters, and the doctor's voice, off camera, begins describing to the nurse the case of Elisabeth Vogler. The narrative begins.

The prologue, along with the shorter epilogue and the brief interlude that interrupts the narrative, establishes a metacinematic frame for the film. The film is not only a story about a relationship between two women but is a film about its own telling. Bergman himself has spoken of the film's "impatience to get started,"[12] as if it had a will of its own. This is reminiscent of Pirandello's attribution of will to the characters he conceived, though in this case it is the film itself that is the willful character. The film's struggle to manifest itself is, as Kawin notes, analogous to the struggle of an individual "self" to realize itself by assuming a "mask."

At one point in the film Alma says that she, with great effort, could become like Elisabeth, but that Elisabeth, on the other hand, could easily perform Alma. But if Elisabeth did perform Alma, Elisabeth's soul would be too big for the character and would quickly break out. Similarly, at one point the "soul" of the film seems too big for its "mask." This occurs during the "break-up" of the film, the interlude that takes place just after the turning point in the narrative—after Alma reads the letter and Elisabeth cuts her foot on the glass intentionally left in her path. It is as if the feelings the film wants to represent are too big for the capacity of film to represent. Again, one is reminded of Pirandello: his notion of a struggle between "life" and "form" and the formal devices he utilized to dramatize this struggle. The interlude interrupts the film's narrative just as members of the play audience interrupt the play-within-the-play of *Each in His Own Way*. A shot of Alma staring out the window—perhaps at Elisabeth, who is outdoors—is interrupted by what appears to be a crack in the film, projected visibly onto the screen. Then a frame seems to burn up, a garbled voice (perhaps a recording of a voice played backwards) accompanies a white screen. Images from the prologue are echoed: flashes of what appear to be a slapstick comedy and a primitive horror film are interrupted by a nail being hammered into the palm of a hand, this time accompanied by agonized groans. There is an extreme close-up of an eye and a slow zoom even closer into its white. This image dissolves into an extremely out-of-focus shot of a room of the cottage. Elisabeth enters, moves across the room, leaves it, and reenters. Focus remains extremely fuzzy and time shifts between an apparent slowed down projection, normal speed, and freeze frames. Time becomes normal, suddenly the image pops into focus, and the narrative resumes. The story cannot be told; the story will be told.

The epilogue is a highly condensed reversal of the prologue. The two quick shots of Elisabeth performing interrupt Alma's departure from the cottage. In the first of these shots Elisabeth is in the midst of a performance of Electra on stage. In the second she is reflected, upside-down, in what appears to be a mirror on the front of a movie camera. This mirror suggests the "reflective" nature of cinematography, and also suggests that we are looking into the lens at the image the camera is "seeing." The camera is on a crane moving down to a shot of Elisabeth on a bed. There is a cut to a shot of the bus on which Alma leaves, the camera pans and tilts down to the ground, and the image dissolves to the shot of the boy moving his hand over the hazy image of the remote archetypal mother. The image in front of the boy fades to white, and there is a cut to a shot of film slipping off the gears of a projector and a reel stopping. Then the glowing carbon rods, which initiated *Persona* and whose light in fact initiates all films, separate and go dim. In contrast to Pirandello's plays, this film has somehow managed to get itself started and, in spite of a major disruption, restarted; it has said what it has to say. Both in the narrative and in the metacinematic frame, there is a sense that in *Persona* something has, indeed, been achieved.

Persona is a film that attempts to give expression to what may be inexpressible. But it is also about that very attempt, about the problem of representation itself, especially when what is to be represented involves imponderable or paradoxical facts or circumstances: extreme cruelty and suffering, and the impossibility of living in the world conjoined with the impossibility of not living in the world. Acting in the world is equated with assuming a mask, and assuming a mask is accepting a sign, a name, a signifier that will never adequately represent its signified, but that nevertheless cannot be dispensed with. A movie is also such a signifier and is caught between the necessity and impossibility of expression. The only thing worse than speech is silence.

Persona's self-referentiality is predominantly Pirandellian. Even the shots of projectors and film—which may, indeed, have a Brechtian effect in reminding us that what we are watching is a film—occur as images inside *Persona* and are part of its illusion, are not a straightforward laying naked of *Persona*'s own machinery. (An authentically Brechtian device would be to move the real projector forward in the theatre so that the audience would continually notice the film image as a projection emanating from a mechanical apparatus.) Nevertheless, Bergman does utilize film devices that are genuinely Brechtian. As in Godard's film, these involve aspects of the editing and camera work that violate the conventions of the traditional, illusionistic, well wrought narrative movie. The film narrative itself (not the metacinematic prologue, interlude, and epilogue) is characterized by extremely long takes. Many scenes are shot entirely in close-ups, with few or no establishing shots that clarify the spatial relationships of the individuals. The editing of scenes involving two individuals (which is most scenes in the film) only occasionally falls into conventional shot/reverse shot patterning, and shots linger for inordinately long periods of time on either the speaker or the listener in the one-sided conversations that take place. Sometimes scenes are done in one shot only, showing only one of the characters: the reverse shot never occurs.

This shooting and editing style tends to focus attention on the performer, and certainly much of the power of the film has to do with the incredible performances of the actors—Ullmann's is remarkable because she must convey her role with no lines at all and Andersson's is remarkable because she has all of the lines. The style also has a certain expressionistic power. Location becomes vague; the predominance of close-ups of faces, along with the uncertainty of spatial relationships, results in a feeling that the two individuals occupy a kind of abstract space. This is especially true of the hospital scenes, where the abstraction of the style is reinforced by the bare, antiseptic environment. The characters seem to hang in space; they could be anywhere or nowhere at all and each of them could be anybody. Hanging in space this way, oppositions and parallels are established between them, and the often noted theme of *doubling*[13] is reinforced by the abstraction.

But the style also creates Brechtian distancing because it violates conventions and leaves gaps in our understanding of the space the film incompletely describes. The close-up is important not only because of what it says but also because of what it leaves unsaid. A scene in which Alma reads to Elisabeth a letter from her husband occurs in the hospital, early in the film. It begins with a shot of Alma's left hand and Elisabeth's right hand, holding the letter. Alma takes the letter from Elisabeth and asks if she would like her to open it. The camera follows Alma's hands as she takes it and opens it, and tilts up to her face as she asks if she should read it aloud. Elisabeth does not speak so we hear no reply to Alma's questions. Furthermore, the film does not give us what we would normally expect: a shot of Elisabeth's face that would let us see the visual answer she is evidently providing. We surmise her "answers" to Alma from Alma's actions, but a tension is created because of the lack of "suture": the scene is not tied together by complementary shots into a visually coherent whole. Alma reads the personal letter, pausing once to ask if she should continue. The fact that she does continue allows us again to surmise what we do not see.

This technically simple scene—which consists up to this point of a single shot—is actually quite complex in terms of the information it provides and denies. Alma's personality is revealed through her desire to be helpful, which conflicts with her hesitation to intrude upon what seems to her to be none of her business. Although we surmise the denotation of Elisabeth's responses, we have no idea of much beyond that: is she eager to hear the letter, indifferent, or anxious about what it may contain? Her decision to remain remote, whatever her emotions are, is emphasized by her invisibility off camera as well as by her silence. The scene also creates a dissonance between visual and auditory, non-verbal and verbal, information. If Alma were speaking as Alma there would be a congruence between the information received through both channels. For the most part, however, Alma does not speak as Alma but reads the letter from

Elisabeth's husband. That letter reveals much about him and more about the relationship between him and Elisabeth, something which is different from the immediate relationship between the women in the scene, though it partly parallels it. Thus, this simply executed scene requires a complex and active attention from the audience—we make determinations about Alma from what we actually see and hear through Bibi Andersson's performance; we make surmises about the silent and absent Elisabeth based on actions of Alma that we understand to be responses to something Elisabeth does; and we learn about Elisabeth's husband and her relationship to him through the words of the letter Alma reads.

Finally a reverse shot of Elisabeth is given. Alma reaches a point in the letter that is perhaps too personal, and Elisabeth grabs it from her. There is a cut to a low angle shot of Elisabeth, appearing cold and angry. From this low angle she looms large and powerful above. Closure is finally established through the reverse shot, but it is provided by means of a fearsome image. The fearsome quality of that image is enhanced by Elisabeth's actions. Alma—her voice off camera now—says that a photo of Elisabeth's son has also been included in the letter. Elisabeth takes it, stares at it for several moments, and then, in a considered, deliberate fashion, tears it in half.

In this scene, as in many of the scenes of *Persona*, Bergman subverts film conventions and creates a Brechtian effect by radically under-editing. Certainly there are many ways this scene might have been shot and edited without seeming so unusual, but the most common would have been to have a more frequent interplay between shot and reverse shot. In this case, the reverse shots would all be "reaction" shots of Elisabeth. The scene could have also been done in long takes, but could have clarified spatial relationships and provided direct visual information about Elisabeth by shooting from a longer range or by moving the camera across space. Alternatively, flashbacks of Elisabeth and her husband could have been included to accompany the letter Alma reads; this would result in a greater congruence between word and image and would seem to utilize the cinematic medium more fully. To leave the camera on a person speaking for an undue length of time is, on the face of it, quite uncinematic, though it is a standard Bergman stylism. Bergman, however, chooses to create distance and lack of closure in the audience by violating normal expectations regarding cinematic exposition. Certainly there is also a dramatic effect to the device as well. A great deal of tension is created through the purely formal device of under-editing so that when the shot of Elisabeth finally comes the closure and resolution that occurs is more intensely felt than that which normally exists when a scene is regularly "sutured"[14] through shot and reverse shot. Still, the satisfaction the audience receives from that closure and resolution is compromised by the awesome content of the shot. Here, as elsewhere, *Persona* locates itself between the formal-expressionist aesthetic of modernism and the self-referentiality of post-modernism.

One of the most striking scenes in the film occurs near the end, when Alma delivers a long monologue describing to Elisabeth Elisabeth's pregnancy, the delivery of her child, and her experiencing her role as mother. This scene is the culmination of the tendency of the two personalities to merge, as suggested by the whole development of their relationship as well as by various other aspects of the film: lines where Alma speaks suddenly, briefly, perhaps accidently, as if she were Elisabeth; a surrealistic scene between Alma and Elisabeth's husband—who appears suddenly and inexplicably at the cottage one evening—in which Alma "plays" Elisabeth perfectly as Elisabeth watches; and the many shots in which Bergman and his cinematographer, Sven Nykvist, create a visual interplay between the faces of the two women.

In this scene the first shot is again a close-up of hands. Shots of hands are an obsessive motif in the film and here Elisabeth's hands are shown covering something. Alma's right hand enters as she asks what it is that Elisabeth has. Elisabeth does not want to reveal it so Alma pries Elisabeth's right hand off a photograph. (Earlier Elisabeth handed the letter to Alma freely.) Alma observes that the hidden object is the photo of Elisabeth's son that she had torn up (though now it seems to be in one piece) and the camera tilts up to both their faces as Alma says that they should discuss the matter. There is a cut to a shot of Elisabeth over Alma's shoulder, and Alma's extended monologue begins. She describes to Elisabeth the circumstances under which Elisabeth decided to become pregnant, her misgivings when she did become pregnant, the fact that she tried to terminate the pregnancy, her hope that the child would be born dead, the unhealthy child's extreme dependence on his mother, and her repugnance for the child. Throughout the monologue it is evident from Elisabeth's reactions that Alma's words are painful and correct. Alma's monologue is delivered entirely as a voice-over, during four shots of Elisabeth listening, each moving to a closer view of her face, from approximately Alma's point of view.

After the monologue is completed, however, the entire scene is repeated, beginning with the shot of the women's hands. This time the four shots are increasingly closer views of Alma, delivering the monologue on camera. As the monologue ends the second time, half of Elisabeth's face is briefly superimposed over the shadowed left half of Alma's (the right half from the viewer's position). Significantly, during the first half of this doubled scene it was Elisabeth's right side (the left from the viewer's position) that was shadowed. These reversed shadows reinforce the interpretation of their roles as complementary; each is the other's darkened half. Alma then asserts that she is not like Elisabeth, she reasserts her role as nurse, and then shouts again that she is not Elisabeth Vogler, "you" are Elisabeth Vogler. Her sentences degenerate into fragments, and the right side of Elisabeth's face is again merged to the left side of Alma's. This time the merger is more permanent and the frozen image lasts for many seconds as the frame slowly fades to white and the scene ends. Because the faces are similar but far from identical, the result is a horrifying asymmetry. Yet the union is complete and both sides are now lit.

The decision to repeat this scene was made during the film's editing. Shots of the two women could have been alternated to produce a single edited version of the scene that would have been organized as something like a conventional shot/reverse shot structure. In fact, Bergman originally cut it this way but felt that "something was missing."[15] Because it is repeated, each performance is seen in its entirety, without interruption. The significance of the scene, which culminates in what might be regarded as the film's climax—the complete merger of the personalities—is emphasized. Moreover, there is a great formality—almost a monumentality—to the way it is done, the second version perfectly balancing and paralleling the first. But the effect is also Brechtian. This is only partly a result of the simple fact that such a repetition is unconventional. To utilize repetition inside a narrative this way is a flagrant subversion of the film's illusionistic power. If the compelling performances and emotionally charged content were to draw the viewer into an excessively strong emotional connection with the scene represented, as indeed they might here, the scene's immediate repetition is a startling reminder that the viewer is experiencing a representation. There is no way to forget the difference between representation and represented when two different representations of the same represented are immediately juxtaposed.

The films of Godard and Bergman illustrate cinematic correlatives to the theatrical techniques of Brecht and Pirandello. Godard is *the* Brechtian film maker. His use of the jump cut in *Breathless* itself stands as a sign for a variety of techniques that he utilized to foreground cinematic artifice. But the film also involves an implied film-in-a-film, parodying the American gangster *film noir* just as its protagonist models himself after the protagonists of those films. The prologue, interlude, and epilogue of *Persona* create an overt metacinematic frame, making explicit the fact that *Persona* is not only a film about two women, but is also a film about a film about two women. Bergman's editing produces audience distance because it is unconventional and because the gaps it leaves in the space that it describes result in a lack of closure and put great demands on the audience. Perhaps Godard is more uncompromisingly postmodern than Bergman. One must ask of Michel Poiccard—as one must ask of Warhol's *Marilyn*—if there is any "self" at all behind the mask. The relationship between Bergman's two women, however, connoting metaphorically "self" and "mask," has clear Platonic and Christian suggestions. Godard and Bergman can be contrasted much as Brecht and Pirandello can be contrasted, the one rigorously skeptical and materialist, the other maintaining a humanist connection and a metaphysical tone.

Films employing techniques related to Brecht's theories are often political in content, as would be expected. This is the case not only in the work of Godard, but also in the work of such film makers as the Yugoslav director Dusan Makavejev, best known in the west for *WR: Mysteries of the Organism* (*WR: Mysterije organizma*, 1970), a film that combines a section on the life and work of Wilhelm Reich, consisting largely of archival and documentary footage, with a narrative section about a young, sexually and politically liberated Yugoslav woman who attempts to fight Soviet domination by living out Reichian theories of the erotic. The juxtaposition of film from diverse sources provokes distantiation, as does as an ending that shifts abruptly into surrealism, thus emphasizing for the audience the arbitrariness of the created narrative. Interestingly, Brazilian director Hector Babenco's *Kiss of the Spider Woman* (1985, based on the novel *El beso de la mujer araña* by Manuel Puig) combines political concerns with a Pirandellian movie-within-a-movie structure. Two responses to political oppression, escapism and action, embodied by two prisoners sharing a cell, are set against each other. Prison life is interspersed with interludes representing a melodramatic fascist propaganda film that the seemingly naive Molina recounts. The film ends with an ironic twist that raises various questions and provides no easy answers. The homosexual Molina, who opted for fantasy, dies trying to aid the comrades of his cellmate; Valentin, the political revolutionary who chose action, dies in a drug-induced dream that is likened to a movie, even, to some extent, to the escapist melodrama Molina told to pass the time.

Cinematic self-reference has also been an aspect of experimental film, especially of those films that have been described as "structural." "Structural Cinema" has involved a more blatant Brechtian declaration of itself as film than anything that would likely occur in narrative, feature films. A great variety of devices have been employed. Splice marks, frame lines, sprocket holes, and even dust particles and scratches on the surface of the film have been intentionally incorporated into the projected image. Sometimes holes have been punched into the film and projected. George Landow, in *Bardo Follies* (1967), elaborated on the frame burning motif found in *Persona*. In that film Landau also optically printed multiple images of the same film loop so that more than one image of the same subject could be seen on the screen simultaneously. Double projection of the same image has also been utilized, thus doing synchronously what Bergman did sequentially in the climactic scene of *Persona*. At times the double projected images have moved at different speeds; at others one of the projections has been a positive and the other a negative image of the same subject. These multiple images, whether existing on the same frame or the result of multiple projection, have the effect of foregrounding arbitrary aspects of the cinematic sign.[16]

On the other side of the spectrum, metacinematic themes and techniques have become popularized, and, in a form more accessible to a mass audience, have occurred in films that are more commercial than those of European *auteurs* such as Bergman and Godard or those of the experimental avant-garde. George Lucas's *Star Wars* (1977) is a seventies remake of what might have been a thirties science fiction serial. It juxtaposes its large screen, color images, stereophonic sound, and highly sophisticated effects and illusions, with the episodic plots, flat characters, and flat performances of the earlier genre. Significantly, *Star Wars* itself is the first film in a series, the first installment of an expanded serial film. *Star Wars* does not look forward but looks backward; it does not "refer to" an imaginary future but to earlier conventions for representing such a future, just as Lichtenstein's paintings are not representations of men and women but representations of depictions of men and women. *Star Wars* is a "Pop" movie that happened to be extremely popular as well.

The second *Star Trek* film, *The Wrath of Kahn* (1982, directed by Nicholas Meyer), begins with a Pirandellian *coup de theatre*; an apparent disaster aboard a space ship is subsequently revealed to be a staged part of a training exercise, much as the murder at the beginning of Truffaut's *Day for Night* is subsequently revealed to be a scene in a film being shot. Richard Rush's *Stunt Man* (1978) is a virtuoso form of cinematic Pirandellianism, filled with art-and-life pyrotechnics. The protagonist is a paranoid fugitive whose paranoia is aggravated when he becomes part of a movie shoot in which the line separating the film and reality is regularly violated by a monomaniacal director willing to do anything to complete his movie. And the film version of *The French Lieutenant's Woman* (1981, directed by Karel Reisz) substitutes a Pirandellian frame for John Fowles's self-conscious narrator. Harold Pinter, who wrote the script, embedded Fowles's Victorian tale of a taboo romance between a gentleman scientist and a fallen woman within a parallel tale of an affair between the twentieth-century performers playing those two characters in a movie.

Notes

1. A projected book by Martin Walsh, to be entitled *The Brechtian Aspect of Radical Cinema*, would have devoted a chapter to Brecht and Godard, but the project was never realized because of Walsh's tragic death. Articles by Walsh relating to the subject of the book along with Walsh's draft outline for the book have been collected and published under the projected title, but the Godard chapter exists only as a short entry in the draft outline. Walsh writes: "Brecht's influence on a seminal group of European film-makers since 1960 has been incalculable, and the central figure is without a doubt that of Godard, whose total *oeuvre* constitutes a superbly 'Brechtian' evolution." *The Brechtian Aspect of Radical Cinema*, ed. Keith M. Griffiths (London: British Film Institute, 1981), p. 130.
2. John Kreidl, *Jean-Luc Godard* (Boston: Twayne, 1980), pp. 99, 123.
3. James Monaco, *The New Wave: Truffaut, Godard, Chabrol, Rohmer, Rivette* (New York: Oxford University Press, 1976), *passim*.
4. Bruce Kawin, *Mindscreen, Bergman, Godard, and First-Person Film* (Princeton: Princeton University Press, 1978), p. 170.
5. Translated in Alfred Guzzetti, *Two or Three Things I Know about Her, Analysis of a Film by Godard* (Cambridge: Harvard University Press, 1981), 143–144. Guzzetti's book consists of a shot-by-shot analysis of the film, including a description of the movement, sound, and music, at least one still from each shot, the French text and an English translation.
6. A good synopsis of Godard's activities and concerns from 1968 through the nineteen-seventies is provided by Colin MacCabe, Mick Eaton, and Laura Mulvey in *Godard: Images, Sounds, Politics* (Bloomington: Indiana University Press, 1980).
7. This metaphoric reading corresponds to that of Robin Wood in *Ingmar Bergman* (New York: Praeger, 1970), p. 147, and contrasts with that of Susan Sontag in *Styles of Radical Will* (New York: Farrar, Straus and Giroux, 1969), p. 136. Sontag sees Alma as the "soul" and Elisabeth as the "persona." Alma's name and Elisabeth's profession lend support to Sontag's position, but the attempt to read other aspects of the film as confirming that position is extremely strained.
8. Sontag, *Styles of Radical Will*, p. 143. Though I agree with Sontag's view of the strength that exists in silence at the outset of the women's relationship, I disagree with her reading of the power shift between the two. Sontag sees Alma having at least an apparent strength at the outset and Elisabeth at least an apparent weakness, with that relation reversing as the film develops. It seems clear to me

that just the opposite is true. Elisabeth clearly dominates the relation at the beginning and, in fact, becomes weakened as the film proceeds, finally becoming completely passive. Alma discovers aggression, no longer stands in awe of Elisabeth, and comes to dominate her. As my reading will make clear, however, I see the film as more resolved and optimistic than do Sontag and most critics, and I believe the ending suggests a resolution of the power struggle and a harmonizing of the two figures.

9. Wood, *Ingmar Bergman*, p. 153.

10. Kawin, pp. 104, 106, *et passim.*

11. Ingmar Bergman, *Bergman on Bergman, Interviews with Ingmar Bergman by Stig Bjorkman, Torsten Manns, Jonas Sima,* trans. Paul Britten Austin (New York: Simon and Schuster, 1973), pp. 195–196, 199. Charles Samuels, *Encountering Directors* (New York: Putnam, 1972), p. 186.

12. John Simon, *Ingmar Bergman Directs* (New York: Harcourt Brace Jovanovich, 1972), p. 30.

13. Sontag, p. 135. Simon, drawing on Sontag, describes *Persona* as a film about "splitting and fusion," p. 216.

14. The device of "suturing" a scene through shot and reverse shot has been the subject of a lively, complex, and subtle discussion and debate among film theorists. Psychoanalytic ideas derived from Jacques Lacan and Marxist ideas derived from Louis Althusser have been utilized in order to argue that the convention is inherently fascist in that it tends to disguise the presence of an "absent-one" who controls the images the audience is allowed to see, as well as their meaning. Two key articles in this discussion appear in *Movies and Methods,* ed. Bill Nichols (Berkeley: University of California Press, 1976), 438–459: Daniel Dayan's "The Tutor Code of Classical Cinema," which first appeared in *Film Quarterly,* 28, 1 (fall 1974) and William Rothman's "Against 'The System of the Suture,'" which first appeared in *Film Quarterly,* 29, 1 (fall 1975). Dayan's article, which elaborates the position characterized here, is largely an explication of the ideas of the French theorist Jean-Pierre Oudart. Rothman's article takes issue with Dayan and Oudart.

15. Samuels, 189.

16. See David Curtis, *Experimental Cinema* (New York: Dell, 1971), 181–191, and Malcom Le Grice, *Abstract Film and Beyond* (Cambridge: MIT Press, 1977), 105–153.

5
WRITING ABOUT WRITING: JOHN FOWLES AND JOHN BARTH

Pirandellian and Brechtian Aspects of the Fiction of John Fowles

John Fowles's *The Magus* (1965, revised version 1977) is a virtuoso performance in narrative Pirandellianism. Nicholas Urfe, a young Englishman teaching on a Greek island, encounters Maurice Conchis, the mysterious owner of a lavish villa, and Julie Holmes, a beautiful young woman living in the villa. Julie's relationship to Conchis is unclear. In Pirandellian fashion, Nicholas hears conflicting explanations of their identities and roles; also in Pirandellian fashion, the story of each casts doubt upon the relative sanity of the other. What begins as a matter of curiosity for Nicholas, intensified by his sexual attraction for Julie, and as a conflict of opposing views regarding Julie's and Conchis's identities is complicated through a series of explanations and revised explanations of what the truth is until it becomes clear that he is being put on by an elaborately contrived non-fourth wall theatre, produced and directed by Conchis. This play in production develops through a seemingly endless sequence of *coups de theatre,* each presenting a new and apparently final truth that reinterprets all that had come before it as part of the illusion Conchis has created. The series of illusions encompassing illusions expands outward from Bourani, the cape on which Conchis's villa is located, insinuating itself into all aspects of Nicholas's life and incorporating even individuals who seemingly could not have had any association with Conchis and the inhabitants of Bourani, individuals such as Alison, a young woman with whom Nicholas had an affair before he came to Greece and who has been eclipsed by the more beautiful and mysterious Julie. Nicholas is transported to unknown locations, abused emotionally, drugged, subjected to sadistic rituals, and intellectually confused to the point that it becomes impossible for him to be certain (like Segismundo in Calderón's *Life Is a Dream*) if any situation he finds himself in is reality or illusion, if he is alone or is being watched by members of the incredible international conspiracy that has been created in order to test him or teach him some kind of philosophical, religious, or psychological lesson.

Conchis describes his "godgame" in terms that acknowledge its debt to the theory of modern theatre:

During the war . . . I conceived a new kind of drama. One in which the conventional separation between actors and audience was abolished. In which the conventional scenic geography, the notions of proscenium, stage, auditorium, were completely discarded. In which continuity of performance, either in time or place, was ignored. And in which the action, the narrative was fluid, with only a point of departure and a fixed point of conclusion. . . . You will find that Artaud and Pirandello and Brecht were all thinking, in their different ways, along similar lines.[1]

And in the final scene in Regents Park, when Nicholas meets Alison again, he cannot know if this reencounter signifies the end of the game or is merely another of its scenes: "I looked round. There were other seats a few yards away. Other sitters and watchers. Suddenly the peopled park seemed a stage, the whole landscape a landscape of masquers, spies" (p. 649).

Although Fowles mentions Brecht and Artaud in *The Magus*, the predominant theatrical inspiration for that novel is clearly Pirandello. Fowles out-Pirandello's Pirandello himself in his creation of a plot structured around a series of shocking revisions of reality models and in his description of a kind of theatre so thoroughly integrated with the world that the participants can never distinguish art and reality and must, in fact, question the very distinction. Also Pirandellian is Fowles's use of a mysterious and beautiful woman around whom questions of character and identity cluster, as a central figure who motivates the protagonist to engage in investigations and speculations regarding what the truth about her really is. (In *The Magus* this figure is complicated by the presence of a second woman, Julie's sister, on Bourani.) Fowles's use of such an enigmatic woman, one who eludes men's attempts to classify her and who thus comes to suggest the larger, metaphysical ineffability of reality, is close to a universal aspect of his fiction and is present in all his novels, from *The Collector* (1963) to *A Maggot* (1985). The Pirandellian point of view is summed up in the following description of a visionary experience that Conchis relates to Nicholas:

But in a flash, as of lightning, all our explanations, all our classifications and derivations, our aetiologies, suddenly appeared to me like a thin net. That great passive monster, reality, was no longer dead, easy to handle. It was full of a mysterious vigour, new forms, new possibilities. The net was nothing, reality burst through it." (p. 309)

Compare this statement with Diego's in *Each in His Own Way*:

What a joy it is . . . when . . . we are able actually to witness the collapse of all those fictitious forms around which our stupid daily life has solidified; and under the dikes, beyond the seawalls, which we had thrown up . . . we are able to see that bit of tide . . . suddenly break forth in a magnificent, overwhelming flood. (pp. 333–334)

If *The Magus* is predominantly Pirandellian, *The French Lieutenant's Woman* (1969) contains a balance of Pirandellian and Brechtian elements—or the narrative correspondences of the theatrical devices of Pirandello and Brecht. Sarah, the mysterious, jilted, "poor Tragedy," functions both thematically and in the narrative/dramatic structure in a manner similar to Pirandello's central female characters, as well as to Julie in *The Magus*, Miranda in *The Collector*, Jane in *Daniel Martin*, the protean muse of *Mantissa*, and Rebecca in *A Maggot*. Various questions revolve around Sarah's character and the facts of her past: Is she victim or victimizer? What really happened between her and Varguennes, the "French lieutenant"? What motivates her manipulative actions in relationship to Charles: love, retaliation against the social class that excludes her, hatred of the male sex? Charles's view of her undergoes numerous revisions, but none of his understandings seems able to contain her or fully explain her actions and character. She exists as a subversive force within Fowles's Victorian society, and affects, for better or for worse, the destruction of Charles's naive positivism. Charles is drawn into a relationship with her in spite of his will and his better Victorian judgment. Ultimately the result is scandal, the breaking of his marital engagement, a lawsuit that disgraces him, his rejection by his own servant, and, in fact, the shattering of his world as he believed it to be: a world in which things, including human emotions and human needs, are explicable and controllable if examined carefully and correctly.

Sarah connotes the "wild," Fowles's term for the ineffable and uncontrollable component of human experience and nature. The wild exists in opposition to all rational, scientific, and Linnaean attempts to explain, classify, objectify, and control. Fowles writes in his philosophical essay, *The Tree*:

> Ordinary experience, from waking second to second, is in fact highly synthetic (in the sense of combinate or constructive), and made of a complexity of strands, past memories and present perceptions, times and places, private and public history, hopelessly beyond science's powers to analyse. It is quintessentially 'wild', in the sense my father disliked so much: unphilosophical, irrational, uncontrollable, incalculable. In fact it corresponds very closely—despite our endless efforts to 'garden', to invent disciplining social and intellectual systems—with wild nature. Almost all the richness of our personal existence derives from this synthetic and eternally present 'confused' consciousness of both internal and external reality, and not least because we know it is beyond the analytical, or destructive, capacity of science.[2]

Sarah is fascinating because she eludes all systems, including the four major Victorian systems featured in *French Lieutenant*: religious morality, social class, male supremacy, and empirical science. The first two are epitomized by the despicable Mrs. Poultney. Charles and Ernestina naively regard themselves as modern, enlightened individuals, Mrs. Poultney's opposites in all respects. In spite of his committment to reason, however, Charles is not at all so free of conventional, if not religious, morality as he thinks, and he is certainly not free of prejudices and presuppositions based on class and sex. And science, for him, is itself a religion, one he shares with Dr. Grogan. When Charles and Grogan confess themselves to be Darwinians, it is as if they are acknowledging membership in a secret sect. Grogan later swears secrecy to Charles, using *The Origin of the Species* as if it were a bible.

The Undercliff, to which Sarah often escapes, is also associated with Fowles's "wild." Once it was common property and, though encroached upon by private owners, it has retained a great deal of its original "wildness." Like Sarah herself it eludes legal and scientific attempts at domestication. Sarah is dismissed from Mrs. Poultney's service because of her refusal to stop walking in the Undercliff, an area associated in Mrs. Poultney's mind with immorality. In the Undercliff Charles searches for fossils and thus attempts to tame nature's own wild through his Linnaean classifying, but in the Undercliff even he is distracted by the "unalloyed wildness" and tempted briefly into "anti-science."[3] And it is in the Undercliff that Charles accidently happens upon Sarah sleeping. When she wakes they stare at each other for a moment, he apologizes for his intrusion, and leaves. But, "in those brief poised seconds above the waiting sea, in that luminous evening silence broken only by the waves' quiet wash, the whole Victorian Age was lost" (p. 81). Later Fowles describes, with considerable sarcasm, Charles's scientific elitism:

Unlit Lyme was the ordinary mass of mankind, most evidently sunk in immemorial sleep; while Charles the naturally selected (the adverb carries both its senses) was pure intellect, walking awake, free as a god, one with the unslumbering stars and understanding all.
All except Sarah, that is. (p. 172)

In spite of Charles's confidence in his own emancipation from prejudice and unreason, his vision of himself as a member of the scientific naturally "select" is, in its arrogance and its oversimplification of the complexity of nature and of human existence, not at all so different from Mrs. Poultney's righteous certainty in herself as a member of the Christian "elect." The partial pun relating the Christian "elect" and Darwinian "selection" is made overt late in the novel when Grogan refers to Charles's desire to be a member of "a rational and scientific elect" (p. 408). Grogan affirms a moral imperative for those who are members of this "elect," and emphasizes the possible abuses that can result when this imperative is not followed. That imperative, Grogan pointedly explains,

is this. That the elect, whatever the particular grounds they advance for their cause, have introduced a finer and fairer morality into this dark world. If they fail that test, then they become no more than despots, sultans, mere seekers after their own pleasure and power. In short, mere victims of their own baser desires. I think you understand what I am driving at—and its especial relevance to yourself. (p. 409)

The Pirandellian tension between the impulse to define and an ineffable reality must remain unresolved because it arises from fundamental metaphysical tensions that are part of the author's philosophy. In *Each in His Own Way* a violent confrontation backstage forces the play to a halt before it can reach its proper conclusion. Fowles does conclude *French Lieutenant,* but in two separate, equal, and opposed ways. A totally imaginary resolution to this metaphysical dilemma is presented in *Mantissa,* where author and muse imagine an unwritable, unfinishable, and endlessly revisable "text without words" that would allow them to "be [their] real selves at last."[4]

Another Pirandellian aspect of *French Lieutenant* is Fowles's assertion—or the assertion of his surrogate, the author-narrator of the novel—that his characters can achieve an autonomy that makes them independent of his intentions and outside his control:

When Charles left Sarah on her cliff edge, I ordered him to walk straight back to Lyme Regis. But he did not; he gratuitously turned and went down to the Dairy. . . . the idea seemed to me to come clearly from Charles, not myself. It is not only that he has begun to gain an autonomy; I must respect it, and disrespect all my quasi-divine plans for him, if I wish him to be real. (pp. 105–106)

In his "Preface to *Six Characters in Search of an Author*" Pirandello wrote of the characters of that play,

They are detached from me; live on their own; have acquired voice and movement; have by themselves . . . become dramatic characters, characters that can move and talk on their own initiative; already see themselves as such; have learned to defend themselves against me. . . . And so let them go where dramatic characters do go to have life: on a stage. And let us see what will happen.[5]

Unlike Pirandello's preface, however, Fowles's commentary on his text is contained within that text, is itself a part of the text. Thus, though its content involves a Pirandellian conceit, its effect is Brechtian; it disrupts the illusionistic flow and produces aesthetic distance.

The Pirandellian aspects of Fowles's fiction—plots structured around questions regarding the truth of a person or situation, female characters who frequently lie at the center of those questions, and an underlying epistemological skepticism informing the plot and characters—"translate" from theatre to fiction with no difficulty. Plot and character are elements shared by both media and can be used in similar ways to evoke similar themes. In addition, the play-within-a-play finds an easy parallel in the embedded narrative: the frame-tale or story-within-a-story. Certainly it would be hard to imagine a kind of fiction that realized the Pirandellian prophecy—that extended outside the page and into "reality" in the literal way experimental theatre and happenings did in the nineteen-sixties and nineteen-seventies. But since that Pirandellian forecast was contained within plays that themselves remained rooted in scripted texts describing characters engaged in dialogue and action, comparisons of his plays with fictional works structured around similar elements are not problematical.

Brechtian devices designed to maximize aesthetic distance involved, among other things, lighting, music, stage design, and performance style, things that do not directly correlate with aspects of fiction. Nevertheless, various aspects of *French Lieutenant* are clearly designed to have a Brechtian effect, are a means that narration can employ to produce a foregrounding of narrative artifice, just as Brechtian staging and performance techniques foreground the artifice of play production. *French Lieutenant* evokes, through its plot, setting, and characters, an earlier era, and Fowles's leisurely yet formal style, together with his use of the intrusive authorial direct address, results in the evocation of an earlier way of writing. However, inconsistencies in this style jar the reader and disrupt the illusion of both a Victorian England and a Victorian novel.

Early in the novel narrational dissonance is achieved through the insertion of anachronistic allusions that are inconsistent with the Victorian style. On the first page, a leisurely description of Lyme Bay connotatively invites the reader to sit back, relax, and begin a gradual process of immersion into an imaginary though life-like world; here, Fowles inserts an allusion to Henry Moore, which momentarily disrupts the illusion of an earlier world and an earlier way of writing. Fowles peppers his discourse with such anachronistic references, including allusions to airplanes, the Gestapo, Marshal McLuhan, computers, and, in fact, Brecht and the "alienation effect" itself. On other occasions the illusion is broken when the narrator comments on his own writing. On one occasion he simultaneously apologizes for and justifies his punctuation : "I am overdoing the exclamation marks. But as Charles paced up and down, thoughts, reactions, reactions to reactions spurted up angrily in his mind" (p. 219).

Furthermore, although Fowles's use of direct address is a revival of a device associated with the earlier style of writing he is evoking, he turns that device against itself so that its effect is opposite that for which it was originally intended. Direct address traditionally is an invitation to the reader to recognize and accept a world and a system of values that he or she shares with the author. The reader so induced will properly draw the correct conclusions and arrive at the correct evaluations regarding the characters the author has created. The major thrust of the device is the implication of a shared world view that is doubted by neither author nor reader. Fowles sometimes uses the device simply to evoke a nostalgic memory of a time when life was presumably simpler and the relationship between author and reader less problematical. At other times, however, he uses it to bring the reader not into a shared world with its assumed certainties but into his own—or his narrator/surrogate's—personal struggle in writing the novel: his thoughts, problems, and limitations regarding his creation. And this world is not one of Victorian certainty but one of twentieth-century doubt and skepticism.

The Brechtian effect, which Fowles had been creating in a relatively subtle fashion in the book's early chapters, becomes overt at the outset of chapter thirteen, when the narrator acknowledges his own ignorance of his characters and affirms their fictional nature. In addition, he makes explicit the gap between the historical setting of his story and the present, as well as that between the narrative conventions he has assumed and those of the contemporary novel. Responding to an apparently rhetorical question about Sarah's identity, asked at the end of the previous chapter, he begins,

I do not know. This story I am telling is all imagination. These characters I create never existed outside my own mind. If I have pretended until now to know my characters' minds and innermost thoughts, it is because I am writing in (just as I have assumed some of the vocabulary and "voice" of) a convention universally accepted at the time of my story: that the novelist stands next to God. He may not know all, yet he tries to pretend that he does. But I live in the age of Alain Robbe-Grillet and Roland Barthes; if this is a novel, it cannot be a novel in the modern sense of the word. (p. 104)

But of course, *French Lieutenant* is a novel "in the modern sense of the word" because Fowles is doing more than reconstructing the style and setting of a Victorian novel. He is, in fact, deconstructing, through the use of such Brechtian techniques, the work he is creating.

One cannot, on the other hand, assume that Fowles is really speaking to us directly and with complete candor; a distinction must be maintained between him and the narrator of *French Lieutenant*. That narrator may be much like Fowles; he is, after all (like Fowles), the author of a novel about Victorian England; it may even be that his philosophy and the various views and opinions he expresses are identical to those of Fowles. It may, indeed, be part of Fowles's Pirandellian game to trick the reader into confusing reality levels and thereby into mistaking narrator for author. Yet, Fowles's narrative intrusions constitute in fact a highly contrived second level illusion. As Linda Hutcheon notes of *French Lieutenant*, "The voice of the narrator is not an exterior authenticating authorial one; it is the voice of a character."[6] Thus, the novel reveals itself to be a frame-tale, a novel about an author writing a novel. From this perspective even the Brechtian devices are part of a larger Pirandellian game. Fowles writes a novel about a fictional author who is writing a novel about Victorian England and who continually betrays the illusion he is creating in that novel.

Fowles, in various ways, tempts the reader to mistake narrator for author. At one point Sarah, using part of the money Charles has given her to begin a new life, buys a Toby jug. Fowles describes this jug in some detail and with considerable affection. He also indicates that ceramics experts (though not Sarah) would recognize its being by Ralph Leigh. (Ceramics experts may also understand why in a later edition of *French Lieutenant* the ceramicist was transformed from Ralph Leigh into Ralph Wood.) He goes on to avow personal knowledge of this particular jug, claiming that it is one that has recently come into his own possession: "the Toby was cracked, and was to be recracked in the course of time, as I can testify, having bought it myself a year or two ago for a good deal more than the three pennies Sarah was charged. But unlike her, I fell for the Ralph Leigh part of it. She fell for the smile" (p. 288). There is, of course, no way of knowing from the novel itself whether the jug is really in Fowles's possession or is merely a fictional object in the possession of his fictional surrogate. But an unwary reader might assume that Fowles has taken a personal possession that he prizes and incorporated it into his novel, thus confusing even more the boundary between Fowles's fiction and Fowles's life. An "object" that is part of a fictional world of 1867 is also a "real" historical object that a hundred years later is in the possession of the author of that fictional world. The affection Fowles seems to feel for the piece is evident, in spite of his claim to have been attracted to it primarily because of its attribution, and one wonders if he is looking at it as he writes. This is, of course, Pirandellian gimmickry, but it is a particularly inventive and ingratiating version of it.

Fowles's placement of his author surrogate inside his novel goes beyond Pirandello's reference to himself as an off-stage character in his plays. On two occasions Fowles's surrogate appears "on-stage" in *French Lieutenant*. The first of these occurs shortly after Charles has committed the irrevocable act of breaking off his engagement, only to discover that Sarah has disappeared. Fowles incarnates himself as a bearded individual who intrudes on Charles's privacy in a train compartment. The two exchange stares and Charles takes a disliking to the stranger, who he decides is "perhaps not quite a gentleman" (p. 415). Fowles's surrogate studies Charles with cold detachment, trying to decide what he is going to do with this character he has created. Fowles, the character (as well as Fowles, the narrator), decides that the solution to his dilemma is to present two distinct and equally valid endings for the novel. The question of which to present first he solves by flipping a coin—a florin—and accepting the result. (Shall we assume the real Fowles flips a coin at his desk?) Charles notices this and decides that the stranger is "either a gambler or mentally deranged" (p. 418). The train enters Paddington station, both exit, and the bearded man disappears in the crowd.

The narrator later reappears, rather changed, outside the house of Dante Gabriel Rossetti, as if observing the final scene between Charles and Sarah that takes place within, the scene the novel presents with two different endings. Fowles excuses the introduction of this new character late in the novel with the claim that he is insignificant. The claim that the character is insignificant, however, is belied by a simile that describes him as "minimal . . . as a gamma-ray particle" (p. 475). Authors writing in the second half of the twentieth century know that gamma rays are not insignificant and affect the course of events, at least of subatomic events, and that human gamma rays—especially when they are writers—affect rather than simply record the lives of those they describe. Moreover, Fowles claims that this character now appears more *"as he really is"* than had the earlier individual, implying that he is not a new character at all. "The once full, patriarchal beard of the railway compartment has been trimmed down to something rather foppish and Frenchified" (p. 475). Thus, this description of the author surrogate turns against itself, stating first that he is a new character and then that he has altered his appearance from that of a previous scene, and asserting that he is a passive observer but implying through the subtle allusion to Heisenberg that the possibility of passively observing events without affecting them is a fiction belied by modern science.

The fact that chance determined the order of the two endings means that one should not be accorded any greater "correctness" than the other. For both endings Charles, having given up everything for Sarah, discovers that she has left, that he has lost her as well. He searches for her, finally gives up, spends two years traveling as an escape, and returns when his solicitor writes informing him she has been located. She is living with the Rossetti brothers and working as a secretary for Dante Gabriel. She has not become the street prostitute that one might have imagined her fate to be but has in fact become the emancipated woman she perhaps always was. In the scene describing their reencounter Charles tries various strategies for persuading her to marry him but she refuses him, justifying her refusal on the basis of her need to be free. In the first version the scene ends with reconciliation, that reconciliation involving the introduction to Charles of his daughter, the product of their earlier passion. The second version ends with no reconciliation, Charles leaving angrily, unaware of the daughter's existence, and Sarah remaining aloof and finally enigmatic. Both endings have a kind of appropriateness, but on entirely different bases. The second, "unhappy," ending seems more consistent with the novel; Sarah remains consistent with the character she has been, consistent even in her need to be inconsistent, if that is what is necessary to elude definition and remain free. But the first ending is appropriate because it conforms to sentimental, "romantic," and moralistic literary conventions. It is highly contrived and involves the "revelation" of a kind of child *ex machina* as a means of doing what the novel could not do if it were fully faithful to its own logic.

There is another, third, ending presented earlier in the novel. But this ending, a "false" ending subsequently revealed to be something Charles imagines, cannot claim the status of the two equally "correct" endings presented later. In this ending Charles does *not* make the fatal error of getting off the train at Exeter, where his relationship with Sarah is consummated. Instead he returns to his fiancé, marries her, and they live unhappily ever after. Ironically, this imaginary ending is probably the most credible of all three, considering what someone in Charles's position in Victorian England would most likely do. In narrating this false conclusion, Fowles's tone becomes increasingly flippant and cursory till it is clear that in some way or another the author is playing an irreverent game with his fiction and with the reader. In addition, his statement that Charles's confession to Ernestina "ends the story" is belied by the fact that there are obviously a hundred pages remaining in the novel at that point. Fowles briefly describes the mediocre future of Charles and Ernestina, Charles having opted against a life of passion and scandal and for a life of conventionality. He summarizes the futures of the other characters, including Mrs. Poultney, whom he follows into the afterlife, and delights in her rejection at heaven's gate and her fall into hell. The beginning of the next chapter reveals that what has been described is something that Charles imagined on the train.

This false ending is, of course, a bit of authorial whimsy in which Fowles flaunts his power and, simultaneously, treats fiction writing with complete irreverence. Charles and Ernestina, he says, "begat what shall it be—let us say seven children" (p. 348). "Sam and Mary—but who can be bothered with the biography of servants? They married and bred, and died, in the monotonous fashion of their kind" (p. 348). And, in contrast to these others, Fowles says of Mrs. Poultney that he "can summon up enough interest to look into the future—that is, into her after-life" (p. 348). He is apparently able to do so because it affords him the opportunity to heap revenge upon the despicable character he has created.

With these false endings and optional endings Fowles lays naked and demystifies, in Brechtian fashion, the art of fictional narration. Still, on another level the illusion is maintained and the artistry remains concealed. On the metafictional level the plot of *French Lieutenant* does not involve the struggles within and between Sarah, Charles, and Victorian society but rather those of a contemporary author in writing a Victorian novel. The struggle of Fowles's surrogate author to write *French Lieutenant* is logically just as fictional as the story of Sarah and Charles, in spite of the fact that Fowles may, indeed, have drawn extensively on his own values and experience in creating that author and even in spite of the fact that in numerous ways he invites the reader to forget the distinction between author and character. The novel Fowles's surrogate writes is characterized by a Brechtian distancing, the result of the gap, the *difference,* in time and culture that obtrudes itself between the time of its action and the time of its writing. But the gap between Fowles and his surrogate author-narrator is much narrower. On that level Fowles plays a Pirandellian game designed to confuse the reader into mistaking his narrator for himself.

The relationship between author and narrator in *Daniel Martin* is similarly problematical. *Daniel Martin* presents itself as the autobiographical first novel of an English ex-playwright who has compromised his artistic integrity by becoming a Hollywood scriptwriter and who hopes to reestablish his integrity and the authenticity of his art by writing this very novel. He frequently thinks of himself as "writing himself," as if his life is like one of his scripts or as if he is writing his life and the novel that describes it at the same time. Daniel, in fact, is probably Fowles's most autobiographical protagonist. Both Barry N. Olschen and Robert Huffaker have made this point in their monographs on Fowles and have noted numerous similarities between Daniel and his author.[7] Significantly, Daniel first intended to name his protagonist Simon Wolfe, and "S. Wolfe" is an anagram for "Fowles."[8] Thus, Fowles is writing about Daniel Martin, a character rather like himself, and Daniel is writing about a character whose name—at least in Daniel's original plan—suggests Fowles's own name. Later Daniel decides to make his book openly autobiographical and use his own name instead. Fowles, significantly, does not make an analogous choice. Nevertheless, his use of the S. Wolfe anagram stands as an open invitation to the reader to commit the intentional fallacy by equating author and character.

Problems revolving around the narrative voice of *Daniel Martin* are complicated by point of view shifts. Daniel writes his novel alternatively in the first and third persons. Furthermore, three chapters and at least one shorter section depart from both these points of view and are written by Daniel's young starlet girlfriend Jenny. Daniel has decided to include these sections in order to provide a view of himself that is presumably more objective than his own. The first of Jenny's chapters is called, in fact, "An Unbiased View." Jenny's sections, however, occupy a very small proportion of *Daniel Martin*, which is a massive, sprawling text, punctuated by schizoid shifts between the first and third person that occur without warning.

The shifts of point of view produce a kind of narrational dissonance similar in effect though different in means to that created in *French Lieutenant*. Shifts in tense further contribute to the distancing effect. Fowles feels that there is a relationship between tense and point of view, but, as Huffaker has noted, there is no consistency in the relationship between person and tense in *Daniel Martin*.[9] Huffaker quotes from a letter he received from Fowles:

Time has always interested me in a philosophical sense—that is, I've always found clock, or mathematical, time the least interesting way to use and experience it. And I feel rather the same about its practical expression in fiction: tense. And tense is bound up with narrating person. I doubt whether all the experiments using these two factors in *Daniel Martin* worked; but that was one reason I found it very enjoyable to write!"[10]

Perhaps because this association between person and tense was "experimental" and not fully thought out or perfected, Fowles, in the novel's last two hundred pages, abandons this experimentation and the novel winds down in a conventional third-person past-tense mode.

Nevertheless, the point of view shifts are interesting as a device not only because of their Brechtian effect but also because they suggest the absence of a firmly rooted sense of self in the narrator (Daniel Martin) as well as a problematical relationship between author (John Fowles or Daniel Martin) and narrator. That problematical relationship has not been resolved by Daniel's (but not Fowles's) decision to defictionalize his work by abandoning his fictional mask and writing a novel the title of which openly acknowledges that it is autobiography.

The "self" in Fowles is always ineffable, the inner correlative of the "wild" of nature, "unphilosophical, irrational, uncontrollable, incalculable."[11] It is this ineffable self that Sarah defended against Charles when she insisted, " 'I am not to be understood even by myself. And I can't tell you why, but I believe my happiness depends on my not understanding' " (p.

464). In *Daniel Martin* the point of view shifts, the use of different pronouns as indexes for the self, suggest something of this shifting selfhood that cannot be pinned down by a word. The novel begins and ends in the third person, and shifts to the first person suggest Daniel's inability to objectify himself in narrative. Sections dealing with particularly disruptive experiences are often accompanied by frequent, schizoid shifts in point of view. One such section describes Daniel's sexual initiation, and occurs midway through the novel. Frequent point of view shifts throughout a forty page chapter dealing with the events leading up to the experience and its abrupt termination enhance the sense of it as psychologically disruptive, both on the boy having it and the man later writing about it. One has the sense of a destabilized self groping for a signifier to hold it in place.

There is clearly a problem in critical distance between Daniel the author and Daniel the character. There may also be a problem in critical distance between Fowles the author and Daniel the author-character. This would account for the fact that, at least in the opinion of this writer, *Daniel Martin* is Fowles's weakest novel. *Daniel Martin* seems to take itself too seriously for a novel that so much narrows the gap between author and character, that does not disguise the connection between the two but flaunts it and tempts the reader to forget the distinction. There is a tongue-in-cheek attitude toward Fowles's inclusion of authorial surrogates in *French Lieutenant*: his arrogant "self" in the train compartment, his Frenchified self standing like a voyeur outside the house where Sarah and Charles enact their final scene, his Brechtian narrator criticizing and defending his use of exclamation points. And if Pirandello included himself as an off-stage character in his plays, he also included critics who detested his work. *Daniel Martin* lacks this tongue-in-cheek attitude. Moreover, certain tendencies in Fowles's fiction, tendencies toward sentimentality and pretentiousness, which elsewhere are held in check and are compensated for by his substantial strengths—his intelligence, his ability to manipulate brilliantly tension and resolution, his well wrought narrations and descriptions, his wonderful erotic scenes—simply get out of hand in *Daniel Martin.*

Nevertheless, *Daniel Martin* is important from the point of view of this study because of the metafictional themes and techniques it shares with other modern and postmodern works: the notion that life itself is something like a novel, play, or film script; the disrupted self groping for a signifier or struggling to "write itself"; the uneasy relationship between author and narrator; the implicit novel-within-a-novel structure; and the utilization of narrational dissonance to create Brechtian critical distance.

John Barth's Hall of Mirrors

There are metafictional aspects to all of John Barth's novels. Barth himself has described *The Sot-Weed Factor* (1960) and *Giles Goat-Boy* (1966) as "novels which imitate the form of the Novel, by an author who imitates the role of Author."[12] Yet, it is with the 1968 publication of *Lost in the Funhouse* that the self-referential aspect of his writing becomes primary. In this "series" of fourteen stories Barth creates narrators and narrations locked inside the "prisonhouse of language," capable only of articulating the walls of that prison, of clarifying its shape and size. These stories describe an ironic impasse in which language struggles to escape from itself, in which the "individual" uses language in an attempt to solve the problems that language creates. And the "individual" is an unknown that lies behind a name or a pronoun, a signified that may or may not be there at all.

Most of the stories comprising the series appear for the first time in it, but a few appeared separately as early as 1963. They range in technique and style from the well-wrought and conventional "Ambrose His Mark" to the comic surrealist allegory "Night Sea Journey" to the absolutely self-referential "Title," a story that is about nothing more than its own unfolding. The various stories, an author's note indicates, are intended to be presented in various modes: to be read silently; to be read aloud; to be heard on a monophonic recording; to be heard on a stereophonic recording; or to be heard in a combination of live and recorded presentation. Some can be presented in more than one of these modes. In spite of the variety in these stories—both in terms of their narrative style and structure and in terms of their ideal mode of presentation—they are united around certain themes: the deferment of reality by language and the paradoxical struggle of the linguistic self to emerge from language's prison. These themes inform the structure and narrative voice of many of these stories in new and radical ways. If there is no transcendental "self" that lies behind the play of language, then a person is rather like a text and the idea of a story being self-conscious, talking to itself about itself, is not so absurd; such a "story" finds itself in a situation that is not so different, after all, from the situation in which a person finds himself or herself.

Such themes suggest a kinship between Barth's ideas as implied by his fiction and ideas of structurists and poststructuralists. Although there is this kinship—whether through direct influence or simply the result of a convergence of interests—Barth is not quite a complete structuralist. His first two novels, *The Floating Opera* (1956) and *End of the Road* (1958), were existential and humanist in orientation, although they contained the seeds of his later developments. Barth maintains a humanistic component even in the midst of his later, more radical treatment of language and the self. In fact, what saves, or at least partly saves, some his more overtly self-referential works—his *Lost in the Funhouse* and *Chimera* (1972) stories and the novel *LETTERS* (1979)—from intellectual and formal sterility, from being the mere working out of clever but tiresome conceits, is Barth's ability to *humanize* the struggle of language to transcend its limits. To reduce the self to a text may seem dehumanizing, but for Barth the struggling text is itself an object of compassion and empathy. Thus, at points within some of his most convoluted and narcissistic tales there are moments of poignance. In spite of his challenge to traditional notions of the self, Barth remains a humanist, perhaps just barely, but a humanist nonetheless. Fowles described the novel as a "humanistic enterprise,"[13] and Barth has said of his *Lost in the Funhouse* stories,

If my writing was no more than the intellectual fun-and-games that *Time* magazine makes it out, I'd take up some other line of work. That's why one objects to the word *experiment*, I suppose: it suggests cold technique, and technique in art, as we all know, has the same sort of value that it has in love: heartless skill has its appeal, as does heartfelt ineptitude; but passionate virtuosity's what we all wish for, and aspire to. If these pieces aren't also moving, then the experiment is unsuccessful.[14]

The first story in *Lost in the Funhouse*, "Frame-Tale," signals what is to come. It consists of a strip of paper indicated by a dotted line along the edge of the page; the reader is instructed to cut out the strip, twist it, and fasten its ends together, thus forming a moebius strip. On one side of the strip is written "ONCE UPON A TIME THERE" and on the other side is written "WAS A STORY THAT BEGAN."[15] The twisting and fastening of the strip has merged the two sides to form a single continuous narrative, an infinite regress of stories inside stories with no beginning and no end: ". . . once upon a time there was a story that began once upon a time there was a story that began once upon a time. . . ." The story is the logical equivalent of Escher's *Print Gallery*. Simultaneously the shortest and longest story in the collection, consisting of only ten different words, it can never be read in its entirety, nor even begun at its beginning. It simply and elegantly illustrates the dilemma of the metalanguage. If metalanguages are created in order to provide a vantage point from which to view "object languages," they themselves are then languages with no claim to finality, and can also be examined by higher level metalanguages. One escapes one "prisonhouse" only to find oneself in another. Metaphorically, it is not only the dilemma of the metalanguage that is implied here but of self-consciousness itself—the consciousness that seeks to locate, identify, and objectify itself, to domesticate itself and protect itself from the Fowlesian "wild." But each new vantage point is another invisible center that can only be domesticated by another new self-conscious level.

Metafictional series occur frequently in *Lost in the Funhouse.* "Menelaid" consists of fourteen sections (conveniently echoing the number of stories in the collection), the first seven numbered one through seven and the second seven numbered seven through one. The numbers of the sections do not indicate their order in the story but the number of narrative levels present in each section. A series of stories-inside-stories builds up incrementally during the first half of "Menelaid" and then subsides incrementally during the second half. Each internal story is enclosed in quotation marks so that during both section sevens there are up to six sets of quotation marks framing the words of the narrator on the deepest, seventh level. In addition, at any point in the story, conversation on any of the "framing" levels can interrupt the progress of any "framed" story. In both section sevens, therefore, interjections can occur that are contained within fewer than six quotation marks or within no quotes at all. When this happens the reader must rethink the entire structure of "Menelaid" in order to determine from which narrative level the interruption arose. Finally, logic would seem to require that interruptions could only move in one direction; that is, narrators and listeners could comment on any of the tales they frame but could not comment on the tales that frame them: a speaker or listener can interrupt a story, but a character in a story can't interrupt the story he or she is part of, presumably. But Barth violates even this rule of logical levels so that speakers in stories do respond to their narrators, or their narrators' narrators, or their narrators' narrators' narrators. This is possible because some characters in framed tales are seers and know the future; therefore they are aware of the stories that will be told about them, can say things about those not-yet-told tales, and those comments will have to be incorporated into those stories when they finally are told. "Menelaid," then, is, quintessentially "messy": framed tales loop back to comment on the tales that frame them. Clearly, a most patient and committed reader is required to keep the narrative levels straight.

The first and "highest" metafictional level in "Menelaid"—that surrounded by no quotation marks—is Menelaus's disembodied voice, all that remains of him, speaking as if to himself, the solipsistic remnant of great human events, great wars and great loves; this voice suggests the discourse of literature itself that remains when its subject no longer exists.

(The voice is later revealed to be actually that of Proteus, the sea god whom Menelaus fought and who assumed Menelaus's own form and voice.) Menelaus quotes himself telling a tale to Telemachus and Peisistratus, sons of his old comrades, during his non-heroic middle age with Helen, after the war. Thus begins "Menelaid" 's weaving into deeper and deeper metafictional levels.

Like Ambrose, protagonist of several other *Lost in the Funhouse* stories, Menelaus embodies Barth's recurring theme of the self-conscious artist, caught in narcissistic convolutions, dissociated from life, the opposite of the man of action: Paris who sweeps Helen away without a thought. The artist's immortalizing in literature becomes a record of his frustration, the trace of his desire to escape the tale he is compelled to tell. In "Menelaid" we learn that Helen has left Menelaus for Paris because Menelaus could not accept her love without questioning it. His self-consciousness, which compels him to articulate his experience, is simultaneously the cause of his alienation from life and the mode of his struggle to overcome that alienation: the story is the story of the struggle to escape from the story. In spite of this absurdity—the means themselves being the cause of the condition they are intended to overcome—Barth is able to conclude on a consoling note; the struggle remains, nevertheless, the struggle of love:

Menelaus was lost on the beach at Pharos; he is no longer, and may be in no poor case as teller of his gripping history. For when the voice goes he'll turn tale, story of his life, to which he clings yet, whenever, how-, by whom-recounted. Then when as must at last every tale, all tellers, all told, Menelaus's story itself in ten or ten thousand years expires, yet I'll survive it, I, in Proteus's terrifying last disguise, Beauty's spouse's odd Elysium: the absurd, unending possibility of love. (p. 167)

Barth's genius lies in his ability to wrench poignancy out of such intellectualized and manneristic conceits as that which informs the structure of "Menelaid." He is not always successful in his attempt to achieve the "passionate virtuosity" he strives for—there are times when his work does seem uninspired and empty, although clever—but when he does succeed he is able to humanize the postmodern without compromising rigor or slipping into sentimentality. The postmodern obsession with language, narrativity, and artifice emerges as not *necessarily* a decadent indulgence but, at its best, a grappling with problems, questions, and paradoxes of linguistic beings.

A metafictional series also informs the structure of "Life-Story." An author begins to wonder if he himself may be a character in a work of fiction. Being a writer, he decides to write a story about someone like himself, a writer who wonders if he is a fictional character who decides to write about it. The result is an implied series of writers writing stories about writers writing stories. The various author-characters are given no names but are identified by letters; alphabetical order is used to suggest the position of these characters on the metafictional chain. Thus, the character created by the first narrator (himself referred to only as "he") is called "D" and D's character is "E." By implication, then, D's author, the "he" of the beginning, is "C" and C's author is, appropriately, "B"[arth]. B[arth]'s own author is, of course, "A," the original A[uthor], the first letter and first mover of the fictional series. Barth freely shifts metafictional levels throughout the story, indicating the different protagonists by different letters of the alphabet at different times. This does not, however, result in any confusion since all authors and stories are the same. Ironically, all these author-characters wish they were writing a different story and, simultaneously, that they were characters in a different story, a more conventional story with a traditional hero and a straightforward plot, instead of an avant-garde story that can't seem to get itself moving. "It's particularly disquieting to suspect not only that one is a fictional character but that the fiction one's in—the fiction one is—is quite the sort one least prefers" (p. 118).

Of course, we cannot really assume that Barth *is* B, the author of C, the character of A, any more than we can assume that Fowles is the narrator of *French Lieutenant,* as much as both authors may tease us into identifying author and character. Barth continues his tease by footnoting various mentionings in the text of the narrator's present time with specific times and dates. These footnotes help create an illusion of documentary authenticity for the story. They indicate that it was begun at 9:00 A.M. on Monday, June 20, 1966. The last such footnote is for 11:00 that evening and the story ends shortly after midnight, when the author's wife enters to congratulate him on this thirty-sixth birthday. Just as one is tempted to believe Fowles owns the Toby jug he described in *French Lieutenant,* one is here tempted to believe that Barth wrote "Life-Story" on the day the footnotes indicate. It is possible that he did, given the 1968 publication of *Lost in the Funhouse* and the fact that "Life-Story" is not one of the stories that had previously appeared. Still, it makes no difference whether or not he did; the Pirandellian confusion of the gap between author and character exists no matter what the exact "truth" happens to be. All that is required is that fiction and reality are close enough to create some confusion for the reader or audience. The narrowness of that gap is also suggested by the birthdays of author and character. The thirty-six-year-old character must have been born on June 21, 1930, but Barth was born (according to *Contemporary Authors*[16]) on May 27, 1930, twenty-five days before his character. This gap between Barth and his surrogate—like the gap that is articulated in Genet's theatre when characters and performers are of different sexes, the gap between Norma Jean Baker and Marilyn Monroe, and the gap between art and life in which Rauschenberg tries to work—is another suggestion of the *differance* that always must exist between signifier and signified. Of course B is manifestly fictional but Barth's confusing the line between himself and his fictional construct—without abandoning fiction and resorting to autobiography—stands as a reminder of a similar gap in all naming and sign making. Twenty-five days is not much difference between an author and a character, but it is enough of one to keep them irrevocably separated.

In "Life-Story" Barth uses ellipses and expressions such as "et cetera" and "fill in the blank" as indications that the reader should, at certain points, insert appropriate words or phrases. To some extent Barth is here devaluing the creative process much as Fowles did in his flippant "false" ending for *French Lieutenant*. Writing out certain obvious words and phrases is tedious and the reader, once he or she gets the idea, should be able to supply them himself or herself. But this device also gives Barth the opportunity to create logical loops and new hall of mirrors effects. The expression "et cetera," for example, takes on a function similar to the "GO TO" command used in computer programming. It suggests that the reader should insert a word or phrase from a similar, parallel construction used earlier:

Why is it L wondered with mild disgust that both K and M for example choose to write such stuff when life is so sweet and painful and full of such a variety of people, places, situations, and activities other than self-conscious and after all rather blank introspection? Why is it N wondered et cetera that both M and O et cetera when the world is in such parlous explosive case? (p. 120)

The first sentence expresses L's frustration over the inability of both his character (M) and his author (K) to write anything but avant-garde fiction when there are interesting and important things to write about. The second sentence shifts up two metafictional levels to N, wondering the same thing about his author and character (M and O). Rather than restate the entire sentence, Barth inserts two "et cetera"'s, the first to be filled in by the phrase "with mild disgust" and the second with the phrase "for example choose to write such stuff."

The paragraph continues, utilizing even more "et cetera"s, and concludes,

> Am I being strung out in this ad libitum fashion I wondered merely to keep my author from the pistol? What sort of story is it whose drama lies always the next frame out? If Sinbad sinks it's Scheherazade who drowns; whose neck one wonders is on her line? (pp. 120–121)

Fiction is essential to the author's survival; it is what keeps him "from the pistol." Yet the story always aims at a completion that can never be achieved, that "always lies the next frame out." Scheherazade's situation is one of Barth's favorite motifs, both because of the frame-tale structure of the work in which she occurs and because her survival is dependent upon her ability to tell stories. He has described her problem as "every storyteller's problem: to publish or perish."[17] Later in "Life-Story" the author delays the suicide he intends only because he is "in the process of completing a sentence" (p. 124).

"Life-Story" also engages in direct address of the reader and authorial intrusion that is more violent and disruptive than Fowles's thirteenth chapter of *French Lieutenant*. The third section of the story begins with a spontaneous outburst against the reader, interrupting the flow of the story—to the extent that any "flow" has in fact been established in "Life-Story."

> The reader! You, dogged, uninsultable, print-oriented bastard, it's you I'm addressing, who else, from inside this monstrous fiction. You've read me this far, then. Even this far? For what discreditable motive? How is it you don't go to a movie, watch TV, stare at a wall, play tennis with a friend, make amorous advances to the person who comes to your mind when I speak of amorous advances? Can nothing surfeit, saturate you, turn you off? Where's your shame? (p. 127)

The author's rage over his circumstances turns against the reader, who, he believes, could end this absurd story. Just as he asks himself why he is compelled to write such fictions when so many more worthy topics are available, so he asks why the reader insists on reading such fictions when there are so many satisfying things to do. Clearly there must be a "discreditable motive" involved. Utilizing a form of Barthian sophistry, Barth places our morals and character in an untenable position when he dares us to stop reading and then to deny that we have continued. Such a denial would provide irrefutable evidence that we are liars.

But as he longs to die and can't without your help you force him on, force him on. Will you deny you've read this sentence? This? To get away with murder doesn't appeal to you, is that it? As if your hands weren't inky with other dyings! As if he'd know you'd killed him! Come on. He dares you. (p. 128)

The author does come to an apparent resolution of his dilemma. He uses a certain logic to determine that he cannot, after all, be a character in a work of fiction, and if he is not a fictional character the entire metafictional dilemma collapses. No fictional character the author is aware of ever became convinced of the fact that he was a fictional character. Since the author has become so convinced, he must not be a character in a work of fiction, or so he reasons. Yet if we accept the premise that a character in a work of fiction cannot believe himself to be a character in a work of fiction, then "Life-Story" ends with an implication of the Epimenides paradox. The author is saved from this paradox only because he does not fully think through his situation. Having reasoned that his belief that he is a fictional character precludes the possibility of his being one, he no longer does believe that he is fictional and thus, ironically, it becomes again possible for him to be fictional.

The most purely self-conscious story in *Lost in the Funhouse* is "Title," which is nothing more than a narrative voice commenting on its own struggle to become a story and, at the same time, on the condition of contemporary fiction. As in "Life-Story" Barth elides words and phrases which the reader is supposed to fill in. Here those ellipses are indicated by the phrase "fill in the blank," the word "blank," or words indicating parts of speech, grammatical constructions, or parts of the sentence. Thus, the sentence, "Try to fill in the blank," could become for the reader, "Try to think" or "Try to act," given the context in which it appears. "Among the gerundive" may suggest "Among the living." Sometimes such phrases turn back on themselves and themselves provide the "content" they request, as in, "otherwise I'll fill in the blank with this noun here in my prepositional object." The reader can make appropriate substitutions for "fill in the blank," "noun," and "prepositional object." But since "fill in the blank" is a predicate and a predicate is what is required at that point, since "noun" is a noun, and since "prepositional object" is here a prepositional object, the sentence fills in its own blanks and the reader can also accept it as it appears, empty though it be. The title of the story, "Title," is not so much the story's "title" (though it may be that too) as an indicator of where the title of a story goes, and the reader can fill in any appropriate title he or she chooses. Utilizing this conceit—using "blanks" where content might be—Barth is able to create a story that approaches non-objectivity, a story that comes close to having no narrative content whatsoever.

Lacking such content, the story becomes a lament on its own deficiencies as a story, on the state of contemporary fiction, and on the state of contemporary culture in general, carried out by a narrative voice talking as if to itself. Sometimes that voice fragments into a "he" and "she" who engage in various verbal exchanges, but no quotation marks are used, confirming the tendency to read both "she" and "he" as different parts of the same solipsistic narrator.

On various levels, the story implies that self-consciousness has the effect of impotence and removal from engagement with life, a standard Barthian theme. This is, of course, a variant on the old contrast between the active and contemplative lives, with a contemporary emphasis on the centrality of language to thought and selfhood. On the most literal level it is a self-conscious narration, a story about its own unfolding, and not about human beings engaged in conflict and action—thus, it is an impotent form of literature. On another level it is about the general self-conscious state of modern literature which, extremely aware of its history and development, orients itself to questions of art rather than of life, turns in on itself, and becomes criticism as much as literature. Finally, the self-conscious story functions as a metaphor for the self-conscious individual who—like Barth's Ambrose and Menelaus—is so involved in contemplating life that he cannot become involved in life. "Historicity and self-awareness, he asseverated, while ineluctable and even greatly to be prized, are always fatal to innocence and spontaneity" (p. 110).

Yet this empty story struggles for a humanistic content:

Take linear plot, take resolution of conflict, take third direct object, all that business, they may very well be obsolete notions, indeed they are, no doubt untenable at this late date, no doubt at all, but in fact we still lead our lives by clock and calendar, for example, and though the seasons recur our mortal human time does not . . . people still fall in love, and out, yes, in and out, and out and in, and they please each other, and hurt each other, isn't that the truth, and they do these things in more or less conventionally dramatic fashion, unfashionable or not, go on, I'm going, and what goes on between them is still not only the most interesting but the most important thing in the bloody murderous world, pardon the adjectives. And that my dear is what writers have got to find ways to write about in this adjective adjective hour of the ditto ditto same noun as above, or their, that is to say our, accursed self-consciousness will lead them, that is to say us, to here it comes, say it straight out, I'm going to, say it in plain English for once, that's what I'm leading up to, me and my bloody anticlimactic noun, we're pushing each other to the fill in the blank. (pp. 112–113)

Barth argued earlier that the attempt to create a completely abstract literature was unlikely to be successful because of the linguistic medium that is the basis of literature: "wood and iron have a native appeal and a first-order reality, whereas words are artificial to begin with, invented specifically to represent" (p. 112). Here he suggests that the attempt is also futile because it removes literature from life and life is, after all, more like a conventional story than an avant-garde self-referential piece. It is at this point in "Title" that Barth's humanistic center is made explicit. Barth writes a story that, perhaps as much as any story ever written, subverts narration and becomes nearly content free, or at least so it seems. But he also subverts his own subversion, lamenting the condition of literature and the condition of the very story we are reading.

The result is a tension between the story's tendency toward abstraction and its need to manifest some content. That tension itself becomes the story's conflict and to the extent that it does in fact involve a conflict and a mounting struggle toward resolution, the story is, after all, conventional. Not that it *provides* resolution, however: it is a struggle of the story itself, or a conflict of two tendencies within the story, rather than the struggle of a character or a conflict between characters in the story. But if human beings are more like texts than existential agents, the story is more mimetic than at first it seems. The paragraph just quoted might, indeed, be regarded as the climax of the story, where the narrative voice gropes to find the words that would satisfactorily articulate a humanistic content in the face of its apparent dehumanization. Nevertheless, the story is not so conventional as to provide us with a resolved conclusion and the paragraph ends appropriately and ambiguously with a perfectly placed "fill in the blank." Barth makes a humanistic statement through the struggle of the story to engage human reality and the story's assertion that fiction must find a way of doing so; but through the final "fill in the blank" he remains faithful to the posthumanistic conceit that informs the entire story. There is both rigor and poignance, and, in this case at least, "passionate virtuosity." The story ends,

Oh God comma I abhor self-consciousness. I despise what we have come to; I loathe our loathesome loathing, our place our time our situation, our loathesome art, this ditto necessary story. The blank of our lives. It's about over. let the *denouement* be soon and unexpected, painless if possible, quick at least, above all soon. Now now! How in the world will it ever (p. 113)

The ambiguity and lack of resolution is perfectly maintained. Is this indeed the end of man, an end that takes place not with a bang but a whimper, or is there something to come, something language has no way of coming to terms with? The story stops but the word "end" is suggested only by a real blank and there is no period.

In contrast to these stories, "Ambrose His Mark" is rigorously conventional. It is the first of three stories in the collection that center on the character Ambrose. "Ambrose His Mark" and "Water Message" (the second "Ambrose" story) were first published in 1963, the earliest stories Barth included in *Lost in the Funhouse*. In spite of the fact that "Ambrose His Mark" is the most conventionally structured and narrated story, it nevertheless articulates the major themes of the entire collection. It is clearly organized, containing an obvious exposition, development, climax, and denouement. The incidents of the story fit into this classical narrative/dramatic pattern the way the themes of a sonata fit into that structure—far more perfectly than is generally the case in narrative art. The exposition describes Ambrose's family and circumstances during his early infancy, the development accelerates toward a slapstick climax, and the falling action or denouement delineates the aftermath and the two major consequences for Ambrose of the story's events: his weaning and his finally receiving a name. (Ambrose's naming has been delayed as a result of the "hectic circumstances" of his birth; his father became convinced that someone else fathered Ambrose, invaded the delivery room in a crazy fit, and has been institutionalized.)

The story contains an elaborate network of related images, the most significant of which are bees, honey, wine, mother's milk, and, of course, the name "Ambrose" (suggesting Ambrosia) itself. At the climax of the story a swarm of bees descends on Ambrose and Andrea, Ambrose's indolent and wanton mother. Ambrose is at his mother's breast, having drunk himself into a drowsy, erotic intoxication. Andrea, who has teased her sister and brother-in-law by openly extolling the erotic aspect of nursing, is in a similar state. A brawl ensues between Ambrose's grandfather—who wants the swarm so that he can make mead from the honey it will produce—and Willy Erdman, the neighbor whose hive the bees have left. Both believe they have a legitimate claim to the bees, which literally cover the infant and Andrea's breasts. Violence erupts, the bees are enraged, but mother and child are nevertheless saved. One bee, however, has managed to remain hidden beneath Andrea's kimono after the remainder of the swarm has been removed and it stings her directly on the breast.

As a result, Andrea refuses to nurse the child any longer and abdicates all responsibility for him, abandoning him to the care of her sister Rosa. As a result of the bee incident, Rosa notices—or imagines—that a wine-colored birthmark on Ambrose's face has the shape of a bee. Konrad, Rosa's shy and intellectual husband, interprets the incident as a "naming-sign" and is provoked to research the history of similar swarming incidents. He discovers a substantial mythology surrounding such incidents, one associating men of thought, language, and eloquence with similar contact with bees in infancy. Such stories associate bees with Plato, Socrates, Xenophon, and St. Ambrose. Andrea balks at the first three names, but finds "Ambrose" not unpleasant, at least in comparison to Xenophon.

It is possible to argue that "Night Sea Journey," probably the best known story in the collection, is really the first Ambrose story. It is a brilliantly executed tale structured around a far-fetched conceit: the musings of an introspective and philosophical spermatozoon provide a vehicle for an existentialistic examination of the absurdity of life. Since "Night Sea Journey" ends with the sperm successfully achieving consummation by penetrating an egg (in spite of his decision that the struggle of life is not worth it and that it would be better to end the cycle of lives and night-sea journeys), and since "Ambrose His Mark," which immediately follows, begins with the words, "Owing to the hectic circumstances of my birth, for some months I had no proper name" (p. 14), it is very easy to read "Night Sea Journey" as the story of Ambrose's conception, his receiving his genetic identity. "Ambrose His Mark," then, is the story of a second conception: he receives his name and, with it, his social and cultural identity. From this perspective there are, in a sense, four rather than three "Ambrose" stories in *Lost in the Funhouse*. But only in a sense; in "Night Sea Journey," "Ambrose" not only has no name, he has only half his genetic make-up. Ambrose is not yet Ambrose.

From a psychoanalytic perspective, "Ambrose His Mark" delineates the sublimation of the literary artist's attachment to the breast to his attachment to language. The milk and honey of infancy become the "honey'd" language of the poet. The psychoanalytic reading of Barth conflates with the structuralist reading, here. The artist, the self-conscious individual, sings, speaks, and thinks in order to overcome his separation from an erotic object that song, speech, and thought ensure will remain inaccessible to him. Language struggles for a meaning it defers. The story ends with the newly named Ambrose frankly in the gap between an existential and a structuralist self, "knowing well that I and my sign are neither one nor quite two" (p. 34).

The volume's title story, the last Ambrose story, deals with Ambrose's experience of getting lost in the funhouse at Ocean City on Independence

Day during the Second World War, when Ambrose is thirteen years old. Throughout the story the narrative flow is regularly interrupted by authorial intrusions that comment on the progress of the story or remark generally on the craft of fiction; by point-of-view shifts from a conventional third-person narrator aware of Ambrose's thoughts to a voice more fully identified with that of Ambrose; and by abrupt time shifts that move the narration back and forth among various moments and events during the day of the family outing. The result is a severely dislocated narrative. Although narrative development is not absolutely absent, the classically perfect structure of "Ambrose His Mark" is. This discrepancy between "Lost in the Funhouse" and an ideal narrative is noted numerous times throughout the story itself and is made most explicit when, during one of the authorial intrusions, the following diagram representing a "conventional dramatic narrative" is given:

This structure, with AB representing the exposition, BC the rising action, C the climax, and CD the denouement, is precisely the structure of "Ambrose His Mark." Barth's purpose here, of course, is not to clarify (except perhaps indirectly) how perfectly his earlier story matches the conventional ideal but to comment on how far short of that ideal the story-in-progress falls.

Authorial intrusions early in the story are mini-lectures on the craft of fiction. Devices the story employs are used as illustrations of means by which a writer can create an illusion of reality. The effect of such intrusions is Brechtian; the illusion that the identified techniques might have created is destroyed.

En route to Ocean City [Ambrose] sat in the back seat of the family car with his brother Peter, age fifteen, and Magda G ———— , age fourteen, a pretty girl an exquisite young lady, who lived not far from them on B ———— Street in the town of D _____ , Maryland. Initials, blanks, or both were often substituted for proper names in nineteenth-century fiction to enhance the illusion of reality. It is as if the author felt it necessary to delete the names for reasons of tact or legal liability. Interestingly, as with other aspects of realism, it is an *illusion* that is being enhanced, by purely artificial means. (pp. 72–73)

On another occasion Barth begins a paragraph with a discussion of the descriptive technique of using details that appeal to various senses. He then returns to the story but leaves certain sentences unfinished, as if completing them is a simple matter of applying the principle he has outlined. The reader can complete them as he or she wishes. Fiction making—even highly crafted fiction making—is a matter of using techniques that anyone can learn.

When the story moves into Ambrose's mind it presents his perceptions, thoughts, and fantasies with varying degrees of distance between the voice of the narrator and the inner voice of Ambrose. Sometimes moderate distance is maintained, in a manner consistent with the recording of a character's thoughts in a conventional third-person narration. On other occasions distance is diminished and the narration assumes something like a modern stream-of-consciousness point of view. At still other times, and more frequently as the story progresses, all distance is lost and the narrative voice seems fully identified with the consciousness of the protagonist. On one such occasion a direct quotation of Ambrose modulates into an authorial commentary; the youthful "voice" of the protagonist becomes the adult voice of the narrator, both somehow contained within the same set of quotation marks. On another occasion the narrative voice ambiguously describes the progress of the story and Ambrose's thoughts when he is lost in the funhouse. By the end of the story there has been an effective merger of narrator and character and even in the third person one feels that Ambrose himself is the story teller.

Time shifts regularly occur between events leading up to Ambrose's becoming lost in the funhouse and his actually being lost in the funhouse. These time shifts help create the impression that his experience of being lost is ambiguously an incident that occurred in the past that can (or might) be narrated and an abiding state or condition of his mind that does not "develop" and cannot be narrated. The story proceeds associatively, as if articulating a certain psychological field—Ambrose's psychic ecology of sex, fantasy, language, and contemplation; at the same time, it struggles to become the narration of a possibly real incident that helped crystallize that ecology. These two views of Ambrose's being lost—as an incident or as a psychological condition—correlate with the two endings for the story.

Ambrose remains lost in the funhouse and dies of starvation, "telling himself stories in the dark" (p. 95), but he also escapes from the funhouse and returns home with his family.

Ambrose dies telling himself stories, but he is unaware of the fact that those stories have been secretly recorded by the funhouse operator's daughter, who eavesdrops on his solipsism, is deeply moved, and writes them down from behind a partition to preserve them for posterity. The identification between "Lost in the Funhouse" and the narration she transcribes, the identification between the narrator of "Lost in the Fun- house" and Ambrose, is suggested by the following infinite regress: "Quietly she kissed the rough plyboard, and a tear fell upon the page. Where she had written in shorthand *Where* she had written in shorthand *Where she* et cetera" (p. 96). If "Lost in the Funhouse" is itself the story—or one of the stories—the girl transcribes, then the tear falls on the very sentence that begins "Where she had written in shorthand. . . ." In order to complete that sentence she must include it within itself, and such efforts at self-reference produce infinite loops from which there is no logical escape. Barth exits from the loop with an "et cetera," leaving its infinite regress implied, but allowing him to go on with the story.

In the second ending, Ambrose does get out of the funhouse and the story concludes with his thoughts as the family returns home. This second ending is more like the conclusion of a traditional narrative, the de- nouement of a story about a boy who gets lost but is somehow found. In this respect Ambrose's loss within the funhouse can be narrated and concluded, in contrast to the funhouse as neurotic state of mind suggested by the infinite regress in the first ending. Yet, even in this second ending the other implication of the funhouse is suggested. Although Ambrose's literal loss in the funhouse may be over, he remains psychologically inside it; the experience has crystallized certain awarenesses of himself as different, as an artist, as one incapable of entering the funhouse the way others do—unselfconscious lovers, for example. Ambrose has gotten lost in the funhouse, and while there has seen the funhouse operator through a crack in the wall and has discovered the illusionistic mechanisms that make the funhouse work. He is doomed or blessed to go through life as an individual who thinks about—and creates—funhouses, rather than as one who enjoys them.

Ambrose's loss in the funhouse is not the cause of his contemplative disengagement but is the experience that provokes him into clearly recognizing it and making a crucial decision in response to it. On a few occasions in the story Ambrose recalls a significant experience that took place three years earlier and that was another manifestation of his disengagement. Magda, the girl accompanying the family on the outing, a year older than Ambrose, surprised Ambrose by performing a sexual act on him in a woodshed in the midst of a child's game. Although he feigned ecstasy, Ambrose self-consciously asserted to himself, *"This is what they call* passion. *I am experiencing it"* (p. 84), words that belie what they assert, since anyone really experiencing ecstasy would not be articulating the experience, at least not at the moment of its occurrence. Ambrose resorts to language in an attempt to grasp passion and only succeeds in holding passion at bay.

The story ends with Ambrose's full realization that he is an artist, a creator of funhouses, and not one of the lovers who enter and enjoy them.

> He envisions a truly astonishing funhouse, incredibly complex yet utterly controlled from a great central switchboard like the console of a pipe organ. Nobody had enough imagination. He could design such a place himself, wiring and all, and he's only thirteen years old. He would be its operator: panel lights would show what was up in every cranny of its cunning of its multifarious vastness. . . .
>
> He wishes he had never entered the funhouse. But he has. Then he wishes he were dead. But he's not. Therefore he will construct funhouses for others and be their secret operator—though he would rather be among the lovers for whom funhouses are designed. (p. 97)

The funhouse that Ambrose imagines is, in fact, a valid description of Barth's own *oeuvre*—a vast maze, a labyrinth of such complexity that only its creator could understand all its intricacies, a "floating opera" of which one catches only segments, comprehending some, not comprehending others, but aware that they are all part of some large artifice—a universe whose coherence one can only partly grasp.

LETTERS and the Metafictional Impasse

Barth has described Borges's imaginary *Encyclopaedia of Tlon* as "a coherent alternative to this world complete in every respect from its algebra to its fire."[18] He says that it was not necessary for Borges to *write* this encyclopedia of an imaginary planet but only to allude to its existence. Yet Barth's own novel *LETTERS*, a massive, complicated, "epistolary" novel, seems not simply to allude to such a "coherent alternative" to this world but to actually write it, to describe it in all its aspects, including its algebra and fire. The world so described is not, of course, the culture of the people of an imaginary planet, but is Barth's own fictional world. *LETTERS* attempts to sum up, "recycle," and consolidate Barth's entire *oeuvre* up to the writing of *LETTERS*. The seven correspondents whose letters comprise the novel consist of five characters (or their descendents or counterparts) from Barth's previous fiction, one entirely new character, and the "author" himself. *LETTERS* thus functions as a sequel to all of Barth's previous works and is an attempt to synthesize their plots, major characters, and themes. The ambition of this project is made evident when one considers the diversity of Barth's fiction, ranging as it does from the historical to the fantastic, from the traditional to the highly experimental.

Although various statements by Barth indicate his belief that fiction should strive to speak to humans about human issues, *LETTERS* does, on the most obvious level at least, present itself as a huge personal intertextuality, an elaborate Barthian solipsism, a "coherent alternative" to the world that points not to the world but to itself and to other works by Barth. Although Barth claims—or seems to claim, through the "Barth" of *LETTERS*—that acquaintance with his previous novels is unnecessary for an appreciation of *LETTERS*,[19] the substantial difficulty of the novel would be inevitably compounded for a reader who had no prior knowledge of Barth's world. *LETTERS* is a fictional prisonhouse of language that cannot escape from its intertextual limits, but which does enlarge the size of its cell through baroque and mannerist variations on Barthian themes and characters. Nevertheless, as in "Menelaid" and other *Lost in the Funhouse* stories, the struggle of language to transcend language may itself provide a humanistic content for the novel.

The struggle of *LETTERS* may seem, at first, to be not much different from that of Didi and Gogo in *Waiting for Godot,* who also get caught up in solipsistic ruminations and who also do a lot of talking, most of which has little meaning. But in *Waiting for Godot* there is still the sense of Didi and Gogo as existential agents who *use* language, perhaps not to communicate, but at least to kill time and to avoid fully confronting their condition. In *LETTERS* the struggle is one of language itself. Barth comes closer than Beckett to the structuralist vision of self as linguistic construct. The whole structure of *LETTERS* and the relation of that novel to the rest of Barth's *oeuvre* suggest the view that language is not simply a problematical mediator between "selves" and "realities," but that language is the reality itself. Barth stops just short of fully embracing this position, however, and periodically asserts a humanistic center and purpose. Ambrose and his sign are not quite two, but they are not quite one either.

The new character introduced in *LETTERS* is Lady Amherst (Germaine

Pitt), widow and acting provost of Marshyhope State University in Maryland. The first letter in the novel is her invitation to John Barth to come to Marshyhope in order to receive an honorary doctorate. Her invitation is an aspect of a larger internal political struggle within the university in which she is pitted against the president, who would prefer to confer the honor upon a conservative rhymer, A. B. Cook VI, "self-styled Laureate of Maryland"; Cook is a descendent of the Cookes and Burlingames of *The Sot-Weed Factor* and may, in fact, not be a reactionary poet at all but the political revolutionary Henry Burlingame VI; he may also be the French Canadian Andre Castine, of Castine's Hundred, Ontario, Lady Amherst's own old lover in disguise. The connection between this Burlingame-Cook-Castine and the similarly protean Henry Burlingame of *The Sot-Weed Factor* is evident. In other sections of the novel letters written by A. B. Cooke VI and his ancestor A. B. Cook IV trace the entire history of the Cookes, Burlingames, and Castines from the seventeenth-century setting of *The Sot-Weed Factor* to the contemporary setting of *LETTERS*.

Barth declines Lady Amherst's invitation, but asks her instead if she will help him with his current novel by sharing with him the details of her life, one that involves not only campus politics but also affairs with numerous major writers of the twentieth century, including one writer from Barth's own fiction. Lady Amherst is involved in a passionate relationship with Ambrose Mensch, the Ambrose of the *Lost in the Funhouse* stories, now himself a writer of experimental fiction and another of the contributors of letters to Barth's novel *LETTERS*. Later Ambrose decides that he wants Germaine to bear his child, though she is nearly menopausal. She does finally become pregnant, though there is some question regarding the child's paternity. In Ambrose's letters, he gives Barth some good advice about writing and makes numerous suggestions that Barth incorporates into his work, even into the novel *LETTERS* itself. *LETTERS* is messy. It is premised on a violation of narrative levels. Fictional characters speak to their author, who is himself inside a work of fiction; stories inside stories loop around like moebius strips in an attempt to surround the stories that surround them.

Other characters who contribute to *LETTERS* include Todd Andrews from *The Floating Opera*, Jacob Horner from *End of the Road*, and Jerome Bray, who appeared in the "Bellerophoniad" novella of *Chimera* but who is also connected in some way to the Harold Bray of *Giles Goat Boy*. Jerome Bray is a piece of inspired surrealism, a paranoid and delusionary environmentalist, computer maniac (perhaps part computer himself), utopian abstract novelist, revolutionary, and (perhaps) part honeybee, a drone who wishes to help usher in a "New Golden Age" by fertilizing all the major women in *LETTERS*. He also believes that through a blood connection with Napoleon he has a legitimate claim to the French throne and that John Barth, whom he is trying to sue, has plagiarized his novels from Bray. The women he finally seduces include the actress Bea Golden (actually Jeannine Mack, daughter of Jane Mack from *The Floating Opera*), Merope Bernstein (Jane's stepdaughter), Marsha Blank (Ambrose's ex-wife), possibly Lady Amherst herself, and possibly Angie Mensch, Ambrose and Marsha's retarded daughter. Bray uses his computer, LILYVAC, in an attempt to create an ideal novel that will consist of numbers rather than letters and that will render obsolete even the conflict between fiction and film that also figures in *LETTERS*. Bray's planned work in "numerature" is Barth's image of the logical extreme of formalist writing, a vision of a true "writing degree zero."

It is impossible to summarize all the complicated and interrelated plots, subplots, stories related in flashback, and recapitulations of earlier works of Barth included in *LETTERS*. Eventually nearly all the characters become involved in the making of a film based on all of Barth's works. The maker of this film, Reg Prince, speaks primarily in interjections, exclamations, and short phrases, and is determined to make a film that will not at all be dependent on language. He and Ambrose, the film's scriptwriter—who will also be playing the role of the author in the film—enact between them a war between literature and film, verbal and non-verbal forms of communication. The film is vertiginously self-referential since in it various characters of Barth end up playing themselves or other of Barth's characters. The idea of making a non-verbal film based on Barth's works—a film that is supposed to remain true to his spirit though completely free in its filmic adaptation—is brilliantly ludicrous and ironic. Since so much of Barth's work is concerned with the problems of language and since linguistic manipulation is involved in so much of his technique, a non-verbal work based on his fiction and true to his themes is unimaginable.

LETTERS is a novel obsessed with letters. The "letters" of the book's title suggest written correspondence, the alphabetical letters that are the elemental units of writing, and the whole domain of *belles lettres*. But it is also a novel obsessed with numbers. The seven correspondents write a total of eighty-eight letters during seven months (March through September) of 1969. A calendar covering this period appears in its entirety near the end of the novel and in one-month segments preceding each of seven sections. Each section is comprised of the correspondence of the month of the calendar that precedes it. Alphabetical letters are placed over the dates of each month that correspond to dates of letters in the section that follows. Individually, these alphabetical letters spell out the novel's subtitle: "An OLD TIME EPISTOLARY NOVEL BY SEVEN FICTITIOUS DROLLS & DREAMERS EACH OF WHICH IMAGINES HIMSELF ACTUAL." Moreover, the positioning of the letters of this subtitle on the calendar months creates the shapes of seven larger letters, those of the novel's main title, one large letter for each of the seven months. On each calendar the names of the seven correspondents are aligned with the seven days of the week; each correspondent writes letters only on a particular day of the week, wherever alphabetical letters aligned with his or her name are placed. In each monthly section letters from each of the seven correspondents are included, always in the same order. Although more than one letter by any of them can be included, the order cannot be violated. The presence of a correspondence by a given writer on a given date is necessitated by the calendar that spells out the novel's title and subtitle.

Thus Barth, in structuring *LETTERS*, has set up a system of rigid numerical rules and constraints under which he must work, a system something like the rules for composing music. The musical association is heightened by the fact that there are seven notes in the diatonic scale, corresponding to the seven letter writers, and eighty-eight keys on a piano, corresponding to the eighty-eight letters comprising the novel. (Barth himself briefly attended the Julliard School and is reputed to be a very competent jazz musician.) In contrast to the diatonic seven, however, the arrangement of the correspondents within each section produces a series of writers somewhat like a tone row in serial composition. Barth maintains the order of the "row" of correspondents he establishes, as if they were notes in a musical series. Like the notes of such a series, correspondents can contribute more than one letter during a given section, provided it is during their "turn"; once that "turn" is passed they will not be heard again until the next section—the next time the series is sounded.

As with musical composition, Barth does make some adjustments or "compromises" with his system. The requirement that he cover all the historical ground between *Sot-Weed Factor* and *LETTERS* results in the necessity for there to be two A. B. Cooks instead of one, but they must be regarded as in some sense a single persona if the novel's correspondents are to be limited to seven, as indicated by the subtitle. In addition, the letters of the first Cook are written on the correct dates, but in the year 1812 instead of 1969.

Barth's generally rigorous formalization of form connects *LETTERS* with Jerome Bray's/LILYVAC's *NOVEL*. *NOVEL* is the logical extension of the formalist and self-referential tendencies of literature, tendencies that dominate *LETTERS*. Furthermore, in a novel filled with anagrams, codes, number games, puns, and cabalistic symbols, the fact that the initials of Jerome Bray, the novel's prince of darkness, are the same as those of the novel's author is certainly no coincidence. Bray's planned work is, of course, a large step beyond *LETTERS* since he abandons letters (and thus language as well) and resorts to numbers, which have no referential significance in his work but function merely as units for formal play.

Besides the numerical patternings that guide the overall structure of the novel, many of its characters are involved in the creation or discovery of mathematical patterns in their lives or their art, patterns related sometimes to occult mystical and magical numbers and sometimes to numbers and ratios that intrigue scientists, mathematicians, and artists: the golden section, the golden spiral, the Fibonacci series, and the proportions of certain natural structures. All the novel's major characters, including "Barth" himself, are in some way involved in the repetition and recycling of aspects or stages of their lives. One of the major themes of *LETTERS* is that of recycling and the novel itself is a recycling of the previous work of Barth. Ambrose sees the development of his affair with Lady Amherst as recapitulating the stages of his earlier love life. Jacob Horner, still an inmate at the Remobilization Farm (though it has changed locations since the time of *End of the Road*) must engage in "Der Wiedertraum," a theatrical reenactment of the events of that earlier novel, as a form of therapy and atonement. Todd Andrews sees his later life as a recycling of the stages of his earlier life, remains obsessed with his father's suicide (as he was in *The Floating Opera*), experiences a reenactment of his affair with Jane Mack as well as a new affair with Jeannine Mack (who may be his own daughter), and plans and carries out a new suicide attempt, this one probably successful, in contrast to the failed attempt on the showboat that provided the name for Barth's earlier novel. Most significantly, perhaps, generation after generation of Cooks and Burlingames reenact the themes of Oedipal rebellion, political intrigue, disguise, and duplicity.

One of the more comically Pirandellian parts of *LETTERS* is Todd Andrew's description of the insanity of Harrison Mack, Jane's husband, who died a month before the first letters of the novel were written. Like Pirandello's Henry in *Henry IV* (*Enrico IV*, 1922), Harrison comes to suffer from the delusion he is a great king, George III. As in Pirandello's play, the crazy man's household engages in an elaborate masquerade (directed here by Lady Amherst) in which various individuals play the roles of historical figures in order to humor him in his madness. The irony in *Henry IV* results from the fact that Henry has actually been sane for a number of years; his friends are thus made to appear crazier than him because of their willingness to serve his fantasy through their elaborate theatrical game. Barth's irony is, if anything, even more elegant. Harrison comes to believe himself to be not George III sane but George III mad. And George III mad believes himself to be Harrison Mack. Thus, Harrison Mack, hopelessly locked in a reality that is pure delusion, is able to carry out his business affairs with complete lucidity and good sense.

The theme of a duplicitous reality that allows for a multiplicity of mutually exclusive interpretations that explain the facts equally well is central to *LETTERS*. Is Harrison Mack really sane and faking it or is he suffering from a double-leveled insanity that allows him to behave in a manner indistinguishable from sane behavior? Situations analogous to this one are reiterated throughout the novel, especially in the extended historical sequences involving the Cooks, Burlingames, and Castines. Every revolutionary may be a reactionary in disguise, and vice-versa. Sons rebel against what they believe their fathers represent only to discover that their fathers have been deceiving them regarding their beliefs and commitments; but this apparent discovery may itself be the result of a deception. At one point the following list of possible interpretations of A. B. Cook VI is offered by his son:

1. He wishes the Revolution to succeed and hopes that I shall support it, since he believes me a "winner"; therefore
    a. he works for it himself, because he considers himself also a "winner" and does not believe that I shall rebel against him; or
    b. he works *against* it, because he regards himself (as he regarded his namesakes) as a "loser," and/or because he believes that I shall work against him.
2. He wishes the Revolution to succeed and hopes that I shall oppose it, since he believes me a loser; therefore
    a. he works for it himself, considering himself a winner and trusting me to rebel against him; or
    b. he works *against* it, believing himself a loser and trusting me *not* to rebel against him.
3. He *opposes* the Revolution and wishes me to do likewise, inasmuch as he considers me a winner; therefore
    a. he works *against* it, believing that he is a winner and that I shall not rebel against him; or
    b. he works *for* it, thinking himself a loser and that I *shall* rebel against him.
4. He opposes the Revolution but wants me to support it, believing me to be a loser; therefore

a. he works against it, thinking himself a winner and that I shall rebel against him; or

b. he works for it, thinking himself a loser and that I shall *not* rebel against him. (pp. 753–754)

Earlier in the novel Lady Amherst, in a letter to Barth, described the advice she received from Ambrose for dealing with the Cooks and Burlingames: "The skill and subtlety of those circumambient impostures over so many generations, the welter of obscure purposes and cross-purposes, made a kind of radical positivism the only possible approach to, or bridge over, the vertiginous quicksand of history" (p. 351). Such a "radical positivism," we can assume, would eliminate all speculation about realities beyond observable fact. Thus, actions by any member of the Burlingame-Cook-Castine line could be described, but any speculation regarding that individual's "true" motives and ultimate purpose would be futile. It is the same epistemology as that voiced by Warhol when he suggests that all he knows or is interested in are surfaces.

Much of *LETTERS* is brilliant, bawdy, comic, and poignant. Some parts do manage to synthesize emotion and technique so that Barth achieves the "passionate virtuosity" he seeks. Unfortunately, many other parts are labored workings-out of Barthian conceits. Some sections of the novel are more interesting when paraphrased than when actually read. This is especially true in the extended A. B. Cook letters. Barth successfully mimics the style of the historical memoir, but that style, combined with the intentionally repetitious nature of the characters and experiences of the various members of the Burlingame-Cook-Castine line, produces a narration destined to test the patience of even the most devoted readers.

In "The Literature of Replenishment" Barth describes the ideal postmodernist author as one who "has the first half of our century under his belt, but not on his back."[20] Barth sees the goal of postmodernism as overcoming the dichotomy between modernist writing and traditional "bourgeois" realism, and as creating a new kind of fiction that is more accessible than "modern" fiction, one that will require less explication by specialist professors. Examples of writers whom he mentions as successfully operating in a postmodernist idiom include Italo Calvino, whom he says manages to keep one foot in the Italian narrative past and another in the Parisian structuralist present, and the Colombian Gabriel García Márquez, whose first lines of *One Hundred Years of Solitude* Barth quotes as a model of postmodern writing. *One Hundred Years of Solitude* obviously was an influence on *LETTERS*. The two geneological tables describing the

Cooks and Burlingames parallel a similar table in García Márquez's novel, as do the recurrences of names (Cooks and Burlingames, Arcadios and Aurelianos) and the recurrences of similar incidents and situations in the lives of similarly named characters. However, García Márquez's novel is suffused with such rich and varied poetry and imagery that the repetitiousness does not result in sterility but functions to bring a necessary unity into the narrative. Barth is fully capable of poetry, but his novel is much more uneven. Furthermore, the novel's complexity and its relationship to Barth's previous work make it all but inaccessible to individuals unacquainted with his literary universe. In spite of himself Barth has created a novel for specialists.

But Barth is right to choose *One Hundred Years of Solitude* as a model. It manages to achieve what many North American and European novels rarely achieve so perfectly: it is a novel that is fully contemporary stylistically and formally and is, at the same time, accessible to a wide audience and is even, to some extent, engaged socially and politically. Its vast imaginary panorama includes (along with nearly everything else) descriptions of relations of economic exploitation, and it ends with a Pirandellian twist, the entire novel revealing itself to be a manuscript on parchment that the most recent Aureliano is deciphering: it is the entire history of his family, in complete detail, up to his very reading of the history he is reading, culminating with his completing the reading which is, at the same time, the moment of his death and the end of the novel.[21]

Embedded narratives and narrative convolutions are favorite devices of other Latin American writers of recent decades. Julio Cortazar's "Continuity of Parks" is a story about a man reading a novel that contains him as the imminent victim (obliviously engrossed in his reading) of a romantic, melodramatic murder. Cortazar's "Blow-Up" (on which Michelangelo Antonioni loosely based his 1966 film), a story self-consciously aware of its telling, contains contradictions and ambiguities involving the relationship between reality and reality narrated and photographed.[22] Mario Vargas Llosa's *Aunt Julia and the Scriptwriter* is the story of a not quite incestuous romance between a young writer and a divorced aunt by marriage. It contains embedded within it narrative versions of popular radio melodramas that begin to emulate modern literature as their scriptwriter approaches senility and loses track of his plots and characters.[23]

Oedipa Maas, the protagonist of Thomas Pynchon's *The Crying of Lot 49*, is unsure whether she discovers or invents paranoically the conspiracy she is investigating, whether the "reality" of that conspiracy is something objective and separate from her or is her own creation. The novel contains an embedded play, *The Courier's Tragedy,* a brilliant and hilarious parody of a Jacobean revenge play, that contains clues to the conspiracy she discovers or projects.[24] Robert Coover's metafictional collection, *Pricksongs and Descants,* dedicates one of its sections to Cervantes; Coover explicitly takes him as his model. "The Magic Poker," from that collection, blatantly presents itself as an invention and playfully reworks ideas and images, experimenting with different ways of modeling the same material and, at the same time, flaunting the fictitiousness of the fiction. The result is a story that is structured not in terms of narrative consistency but more like a musical theme and variations.[25]

Alain Robbe-Grillet's *Project for a Revolution in New York* is a novel whose point of view regularly shifts to the inside of reflections or representations. Scenes left behind as a result of these shifts are often rediscovered, now inside the reflections or representations they previously contained. Usually such rediscovered scenes are not exact recreations of earlier ones but are variants, somewhat in the manner of Coover's "The Magic Poker." The novel parodies various sources: urban crime thrillers, spy novels, and sado-masochistic exploitation films, all relayed through an extremely effaced narrative voice (in ironic contrast to the sometimes highly charged material) that moves through a Pirandellian hall of mirrors. Robbe-Grillet's title notwithstanding, the novel seems not to have any political purpose but seems to be an elaborate, self-contained narrative labyrinth. It is postmodernism at its most removed from anything referential, apart from the references to art itself.[26]

Fowles and Barth are humanistic postmoderns. They share with structuralists and poststructuralists a recognition of the role of language in creating human reality and in constituting the sense of self. At the same time, they are not prepared to completely abandon the individual and feel that the work they do must finally find its value and justification in its relevence to human beings. If their goal is somehow balancing a humanist and a posthumanist position, of creating an authentic contemporary literature that engages human beings, their respective weaknesses lie in opposite directions. When Fowles loses balance he lapses into sentimentality; sometimes his self-referential devices seem to be simply imposed upon what is really a traditional romance. When Barth loses balance the effect is the opposite; sentiment is lost and his narratives become elaborate, clever, but sterile workings out of overly intellectual conceits. Significantly, both writers, after major but imperfect works—*Daniel Martin* in 1977 and

LETTERS in 1979—seem to have given themselves "sabbaticals" by writing shorter, less ambitious novels. The title of Fowles's *Mantissa* (1982) suggests that the work is, in the words that the novel itself quotes from the Oxford English Dictionary, "an addition of comparatively small importance, especially to a literary effort or discourse" (p. 188, n.). The title of Barth's *Sabbatical,* published the same year as *Mantissa,* similarly suggests that the work may be a means of rest or regeneration and is less ambitious than some of the author's other works. Fowles's *A Maggot* (1985) is more interesting and ambitious; it utilizes a legal inquiry as a means of presenting a variety of points of view regarding an elusive truth that is sought. In *Tidewater Tales* (1987) Barth once again writes a long novel. A writer and his wife share tales of their past during a risky cruise they take during her last few weeks of pregnancy; additional embedded stories are provided by various people they meet, who include the couple from *Sabbatical,* a novel closely related to *Tidewater Tales* in theme, situation, and technique. There is nothing new, perhaps, in these later novels, and they do not seem to aim quite so high as the major earlier works of these authors, but they are comfortable variations on postmodern devices and comfortable incorporations of postmodern themes into novels that are, in fact, fairly accessible.

Notes

1. *The Magus, A Revised Version* (Boston: Little, Brown, 1978), p. 404. Revised version first published London: Jonathan Cape, 1977. Original version first published in 1965 by Jonathan Cape (London) and Little, Brown (Boston). Future citations in parentheses.

2. John Fowles (text) and Frank Horvat (photographs), *The Tree* (Boston, Toronto: Little, Brown, 1979), unpaginated. An excerpt from this essay was published as "Seeing Nature Whole," *Harpers* (November 1979), 49–68. This quote appears on p. 53 of the *Harpers* excerpt.

3. John Fowles, *The French Lieutenant's Woman* (Boston: Little, Brown, 1969), p. 77. Future citations in parentheses.

4. John Fowles, *Mantissa* (Boston: Little, Brown, 1982), p. 161.

5. Trans. Eric Bentley, in *Naked Masks,* p. 366.

6. *Narcissistic Narrative, The Metafictional Paradox* (New York and London: Methuen, 1984), p. 63.

7. Olschen, *John Fowles* (New York: Ungar, 1978), p. 112. Huffaker, *John Fowles* (Boston: Twayne, 1980), 36–39.

8. Olschen, p. 112. Olschen cites David H. Walker, who made this observation in his paper "Subversion of Narrative in the Work of André Gide and John Fowles: From Ironic Monologue to Self-Conscious Novel," delivered to the annual conference of the British Comparative Literature Association, December 1977.

9. Huffaker, p. 42.

10. Huffaker, p. 42. Letter dated July 7, 1978.

11. "Seeing Nature Whole," p. 53.

12. John Barth, "The Literature of Exhaustion," *The Atlantic* (August 1967), p. 33.

13. Quoted in Huffaker, p. 35. The quote is from a letter to Huffaker dated July 16, 1977.

14. Quoted in David Morrell, *John Barth, An Introduction* (University Park: Pennsylvania State University Press, 1976), p. 96. Barth made these remarks at an address delivered at the Library of Congress on May 1, 1967.

15. John Barth, *Lost in the Funhouse, Fiction for Print, Tape, Live Voice* (Garden City, New York: Doubleday, 1968), 1–2. Future citations in parentheses.

16. *Contemporary Authors,* new revision series, Vol. 5, ed. Ann Evory (Detroit: Gale Research Company, 1982), p. 38.

17. John Barth, "The Literature of Exhaustion," p. 33.

18. *Ibid.,* p. 32. The encyclopedia is described in Borges's story, "Tlon, Uqbar, Orbis Tertius," *Labyrinths, Selected Stories & Other Writings,* ed. Donald A. Yates and James E. Irby (New York: New Directions, 1964), 3–18.

19. John Barth, *LETTERS* (New York: Putnam, 1979), p. 341. Future citations in parentheses.

20. John Barth, "The Literature of Replenishment, Postmodernist Fiction," *The Atlantic* (January 1980), p. 70.

21. Gabriel García Márquez, *One Hundred Years of Solitude,* trans. Gregory Rabassa (New York: Harper & Row, 1970).

22. Julio Cortazar, *End of the Game and Other Stories,* trans. Paul Blackburn (New York: Random House, 1967).

23. Mario Vargas Llosa, *Aunt Julia and the Scriptwriter,* trans. Helen R. Lane (New York: Farrar, Straus and Giroux, 1982).

24. Thomas Pynchon, *The Crying of Lot 49* (Philadelphia: Lippincott, 1966).

25. Robert Coover, *Pricksongs & Descants* (New York: Dutton, 1969).

26. Alain Robbe-Grillet, *Project for a Revolution in New York,* trans. Richard Howard (New York: Grove, 1972).

6

POSTMODERNISM, POSTHUMANISM, AND POLITICS

It has become a commonplace assumption that the present is a posthumanist era. As early as 1935 José Ortega y Gasset spoke of art's "dehumanization."[1] Although remarkably prophetic in many respects, Ortega y Gasset, as the title of his famous essay implies, was discussing a new notion of art more than a new notion of humankind. More recent writers have elaborated more fully the implications of his insights and have explicitly suggested that a major shift in the concept of the human individual has occurred in recent decades. They have argued that something fundamental has happened that has disrupted, radically extended, or transcended the humanist tradition that has served Western humanity for at least half a millenium.

Ihab Hassan, for example, uses the terms "posthumanism" and "transhumanism" to suggest both the disruption of the notion of a self firmly rooted in the Cartesian *cogito* and a new, expanded notion of a transcendent self, a "cosmological extension of human consciousness" related to the ideas of thinkers such as Pierre Teilhard de Chardin and Henri Bergson.[2] Jonathan Culler discusses the anti-humanistic implications of semiotics and structuralism, which suggest that "the self is dissolved as its various functions are ascribed to impersonal systems that operate through it." The individual ceases to be centered in an *a priori* "self" but becomes instead a locus where various signifying systems intersect.[3] Richard Schechner gives a book on contemporary theatre the title, *The End of Humanism*: *postmodern* performance signals the end of what is for him the arrogance of the humanist tradition, with its faith in the individual and in the power of human reason; in its stead he imagines a "holistic" perspective, seemingly mystical in nature, reminiscent of Hassan's "trans-humanism," yet somehow connected in his mind with sociobiology, computers, and multinational corporations.[4]

Jacques Derrida, leader of deconstruction—the poststructuralist theory rooted in radical skepticism applied to the reading of texts—writes of a view that "is no longer turned toward the origin, affirms play and tries to pass beyond man and humanism, the name of man being the name of that being who . . . has dreamed of full presence, the reassuring foundation, the origin and the end of play";[5] the implication is that the latter *is* a dream, that there *is* no "full presence" or "reassuring foundation," and that play is all. The French psychoanalyst Jacques Lacan is similarly anti-Cartesian, rewriting Freud with an awareness of structural linguistics; Lacan sees the adult personality as a product of the entrance into language.[6] Finally, Marxist writers like Louis Althusser and Fredric Jameson attempt to integrate structuralist insights and Marxist materialism and deny the ontological primacy of the individual; Jameson describes ideology as a "strategy of containment" that represses history and creates an estranged subject.[7]

It is clear that the various individuals who speak of a "posthumanist" point of view do not necessarily share common attitudes and philosophies in other respects. The thoroughgoing skepticism of the deconstructionists seems a far cry from the utopian faith of Hassan and Schechner, certainly. Nevertheless, there are some common assumptions held by those who describe the posthumanist perspective, in spite of their differences. The *cogito,* for example, is generally called into question, either in the name of a larger, transcendent self, expressed in quasi-mystical terms, or when subjected to the scrutiny of an uncompromising skepticism that refuses to accept the *a priori* certainty of the conscious self, in spite of its Cartesian and seemingly self-evident basis. For the one the self is transcended through technological and spiritual growth (the two are no longer seen as opposed); for the other it is a logocentric error. Faith and skepticism here arrive at a common conclusion.

A second humanist belief questioned by posthumanists is the belief that the intellect is capable of apprehending any truth beyond its own linguistic maneuvering. Such attitudes lie deep in the fabric of modern culture—in Nietzsche, Wittgenstein, Whorf, and, perhaps most significantly for recent critical thought, Saussure. In *The Will to Power* Nietzsche described the "logical appearance" of reality as a human illusion, something determined by the need to order and classify, a reflection, that is, of the structuring operations of the mind rather than of anything inherent in the objects of human contemplation:

> The form seems to be something enduring . . . but the form was invented merely by ourselves. . . .
> *Form, species, law, idea, purpose*—the same fault is made in respect of all these concepts, namely, that of giving a false realism to a piece of fiction: as if all phenomena were infused with some sort of obedient spirit. . . .
> We should not interpret this *constraint* in ourselves, to imagine concepts, species, forms, purposes, and laws . . . as if we were in a position to construct a *real world*; but as a constraint to adjust a world by means of which *our existence* will be ensured: we thereby create a world which is determinable, simplified, comprehensible, etc., for us.[8]

And Saussure emphasized the dependence of ideas upon the language that expresses them, arguing that without language ideas could not exist: "Without language, thought is a vague, uncharted nebula. There are no pre-existing ideas, and nothing is distinct before the appearance of language."[9]

Skepticism regarding the nature and existence of the self together with epistemological skepticism imply the end of the ancient notion of man as the measure of all things. Man is the measure neither through his position as a psychological-spiritual center situated in a material world with which he interacts, nor in his significance as a being endowed with an intellect that enables him to come to an understanding of that world. No rules of rational thought provide a vantage point from which humans can observe and know a world understood as existing independently of consciousness itself. And the self itself is de-centered, dissolving into a technological oversoul or subsumed by the textual interplay of language.

Postmodernism plays with these ideas, pursuing them with an unprecedented singlemindedness. Epistemological skepticism, the crisis of the self, and a "systemic" or "structuralist" consciousness that views human beings more as aspects of a larger structure than as fundamental entities are recurring themes of the major works discussed in this study. Pirandello's plays attempt systematically to subvert confidence in conventional ways of knowing, and the conflict between the self and the mask occurs regularly in those plays; they also suggest, however, that the "self" that is involved in this conflict may be an illusion, a product of *beliefs* about the self rather than of any essential psychological or spiritual center. The play-within-a-play structure of many of Pirandello's plays is a means of formally dramatizing the theme of reality as theatre, the known as a creation of the knower. Brechtian techniques designed to foreground artifice are attempts to acknowledge the play as a sign and to avoid the illusion that it is a transparent window opening onto a real world. Novels of Fowles such as *The Magus* and *The French Lieutenant's Woman* are Pirandellian in theme as well as style and structure. *French Lieutenant,* moreover, contains numerous narrative correspondences to Brechtian theatrical devices. Pop portraits and self-portraits by Warhol involve a similar skepticism in relation to their subjects, the knowability of those subjects, and even their very existence as entities in themselves. And the disguise motif in John Barth's fiction, along with the recurring ambiguity of motives in his characters, functions ultimately to subvert credence in the existence of a self behind the role played and in the possibility of understanding anything beyond, below, or behind observable facts. A "radical positivism" is perhaps the only attitude that would afford one a degree of assurance in the face of the inscrutability of history. Assuming the posture of radical positivism, one would not interpret motives but simply note actions; one would not attempt to determine if apparently different individuals were really the "same" individual in different guises, but would simply recognize roles as the only truths about individuals that can be known. Barth's "radical positivism" is thus closely related to the epistemology implied by the surface realities of Warhol's portraits.

Structuralism, as well as the various "poststructuralist" critical approaches, contributes to contemporary skepticism regarding the knowability of reality and the nature of the self. Structuralism is sometimes treated as if it were nothing more than a method of semiotic analysis; at other times it is presented as something like a philosophy or, to use the word in its recent, extremely broad application, "theory."[10] Structuralism is, in either case, *at least* a method. Furthermore, if it is not also a philosophy—which it is not if being a philosophy requires laying out arguments for or against philosophical positions—at least it is a method grounded in certain philosophical attitudes, beliefs, and presuppositions. One of the crucial structuralist attitudes is epistemological and ontological skepticism; in addition, structuralism assumes the central role of language in constituting human reality and human understandings of the self.

Much of this skepticism can be traced to Saussure, the founder of structuralism, whose *Course in General Linguistics* is viewed as a pioneer text of modern linguistics as well as of the interdisciplinary textual theories of structuralism, semiotics, and post-structuralism.[11] There are a number of ideas in Saussure used by later writers in support of two significant poststructuralist tenets: that the relationship between texts and their supposed referents is ultimately unknowable, and that the meanings of texts themselves (whatever their referential validity may be) is ultimately unknowable. The latter belief is, from one perspective, simply an application of twentieth-century skepticism to the examination of texts.[12] Texts, especially literary texts, with their ability to layer possible interpretations through the use of metaphor, pun, and other rhetorical devices and their ability to capitalize upon the force of words resulting from the etymological baggage they carry, provide ample opportunity for being "problematized" and for the "deconstruction" of any apparently unambiguous interpretation.

One Saussurian notion frequently cited is the idea of the "arbitrary" nature of the linguistic sign (pp. 67–68). Clearly Saussure did not literally mean "arbitrary" when he used the word but meant, instead, *conventional.* His point was that there is no *inherent* connection between words and the concepts with which they are associated—they are, as a general rule, neither iconic nor indexical signs, to use the terminology of Charles Sanders Peirce.[13] That is, words in no way resemble the concepts they evoke (as a piece of sculpture may have a shape similar to the thing it represents), nor are they causally connected to their referents (as tracks in the snow may suggest an animal). Rather, in language the semiotic bond—the relating of a signifier and a signified—is established by culture. Epistemologically it might not seem to matter whether relationships between signifiers and signifieds are conventional or "motivated." After all, motivated or not, signifiers are not their own signifieds—resemblance or causal connection do not constitute identity—and a gap between the two must always remain. Still, through resemblance or existential association, motivated signs do point toward an extra-linguistic world in a way that arbitrary signs cannot. Arbitrary signs can only be logically related to other signs within their own systems. Language is self-defining, and each term in a language has significance, from the point of view of structuralism, only as it relates to other terms in the system. Such relationships can be syntagmatic (referring to the linear sequence of terms actually present in discourse) or associative (referring to the relation of a term to any number of terms not actually present) (pp. 122–127), the former roughly corresponding to the grammatical and the latter roughly corresponding to the lexical. In either case, words have nothing to relate to except other words in the system of language. Thus, Saussure's emphasis on the arbitrary nature of the linguistic sign, not particularly shocking in itself, has been seen to corroborate and necessitate the essential structural and self-referential nature of language, and has been used to corroborate the more radical skepticism of later poststructuralists.

More significant, however, is Saussure's belief that thought itself is dependent on language and that concepts do not precede the terms that articulate them. Ideas are as amorphous and inchoate as sounds, and the articulation of both into distinct ideas and sounds, together with the joining of those two articulations in the sign, is itself another aspect of the arbitrariness of language.

> Language can also be compared with a sheet of paper: thought is the front and the sound the back; one cannot cut the front without cutting the back at the same time; likewise in language, one can neither divide sound from thought nor thought from sound. . . .
>
> These views give a better understanding of what was said before . . . about the arbitrariness of signs. Not only are the two domains that are linked by the linguistic fact shapeless and confused, but the choice of a given slice of sound to name a given idea is completely arbitrary. (p. 13)

Because language lacks a means of pointing outside itself, its workings and significance are dependent upon relationships established within its own system, upon the articulations it establishes within phonetic and conceptual fields and relations it establishes among and between the terms of each field. Language is structural: it functions by means of distinctions or differences between different sounds and between different concepts. "In language there are only differences without positive terms. . . . The idea or phonic substance that a sign contains is of less importance than the other signs that surround it. . . . A linguistic system is a series of differences of sound combined with a series of differences of ideas" (p. 120).

Poststructuralists inherit this belief in the enclosed, self-referential nature of language, based as it is on differences and oppositions that exist within its own system. But they add something not so evident in Saussure, namely the belief that, in addition to the questionable referential validity of language, language is also problematical in that it is impossible ultimately even to determine what its reference is. To phrase it baldly, not only can we not determine whether what is said is true or not, we can not determine unambiguously what it is that is being said. The former is related to what Derrida refers to as the "metaphysics of presence" in Western philosophy, the belief that there is some final foundation of being that exists and is accessible to language and reason. The latter is rooted in the belief that this problematical aspect of Western metaphysics—its need to "supplement" the absence of a foundation with the assertion of a foundation that compensates for and simultaneously reveals the elemental absence—will be revealed through a close rhetorical analysis of any text. Derrida is thus indebted to Saussure in his emphasis on the arbitrary nature of the sign and his understanding of language as something structured on the basis of a system of differences, but criticizes Saussure as logocentric in that he implies that linguistic systems are codes that can, in the end, be decoded.[14]

When one realizes that any metalanguage that sets as its goal the critical examination of a text must itself be implicated in the grammar and vocabulary of a language—must itself be a language—one realizes that language is a prisonhouse from which there can be no escape. As Christopher Norris expresses it, "There is no language so vigilant or self-aware that it can effectively escape the conditions placed upon thought by its own prehistory and ruling metaphysic."[15] Just as rigorous skepticism doubts that language can have access to an unmediated reality, so must it doubt that criticism can have access to an unambiguous interpretation of any text.

Deconstruction approaches philosophical texts as literary texts, analyzes or "deconstructs" their language, their figures, their metaphors—acknowledged and unacknowledged—and traces the etymologies of their words in an effort to demonstrate that ambiguity exists where things seem clear and that the literal is always figurative, is simply an instance of a forgotten or unacknowledged figurative origin. It asserts the significance of rhetoric above dialectic and treats logic as a special instance of poetics. It "argues" this not in any traditional way—through rational rebuttals or rational arguments for opposed positions—but through a rhetorical analysis of philosophical and literary texts designed to demonstrate that texts are always self-subversive if examined closely enough. To deconstruct a text, therefore, is to demonstrate that it, in fact, deconstructs itself if subjected to close rhetorical analysis. Culler writes, "to deconstruct a discourse is to show how it undermines the philosophy it asserts."[16]

Deconstruction thus approaches texts in a manner somewhat similar to Freudian or Marxist criticism, although it certainly need not ally itself with either of those two systems and does, in fact, subject such texts themselves to deconstructive analysis at times. All three approaches attempt to "second think" texts, to argue that the apparent meaning of a text is never the unambiguous truth about it and that other unacknowledged meanings may be present that are different from or even opposed to the apparent one and which, when discovered, will tend to subvert the text's apparent meaning. For Freudians, slips, inadvertant symbols, and accidental puns may reveal an unconscious content denied overtly by the text. For Marxists, the power relations between classes and class ideology will inform and limit a text even when it claims to present an impartial and "objective" view of reality. Deconstruction discovers *aporias,* irreconcilable contradictions, that exist in texts and are manifestations of a philosophical (as opposed to a psychoanalytic or political) dilemma existing within Western metaphysics. Texts are always implicated in a logocentric "metaphysics of presence," an understanding of "being" as a firm foundation, as a "transcendental signified" that is the goal of understanding and the final referent behind all signifiers.

Texts engage in a variety of strategies designed to conceal the opposite implication—that they are dissociated from any such imaginary reality, that they are essentially about themselves, and that, lacking the firm foundation of a "transcendental signified," their activity can best be described as a kind of "game" or "play" (pp. 49–50). Close analysis will reveal those points where the cover-up occurs, where the presence of a "supplement" that claims to be an inessential addition to something already complete suggests also that the thing supplemented is incomplete and inadequate. Deconstruction does not involve arbitrary readings of texts; nor does it involve denying the existence of an *apparent* "univocal," "naive," or "metaphysical" interpretation of a given text. It does, however, involve the identification of a "deconstructive," anti-metaphysical reading that it sets alongside the apparent reading.[17] This anti-metaphysical reading of a text is derived from a rhetorical analysis of the text itself and is taken as evidence of the basic contradiction and cover-up strategy that is present in the metaphysics of Western language. Just as Freudians might take denial as evidence of the existence of the very thing that is being denied, deconstructionists take metaphysical assertions as evidence of a nihilism that metaphysics denies, but whose existence is betrayed by metaphysics itself.

In "Linguistics and Grammatology" Derrida reads Saussure's suppression of "writing" in favor of "speech" as a logocentric strategy designed to conceal the inherent, irrevocable breach between all signifying practice and any firm and ultimate meaning, a strategy Saussure shares with others in the history of Western metaphysics, including Plato, Aristotle, and Rousseau. In speech it is possible to maintain the illusion of "presence," the illusion that language is simply the carrier of a meaning intended by speakers. In "writing"—where there is a more obvious distance between inscription and meaning as well as between inscription and author—this illusion is more difficult to maintain. This explains the historical subordination of writing to speech. Speech is presented as something natural and present, as having an immediacy in relation to the speaker's meaning that is lost in writing, which exists as merely a representation of speech. Saussure excludes writing from the study of language. His rhetoric describes it as something exterior, something unnatural and "fictitious," and as a "disguise." It is only through a kind of violence, a usurpation, a perversion of the natural hierarchy, that speech can be seen as an imitation of writing or can, in fact, at times emulate writing.

Saussure's anti-writing rhetoric is, in fact, *too* strong and suggests to Derrida that something more is operating than a mere description of the relationship between two modes of discourse; it suggests that a fundamental denial or evasion is at work. It is a denial of the priority of writing over speech and of all the anti-metaphysical, anti-"onto-theological" implications of that priority. In his discussion of Saussure's rhetoric, Derrida acts in a manner exactly analogous to that of a psychoanalyst, who identifies fundamental repressions and unconscious motives that lie below and belie a patient's conscious assertions. Derrida, in fact, mentions Freud as a source for his methodology in deconstructing Saussure (p. 45).

He points out that Saussure cannot carry out his project without violating and casting doubt on the very hierarchy he asserts. Saussure's thesis of the arbitrary nature of the sign mitigates against the so-called naturalness of speech and "must forbid a radical distinction between the linguistic and the graphic sign" (p. 44). In addition, despite his having marginalized writing in favor of speech, Saussure must refer to the sign system of writing—the way in which visual inscriptions are made to stand for words—in order to clarify the way in which the linguistic sign system works (p. 52). Finally, Saussure's emphasis on language as operating through a system of differences mitigates against his assertion that a more natural relationship exists between sound and meaning than between graphic inscription and meaning. As Saussure himself points out, it is the structure of differences that produces meaning and not the substance (phonic or graphic) of the elements structured (Derrida, p. 53).

Derrida's deconstructive reversal of the conventional hierarchy, argued by opposing Saussure to himself, consists of his position that it is writing that is primary and that speech is really dependent on writing rather than vice-versa. Derrida's "writing," however, does not refer simply to visual inscriptions but to a generalized notion of an "arche-writing," a code that always entails a breach between signifier and signified. This *differance,* which differs from and defers any final, foundational meaning, is essential for speech as well as for written inscriptions. Thus "writing," in this generalized sense, is prior to speech and is its necessary precondition. Saussure's metaphysical attempt to obscure the elemental absence of presence, even in speech, is belied by his exaggerated rhetoric, by his own theories of the arbitrariness of the sign and the structural nature of language, as well as by his reliance on the system of inscription as a model for clarifying the system of spoken language. Derrida writes that he "would wish rather to suggest that the alleged derivativeness of writing, however real and massive, was possible only on one condition: that the 'original,' 'natural,' etc. language had never existed, never been intact and untouched by writing, that it had itself always been a writing" (p. 56).

The deconstructive process situates itself between two readings, a metaphysical and an anti-metaphysical reading, or between two terms of a text, one dominant, the other marginalized, and aims to reverse the hierarchy the text seems to establish between those readings or terms. Deconstruction itself, constituted as it is in language—often the same language it deconstructs—can make no higher claim to truth, occupies no privileged position outside of language from which to view texts, must itself embrace the metaphysical terminology of the language it speaks, and is itself subject to deconstructive analysis. Culler states that "the practitioner of deconstruction works within the terms of the system but in order to breach it" (p. 86). Thus, it is impossible to effectively argue with deconstruction. If one questions a deconstructive reading of a text, one simply stands in danger of being deconstructed oneself.[18] If one instead deconstructs a deconstructionist reading, one simply joins those one is opposing. Contradictions and *aporias* may be fatal to those who are incomplete skeptics and dare to make assertions, but they roll harmlessly off the backs of deconstructists who, at the outset, render them innocuous by acknowledging their own dependence on the grammar, vocabulary, and metaphysical implications of the language they share with that of the texts they deconstruct. No answer or rebuttal to deconstruction is possible. The only possible answer would be a new epistemology so compelling that it would set to rest doubt and establish once and for all a consensus of philosophers, literary theorists, and aestheticians regarding the appropriate means humans should employ to arrive at the truth. Since such a theory is unlikely, there will always be a place for rigorous skepticism and no text can be immune to attack from a determined skeptic.

Inevitably, poststructural textual theory, as well as postmodern literature and art—which is rooted in ideas similar or related to those of poststructuralism—are offensive to many. John Gardner, for example, in *On Moral Fiction,* writes a sweeping indictment of nearly all recent fiction and critical theory. Gardner's aesthetic is largely, though not exclusively, classical and Aristotelean, and his evaluations are based on a view of art as mimetic in nature and ethical in purpose. His views are, unfortunately, dogmatically stated, as if the principles he espouses are self-evident or true by nature of their history alone. His book does not even begin to engage in any interesting way those against whom he sets himself. Regarding the postmodern, he writes,

Fiction as pure language (texture over structure) is *in*. It is one common manifestation of what is being called "post-modernism." At bottom the mistake is a matter of morality, at least in the sense that it shows, on the writer's part, a lack of concern. To people who care about events and ideas and thus, necessarily, about the clear and efficient statement of both, linguistic opacity suggests indifference to the needs and wishes of the reader and to whatever ideas may be buried under all that brush. And since one reason we read fiction is our hope that we will be moved by it, finding characters we can enjoy and sympathize with, an academic striving for opacity suggests, if not misanthropy, a perversity of shallowness. . . . Where language is of primary concern, communication is necessarily secondary.[19]

In quotes such as this Gardner summarily discounts a major part of the modern—to say nothing of the postmodern—experience, which does involve a serious consideration of the role of language and other sign systems in constituting human consciousness. To discount that experience in this way is to casually dismiss the ideas of Nietzsche, Wittgenstein, much of modern linguistics, structuralism, and all of poststructuralism, to say nothing of the insights and obsessions of innumerable artists and writers. It is, of course, quite possible that those insights are wrong and that the obsessions are the result of neurosis. But certainly the great number of artists, philosophers, and scientists who have shared these concerns suggests that, right or wrong, they are more than frivolous; they are powerful forces in modern Western culture and therefore, if one wishes to affect the nature of modern literature or change the direction of recent criticism, a more considered reply is necessary. Gardner also argues that all modern and postmodern critical movements, from New Criticism to poststructuralism, are "too neat, too theoretical, too 'scientific' " and that they "ignore the very essence of art, which is emotional affirmation."[20] He goes on to say that criticism, like art, ought to be concerned with "the Good, the True, and the Beautiful," ideas he derives from Aquinas and Ockham. It may not be that Gardner's notions of art and criticism are so wrong; it's just that by neglecting to really engage modern and postmodern art and criticism, by refusing to treat them at least seriously enough to confront them for what they are, and by simply restating instead a traditional theory of art as mimetic and moral, Gardner's book is likely to remain simply an impotent polemic in the face of twentieth-century skepticism, which does not see things so clearly as he does.

Other writers, who are not so categorical in their denunciation of modernism and postmodernism, who are to a great extent sympathetic to postmodernism, nevertheless express a qualified concern regarding its potential pitfalls. Robert Alter, for example, whose *Partial Magic* traces the roots of modern and contemporary self-conscious fiction to origins in Cervantes, Sterne, and Diderot, is concerned that at times contemporary self-conscious writers lose touch with the significant philosophical bases of such writing and their work becomes simply an "arid exercise and indiscriminate invention."[21] And Christopher Butler, in his book on the avant-garde, similarly warns against the "game-playing aspects of literature" that often reflect "a turning away from those deeper responsibilities which have traditionally been seen in moral terms."[22] Butler, whose views on literature and art are in many respects more modern than postmodern—in spite of the fact that he uses the latter term and views postmodernism as a significant break from modernism—echoes Gardner in his emphasis on the moral dimension of literature as well as Alter in his warning of the danger of mere aesthetic play and formal virtuosity.

Alan Wilde argues in favor of a "middle grounds" or "midfiction," which lies between a "realism," rooted in a belief in the possibility of a simple mimesis, and a highly self-referential metafiction, which denies all possibility of literature engaging a "reality" outside of language itself. Wilde uses works by writers such as Donald Barthelme, Thomas Berger, Thomas Pynchon, and Grace Paley as illustrations of this "midfiction," which engages in an interrogation of the world, neither denying it nor asserting that it is ultimately knowable, and acknowledging the significance of language in constituting it for humans. On the theoretical level, Berger attempts a difficult rapprochement between the phenomenology of Merleau-Ponty and poststructuralism. Wilde, relying partly on Norris and partly on Derrida, argues that deconstruction does not really deny the possibility of communication and of "presence" but suspends discussion of them. On the other hand, phenomenology acknowledges that the individual project of "intending" the world is continually threatened by a background disorder that finally eludes any "totalizing" order created by a subject. The "creation of meaning takes place within and against the background or horizon of the world's never wholly recuperable disorder."[23]

A formidable attack on postmodern literature and literary theory is Gerald Graff's *Literature Against Itself, Literary Ideas in Modern Society.*[24] Graff, in contrast to Gardner, Alter, and Butler, seems to have a fairly thorough understanding of the theoretical and philosophical bases of postmodernism and does an excellent critical "reading" of postmodern theory, its jargon, its unquestioned assumptions, and its sometimes moralistic tone (ironic in the context of other attacks on postmodernism as amoral or immoral). Graff acts in a manner repugnant to deconstructionists and deconstructionist sympathizers by placing deconstruction in a historical context and viewing it as a manifestation of a cultural milieu, one connected to earlier movements such as modernism, neocriticism, and romanticism.[25] Graff sees postmodernism as essentially a continuation of modernism, rather than as a sharp break from it, although more coherent than modernism in that it is willing to accept fully some of the less pleasant implications of modernist theory. If, for example, modernists turned to art as a source of consolation in the face of a reality perceived as disordered and lacking in enduring values, postmodernists, more consistent in their skepticism, doubt the capacity of art and literature to provide humans with the order, value, and meaning lacking elsewhere (p. 55).

Graff recognizes the value of structuralism as a "method of analysis" but is unwilling to accept its more radical philosophical aspects. (Whether these are consequences or presuppositions of structuralism is an important question that will be dealt with shortly.) Graff quotes individuals such as Gerard Genette, Edward Said, and J. Hillis Miller, who seem to take the more radical and skeptical aspects of structuralism as givens, as if the philosophical issues involved have been clearly settled and there is no point or necessity in rearguing them (pp. 19–20).

Graff also criticizes some of the excessive metaphysical implications later thinkers seem to find in Saussure.

From the proposition, unexceptionable in itself, that no signifier can mean anything apart from the code or sign system which gives it significance, one infers the conclusion that no signifier can *refer* to a nonlinguistic reality—that, as [Perry] Meisel puts it, "all language is finally groundless." There is, then, no such thing as a "real" object outside language, no "nature" or "real life" outside the literary text, no real text behind the critical interpretation, and no real persons or institutions behind the multiplicity of messages human beings produce. Everything is swallowed up in an infinite regress of textuality.[26]

Certainly Graff is right. There is no doubt that late structuralists and poststructuralists have gotten rather significant skeptical mileage from the relatively innocuous Saussurian insights regarding the "arbitrary" nature of the linguistic sign and the recognition of language as a system wherein meaning is produced through internal relations and "differences." Furthermore, this skepticism, to the extent that it does exist in Saussure, is a presupposition and not a consequence of his understanding of language. Saussure begins with skeptical assumptions and his ideas are at least in part a result of those assumptions, not the other way around. Late structuralists and poststructuralists, however, are inclined to speak as if it was Saussure who *demonstrated* the truth of their skeptical positions. Saussure never attempted to demonstrate anything philosophically—he was not a philosopher but a linguist, after all—but presented a theory of language based on certain epistemological presuppositions he held regarding the relationship between language and ideas. The reverence for Saussure becomes stranger with the realization that his *Course in General Lingistics* is a very indirect representation of his ideas, not a text he wrote but a collection and editing of his ideas based on the notes of seven or eight of his students at the University of Geneva (pp. xiii–xvi).

To be sure, from a post- or late structuralist perspective this latter objection may, indeed, be irrelevent. If language speaks men rather than men speak language, the attribution of the *Course* to Saussure specifically is irrelevent. Moreover, when the skeptical notions implicit in Saussure are seen within the context of a longer tradition of epistemological skepticism in Western philosophy, a tradition beginning at least with Kant and reaching a culmination with Nietzsche, it becomes clear that contemporary skepticism is very little dependent on Saussure, though he is frequently given credit for supposedly demonstrating the validity of that skepticism and his book, a pioneering text of modern linguistics, is frequently treated as holy scripture for contemporary philosophical doubt.[27] Nevertheless, the nearly religious faith in the truth of skeptical presuppositions identified in structuralist texts remains a surprising phenomenon, especially when one considers the rigorous doubt that is applied to all other texts. This curious blend of thoroughgoing doubt and irrational faith, skeptical rigor and thoughtless acceptance, the impulse to debunk and the blind emulation of chosen leaders is, unfortunately, a recurring characteristic of much contemporary textual theory.

Graff argues that the fact that language possesses meaning by means of the internal structure that relates its elements does not necessarily imply that language cannot refer to something besides itself. "The fact that language is always referring to itself does not mean that is *all* it refers to. The fact that meanings are constituted by internal systems of semantic and syntactic rules does not mean they are constituted *only* by these rules and are therefore not answerable to anything external." Similarly, he argues that the fact that signs are arbitrary does not imply that "the *concepts* denoted by these signs are also arbitrary" (p. 196). Probably he is right. To use Saussure's own paper analogy, the fact that a certain conceptual "territory" is cut out on one side (and joined semiotically with a "territory" of sound simultaneously cut out on the other) suggests that the nature of concepts may be somewhat less arbitrary than the relationship between sounds and concepts. If one side represents a mass of thought, the placement of the borders dividing that mass into concepts is arbitrary, but it is still necessary for the concepts themselves to be internally cohesive. The surface is continuous and only adjacent areas can be joined; two areas bordering each other might or might not be part of the same sign-concept, depending on the linguistic system articulating them; but it would not be possible—at least as suggested by this analogy—for an area in the upper left hand corner of the paper to be part of the same concept as an area in the lower right, if other concepts existed in between. By analogy, at least, the suggestion here is that there are limits on the malleability of concepts. Eskimos may have many words for snow (indicating a highly refined ability to create discriminations within what we regard as a single category) and the ancient Greeks may have had a single word for black and purple (suggesting a less refined discrimination of colors, in this particular instance); nevertheless, it would be difficult to conceive of a language in which slush, sleet, rain, and fire were included in a single concept that excluded light snow, or a language in which orange, pink, and blue were included in a single concept that excluded red. While there is no doubt that our concept of reality is greatly controlled by our language, it is highly unlikely that language has complete license in its creation of concepts. The relationship between language, thought, and reality is clearly complex and understood only to a small degree; furthermore, the fact that we understand *in language* suggests that the attempt of language to understand language can never be wholly successful. As human beings it may be necessary for us to content ourselves with a forever partial, imperfect, and sometimes contradictory notion of what is. Still, the assumption that language is somehow the sole or primary determiner of human reality, or the suggestion that it is in no way or very little accountable to something outside itself, has no more justification than a naive realism that assumes that linguistic concepts are always perfectly correlated with natural divisions existing in the universe.

Norris criticizes Graff for his "moralistic line," his failure to engage his opponents, and his historicist reductionism. Discussing those who criticize deconstruction, Norris writes,

> Other objectors have taken a flatly moralistic line. Gerald Graff, for one, has denounced deconstruction as a culpable retreat from the problems of modern society, a kind of textual fiddling while Rome burns. . . . The trouble with Graff's toughminded stance is that it doesn't engage with his opponents in any real argumentative way. He lumps them all together, critics and novelists alike, as self-condemned enemies of reason, without seeing—or allowing himself to see—the force of their case. (p. 131)

These objections seem far more appropriate to a writer like Gardner than Graff. Certainly there is a moral dimension to Graff's argument, but his argument is not limited to moral outrage or dogmatic rejection of those he opposes. Graff makes numerous significant arguments suggesting that contemporary theory is not always fully thought out, involves at times invalid logical leaps from structuralist principles, and is often a matter of faith and unquestioned acceptance rather than of the intellectual rigor it espouses. Norris continues his criticism of Graff:

> Wittgenstein is always at hand with a knock-down argument against thoroughgoing scepticism: that "if you tried to doubt everything you would not get as far as doubting anything. The game of doubting itself presupposes certainty" (quoted by Graff 1979, p. 195). But this, once again, is to throw the whole argument back on to a bedrock of flatly commonsense assertion which hardly meets the deconstructionist challenge. (p. 132)

Certainly Wittgenstein himself, a pioneer of modern linguistic skepticism, cannot be faulted with the sin of falling back on a simplistic commonsensical attitude. More to the point here, however, is the fact that Norris flagrantly ignores Graff's clear understanding of the complexity of the issue by isolating his quotation of Wittgenstein from its context. Graff, like Norris, realizes that the issue is too complex to be dismissed on the basis of a quote from Wittgenstein, in spite of the latter's stature as a pioneer of modern thought, and the sentences immediately following the one that Norris quotes read,

> But some further response seems necessary. For it is indeed true, as recent structuralists insist, that meanings are paradigm-bound and system-constituted,

that perceptions are mediated by interpretations, that perceptual reality is in a sense our construction. The question is, what follows from these assumptions? (p. 195)

Norris chooses to ignore this obviously important limitation on Graff's reliance on Wittgenstein and Graff's recognition of the complexity of the problem. Graff goes on to make the arguments, summarized above, that the fact that statements possess meaning only because they are part of semiotic systems does not imply that they necessarily refer to nothing but those systems and that the arbitrary nature of signs does not imply that concepts are arbitrary. Thus, Graff does challenge his opponents in ways that Norris refuses to acknowledge; only by ignoring his real challenge can Norris claim that Graff's argument is rooted solely in moral outrage and simplistic historicism.

Clearly, there *is* a moral dimension to Graff's position, and an important one. It arises—as Norris understands—from a sense that literature, criticism, and critical theory have become disengaged from significant human issues and from a belief that approaches like deconstruction *are* engaged in a kind of "conceptual fiddling while Rome burns."[28] Graff fears that radical skepticism and the notion of literary texts as autonomous—as being solely self-referential and incapable of representing a world external to themselves—renders contemporary criticism incapable of powerful engagement with social, ethical, and political matters. But in contrast to someone like Gardner, he respects and fears his opponents enough to have read them and developed an understanding of them. Norris is wrong when he claims that Graff's objections are *merely* moral outrage and that Graff raises no substantive objections worthy of a response. Indeed, Norris's cursory dismissal of Graff is similar to the dismissal that he incorrectly claims that Graff displays in his response to deconstruction.

Some explicators of deconstruction, such as Culler, believe that, contrary to Graff's opinion, deconstruction has the potential for social and political engagement. Because deconstruction involves performing certain "reversals" in the reading of texts—noting the hierarchical relations texts establish and the ways in which they simultaneously subvert those very hierarchies—it can be used to disrupt the ideological bases of institutions. "In general, inversions of hierarchical oppositions expose to debate the institutional arrangements that rely on the hierarchies and thus open possibilities of change—possibilities which may well come to little but which may also at some point prove critical" (p. 179). Culler himself understands that the potential of deconstruction for political and social engagement is a complex problem and this explains the highly qualified "possibilities *which may well come to little* but which may also *at some point* prove critical." Nevertheless, Culler does want to argue for the possibility of such engagement and devotes one full chapter of his book on deconstruction to discussing that possibility. Still, he realizes that the consequences of the deconstructive project are both distant and incalculable, distant in that they will have little impact on immediate ethical, social, and political issues, and incalculable in that there is no assurance that those effects will be desirable ones, when and if they do occur. Thus, Culler argues—with some support from Derrida—that action is required on two fronts—the deconstruction of philosophical oppositions, which will yield fruits in the distant future, fruits that will *hopefully* be beneficial, and more immediate critical and political action, which is not the same as the first and yet not separated from it either (pp. 158–160).

In this regard, Norris is more persuasive. His discussion of the attempts of some writers to reconcile deconstruction with Marxism could apply to the attempt to reconcile deconstruction with any form of progressive social and political commitment:

As I have argued, it is difficult to square deconstruction in this radical, Nietzschean guise with any workable Marxist account of text and ideology. Such attempted fusions in the name of a Marxian post-structuralist theory are fated, for reasons I shall now pursue, to an endlessly proliferating discourse of abstraction. To deconstruct a text in Nietzschean-Derridean terms is to arrive at a limit-point or deadlocked *aporia* of meaning which offers no hold for Marxist-historical understanding. (p. 80)

Marxists seem to agree, at least when what is being discussed is rigorous, philosophical deconstruction—deconstruction in its "radical, Nietzschean guise"—which insists on subjecting itself to the same rhetorical scrutiny it applies to other texts. Terry Eagleton argues that post-structuralism is an escape from politics[29] and Frank Lentricchia writes, "Politically, deconstruction translates into that passive kind of conservatism called quietism; it thereby plays into the hands of established power. Deconstruction is conservatism by default."[30] Significantly, however, both Eagleton and Lentricchia are willing to accept a less unrelenting form of deconstructive textual analysis, one allied to political purposes and devoted to uncovering the means by which discourse is used to maintain political and social power.

It is clear that any form of rigorous deconstruction must be limited to a purely subversive posture. Deconstruction is an approach, based in a rigorous philosophical skepticism, that regards all texts—at least all Western texts—as rooted in elemental contradictions that can be exposed by close rhetorical analysis. Recognizing itself as a discourse comprised of texts in Western languages, bound to the grammar and vocabulary of Western metaphysics, deconstruction admits to its own limits and the possibility—indeed, the necessity—that it also be deconstructed. Derrida's writings are filled with rigorously controlled, fully recognized and fully layed bare, self-contradictions. This may be remarkably honest and may, indeed, put deconstructionists in a position where they are immune to attack: their self-deconstructions in effect co-opt their critics; furthermore, any successful identification of contradictions they have not themselves acknowledged can easily be appropriated and reinterpreted as confirmation of their own anti-metaphysics. Since political and social systems are rooted in, validated by, even constituted by texts of various sorts, deconstruction *is* a potentially subversive force in relation to any social or political system. Nevertheless, the fact that it can *only* be subversive and provides no grounds upon which to assert anything that is not subversive, certainly provides no grounds for arguing in favor of any ethical, social, or political system, progressive, reactionary, or otherwise, is a severe limitation on its potential for aiding in social change.

Finally, it must be acknowledged that deconstruction is an extremely sophisticated approach to texts, involving an understanding of the history of Western philosophy and literature and incorporating its own highly specialized vocabulary. At best that vocabulary can be seen as sometimes logically rigorous, often poetic (note the highly evocative Derridean terminolology: the "trace," *differance*, "force," "metaphysics of presence," "transcendental signified," and so forth); at worst, it can be seen as a language unnecessarily arcane, one filled with pretentious neologisms that suggest that a game of intellectual and moral one-up-manship is being played, a game designed to intimidate the insufficiently critical reader. The specialized language of deconstruction, the fact that its possible effects are acknowledged to be distant and incalculable, and the fact that it has no basis upon which to assert any ethical or political system, all suggest that there is little likelihood of its functioning as an effective force for social change. In a world where the problems are diverse, complex, and manifold, the involvement in such an enterprise may appear to some as a form of decadence. Norris, somewhat mockingly, describes Graff's moral position as an objection to "a kind of textual fiddling while Rome burns." But one would have to be grossly insensitive to major moral and social issues in the world not to be at least slightly bothered by the gap between the sophisticated exercises of Western intellectuals—most of whom, let it be said, are among the materially privileged of the earth, fortunate enough to possess sufficient time and wealth to engage in the most speculative and theoretical of preoccupations—and problems like mass starvation, poverty, genocide, sectarian warfare, and possible nuclear holocaust. What Butler writes of avant-garde literature could be said of much contemporary critical theory:

The arguments for this type of writing have a certain intellectual appeal, since the attack on idealism, moral absolutes, or the empirical liberalism implicit in realism, has a satisfying traditional philosophical cast. But the claims for the *social* effectiveness of such works will always seem negligible, in proportion to the narrowness of their institutional base, since the dominant ideology they rightfully attack has by definition bigger (or at least better distributed) weapons, like Harold Robbins, Jacqueline Susann, television soap-opera, and so on.[31]

The discourse of deconstruction, with its specialized language, its uncompromising skepticism, and its confinement within academia, has produced a gap between the theoretical and the pragmatic that casts serious doubt on its ability to help bring about beneficial social effects. If one compares the language of the textual theorists of academia with the language used by the "dominant ideology"—that of the popular and commercial arts and of political propaganda—it is quite clear why the latter will always be the winner. Both are immensely sophisticated languages, but, in contrast to the language of the academics, that of the dominant ideology is designed to touch the hearts, minds, and behavior of masses of people. It is for this reason that a politically engaged critic like Lentricchia—who attempts to incorporate some of the key insights of poststructuralism—is willing to take the position that political criticism ought to incorporate the rhetorical strategies of commercial capitalism, strategies previously disdained by such critics.

In addition, pure and rigorous skepticism alone can result in fascism as easily as in progressivism, not only because it subverts the ability of progressives to assert anything with conviction, but because, in itself, it can easily result in an ethics of power. Kuhn discusses the role of pressure from the scientific community in determining what scientific "truth" is at any particular time;[32] that is, scientific truth seems to result, from Kuhn's perspective, more from a kind of social pressure that affects an individual's beliefs than from any "objective" criteria regarding the proper means for apprehending truth. Although Kuhn, in his 1969 "Postscript" to *The Structure of Scientific Revolutions,* does attempt to qualify his relativism, his emphasis on the role of social pressure in determining truth does point towards an epistemology of power and a situation in which individuals could easily justify using their power to attempt to impose their truths upon others. After all, if power is the criterion, why not use one's power to create a world most advantageous to oneself? Thus, that individual or group (whether the group is an aristocracy, an oligarchy, or a majority) that holds the power tends to be legitimized as the individual or group that controls the beliefs of a society. It is not all that surprising that Pirandello, whose plays elegantly dramatize epistemological skepticism, could have become a fascist and could have publically supported Mussolini, even though his plays at times expressed compassion for individuals whose lives were shattered by others intolerant of different points of view. Pirandello was able to imagine Mussolini as a hero who had the courage to understand the relativism of human reality and who therefore had the right to forge reality for himself—and, presumably, for others less courageous than he. In a 1924 interview, Pirandello expressed this view of *Il Duce*:

I have always had the greatest admiration for Mussolini and I think I am one of the few people capable of understanding the beauty of his continuous creation of reality; an Italian and fascist reality which does not submit itself to anyone else's reality. Mussolini is one of the few people who knows that reality only exists in man's power to create it, and that one creates it only through the activity of the mind.[33]

This view was not simply the projection of the views of an intellectual onto a political leader he admired, but was an attitude Mussolini himself understood quite well. Mussolini had a clear understanding of modern skepticism and used it to justify an ethics based on power: "From the fact that all ideologies are equal value, that all ideologies are merely fictions, the modern relativist infers that everybody has the right to create for himself his own ideology and to attempt to enforce it with all the energy of which he is capable."[34] It is common enough to regard fascism as the result of absolutist ideologies, but these statements suggest that it can also be the result of skepticism, one that can subvert the power of progressive forces and that can give those who do possess power license to use it to justify the pursuit of their own ends. This is not to suggest that skepticism be abandoned and traditional values be reconfirmed and accepted on the basis of mindless faith. But it is to suggest that if contemporary skepticism is not to result in either chaos or fascism, it must tempered by a commitment to certain ethical principles, principles that, inevitably, will have to arise from other quarters.[35]

There have, of course, been numerous attempts to create a political poststructuralism in the past few decades. These have been partly a result of a perceived failure of the utopian attempts at political and social change of the nineteen-sixties. This failure has come to be marked by the suppression of the French student and worker's protests in May and June of 1968. Indeed, the significance of that event as a crisis for nineteen-sixties utopianism as well as for radical thought in politics and art is suggested by its frequent abbreviation as simply "May." This abbreviation carries with it the assumption that "May" has resulted in a shift in our whole understanding of what is required for radical change and of the kind of forces involved in maintaining the status quo. The question is, "Why did the sixties fail?" and the answer is that the forces operating against change in the West are generally subtler than guns and have to do with the incorporation of ideology—by language itself, among other things—into the constitution of the subject. The individual itself is regarded as a construct of bourgeois ideology. This insight invites a synthesis of structuralism, poststructuralism, and politically engaged theory, and encourages the ascendence of those thinkers who had already been working along those lines. Structuralism and poststructuralism are utilized in an attempt to fill the gap between psychology and politics. Lacanian psychoanalysis, Althusserian Marxism, the poststructural feminism of Julia Kristeva and Gayatri Chakravorty Spivak, and even Derridean deconstruction—when allied with a political and historical framework that works to recontain it—all are utilized in an attempt to explain why guns are not always necessary to ensure the continuation of a system regarded as oppressive, and to begin working to dismantle the symbolic, linguistic, rhetorical structures that support it. Sherry Turkle writes of the ascendence of Lacan after 1968,

Lacan's theory of the construction of the symbolic order, when language and law enter man, allows for no real boundary between self and society: man becomes social with the appropriation of language, and it is language that constitutes man as a subject. Leftist intellectuals have read this to suggest that the notion of a private self is itself a construct of capitalism. The distinction between private and public, the very touchstone of bourgeois thought, exists only as bourgeois ideology. Alienation is not psychological or social; it is both, and at the same time: society is discovered within the individual.[36]

Politically engaged theory and criticism tend to be contextual and interdisciplinary, emphasizing the ideological mission of literature and art within a social and political context and rejecting the formalist separation of the work of art from other aspects of culture. Such criticism draws on

Marxism, psychoanalysis, and structural and poststructural thought; it tends to view the various forms of art, as well as other modes of cultural expression, as part of a cultural, structural whole, the parts of which are somehow related, though not necessarily in obvious or commonsensical ways. Psychoanalysis becomes less an examination of a conflict between innate drives seated in an individual's "unconscious" and an external "reality" and society that imposes limits on those drives, and more an examination of the way in which language (as well as narrative and the sign systems of the various arts) insinuates itself into and manages itself to constitute the human subject. Liberation is far more difficult when the enemy is not an "other" external to oneself but is, if not quite oneself, at least the very mode by which one apprehends and understands oneself and the world. "Theory" becomes the struggle for a metalanguage that will allow one to examine that mode, the mode of common sense.

Drawing on Foucault and Kenneth Burke, Lentricchia writes that the "compartmentalization" of human capacities implied by the "disciplines" of colleges and universities is not something natural but is itself a product of the will to "control and dominate by dividing and partitioning" (p. 54). Lentricchia here also seems to be echoing and responding to a similar argument of Edward Said. Said had criticized him, Jameson, and Eagleton as "literary Marxists who write for literary Marxists, who are in cloistral seclusion from the inhospitable world of real politics."[37] For Said the emphasis on specialization in academia is a political strategy that eliminates any possibility for a powerful engagement between criticism and significant political and social issues. This strategy, accepted by academics, renders academic criticism complicitous, through its willing acceptance of a marginal role, in the politics of the "Age of Reagan."

At this point most politically engaged critics agree that the techniques of criticism ought to be drawn from diverse fields (Marxism, psychoanalysis, and poststructural rhetorical analysis, among others) and the object of criticism ought to be broadened—both in the sense that objects under consideration should include works not derived from the traditional "canon" and in the sense that works need to be considered in a larger social and political context often conceived in structuralist terms. Jonathan Arac, in his introduction to *Postmodernism and Politics,* draws on Said and similarly calls for a broadened object of academic criticism as an antidote to the apparent impotence of socially engaged criticism: critics should engage in "cultural" rather than "literary" studies and in "criticism" rather than "literary criticism."[38] And Paul A. Bove, in the same volume, urges a disregard of conventional definitions of the proper object of academic criticism, suggesting, as an example, that critical skills developed for the analysis of literary discourse might be applied to media representations of the struggle against apartheid in South Africa.[39]

For Jameson, ideologies are "strategies of containment," structures effecting the repression of history and class conflict; he posits a "political unconscious," a seat of revolutionary energy analogous to Freud's unconscious which is the seat of instinctual energy.[40] Literature is fundamental in carrying out the ideological mission of repression. It is part of a cultural sphere that is an aspect of a social system conceived in *structuralist* terms: all aspects are interrelated even as they maintain a "relative autonomy," and "causality" is a manifestation of the operation of the entire system (as opposed to an orthodox Marxist view of a simpler causal relationship between base and superstructure).[41] In addition, narrative itself is a fundamental *epistemological* (rather than purely literary) category through which history itself is understood. The role of the Marxist literary critic is to engage in a symptomatic analysis that reveals and dismantles the covert ideological content of literary texts, much as a psychoanalyst reveals the latent content below the manifest content of dreams or as a deconstructionist unravels a fundamental philosophical aporia contained within an apparently lucid, consistent, and transparent text.

By locating aporias not in a repressed philosophical/linguistic impasse but in repressed class conflict, Jameson seeks to subsume poststructuralism within a Marxism that incorporates structural and poststructural insights. From the point of view of rigorous deconstruction, Marxism tends to make ontological claims and thus participates in the traditional delusion of Western metaphysics; from the Marxist point of view, deconstruction is itself another strategy for evading history and class struggle. The one skirts full recognition of the impasse implicit in language and "signification"; the other skirts full recognition of its complicity in bourgeois ideology.

Jameson seeks to transcend this dilemma by describing Marxism as a "single great collective story," "a single vast unfinished plot" (pp. 19–20). If Marxism is a fiction, it is, in a sense, the largest fiction, a superior vantage point or "untranscendable horizon" able to subsume other approaches, able to demonstrate the ideological limitations of other approaches to literature and, indeed, all culture (pp. 9–11). Within this largest context or "horizon"—a Marxist view of history conjoined with a structuralist view of social systems—texts do become intelligible, though what they reveal (as in psychoanalysis) is often what they deny.

It is difficult to understand how Jameson can make such claims while acknowledging that the various historical forms of Marxism can themselves be ideologically unmasked; they are themselves strategies of containment, repressing the nightmare of history and offering a utopian vision not entirely unrelated to a religious afterlife; they are, in a word, "theological" themselves. His response is that his view of the Marxist "totality"—a vision of history and social structure—is not so much a positive vision or a view of absolute truth as a methodological standard and an ideal against which to set ideological formations so as to allow their unmasking. Drawing on Georg Lukacs, Jameson writes that totality "must be read, not as some positive vision of the end of history . . . but as something quite different, namely a methodological standard" (p. 52) and that strategies of containment "can be unmasked only by confrontation with the ideal of totality which they at once imply and repress" (p. 53).

The ideological critique does not depend on some dogmatic or "positive" conception of Marxism as a system. Rather, it is simply the place of an imperative to totalize, and the various historical forms of Marxism can themselves equally effectively be submitted to just such a critique of their own local ideological limits or strategies of containment. In this sense, Hegel's great dictum, "the truth is the whole," is less an affirmation of some place of truth which Hegel himself (or others) might occupy, than it is a perspective and a method whereby the "false" and the ideological can be unmasked and made visible. (p. 53)

The "imperative to totalize" stimulates and makes possible a critique of ideological formations, providing a perspective from which to view them, even though any real position one might occupy—even that occupied while operating under the "imperative to totalize"—is going to be vulnerable to a similar critique. Jameson's method is a *via negativa* that he anticipates will, in the end, produce positive results, wresting a degree of freedom from that necessity which is history. This *via negativa*, together with Jameson's acknowledgment that Marxism itself can be deconstructed, brings him perhaps a hair's breadth away from the more unrelenting skepticism of deconstruction. Nevertheless, Jameson maintains his commitment to history, if only as an "absent cause, inaccessible to us except in textual form" (p. 35). If history cannot be known, its existence can be surmised; if we cannot know a truth, we can know that a truth exists; and that limited knowledge together with the acceptance of a provisional Marxist "totality" as a methodological standard are essential if we are to come to an understanding of the ideology that constrains our freedom.

Other Marxist critics feel less compelled to reconcile their work with structuralism and poststructuralism. Eagleton takes the position that poststructuralism is partly the result of a retreat from politics in the post-1968 world, rather than the result of a realization of the need for a more sophisticated approach to politics and political criticism (pp. 142–145). It is likely that there is some truth to both positions, depending on which particular "poststructuralist" is being discussed. It is also true that political critics like Eagleton tend to reserve their harshest attacks for the Anglo-American deconstructionists and are likely to be more qualified in their attacks on Derrida himself, whose political side they often recognize (p. 148). Moreover, even Eagleton is willing to grant a qualified place for structuralist and poststructuralist textual analysis within a political framework.

Structuralism is best seen as both symptom and reaction to the social and linguistic crisis I have outlined. It flees from history to language—an ironic action since as Barthes sees few moves could be more historically significant. But in holding history and the referent at bay, it also seeks to restore a sense of the "unnaturalness" of the signs by which men and women live, and so open up a radical awareness of their historical mutability. In this way it may rejoin the very history which it began by abandoning. Whether it does so or not, however, depends on whether the referent is suspended provisionally or for good and all. (p. 141)

Structuralism's tendency to "suspend" the referent—that is, the whole question of what things mean—can be useful in order to underline the conventionality of language and to analyze the ways in which language changes in history. We can assume, from Eagleton's Marxist context, that he is suggesting that changes in language involve changes in understandings of reality that are ideological and political. But this use of structuralism can only be politically effective if the suspension of the referent is only provisional and if we recognize that once the analysis is carried out the question of meaning and truth must be broached once again. Eagleton further argues that the "truth" imparted by language ought to be regarded as something embodied in the effects of language itself, rather than as something that lies as if "transcendentally" behind the signifiers of language themselves. Responding to Derrida and deconstruction, he says,

Meaning may well be ultimately undecidable if we view language contemplatively, as a chain of signifiers on a page; it becomes "decidable," and words like "truth," "reality," "knowledge" and "certainty" have something of their force restored to them, when we think of language rather as something we *do*, as indissociably interwoven with our practical forms of life. (146–147)

Lentricchia makes some similar points, though he feels compelled to engage structuralism and poststructuralism more fully and to incorporate their insights and techniques into his own theory. In *Criticism and Social Change* he argues that all literature, criticism, and teaching is, in one way or another, political. In this way he aligns himself with Marxists influenced by contemporary structuralist thought, who would take the same position, and he defends his work against more simplistic political activists, who might charge teachers, critics, and literary theorists with irrelevance, at least in comparison with more obvious kinds of political activity. The politics of deconstruction—especially that of Paul de Man—is, unfortunately, conservative by default and, whether it intends to or not, works to support the status quo. Like Eagleton, Lentricchia accepts the role of deconstruction in unmasking what he calls "epistemological fraud." Drawing on the work of Kenneth Burke (Lentricchia's book is largely an explication and development of Burke's ideas), he presents deconstructive style analyses of the traditional understandings of such seemingly fundamental concepts as the subject (as agent), action, and substance.

In a strategy similar to Eagleton's, though more fully developed, Lentricchia suggests that we *accept* the deconstructive insight and replace the lost referent not with a referent reclaimed, but with a referent redefined: that is, if language is power, if all language utilizes rhetoric ideologically, if knowledge is created by rhetorical force rather than being a passive representation of something independent of language, then let us replace the rhetoric we oppose with a pragmatically effective revolutionary rhetoric of our own.

> Deconstruction's useful work is to undercut the epistemological claims of representation, but that work in no way touches the real work of representation—its work of power. To put it another way: deconstruction can show that representations are not and cannot be adequate to the task of representation, but it has nothing to say about the social work that representation can and does do. . . . it has no positive content, no alternative textual work to offer intellectuals. It has nothing to say. (pp. 50–51)

Deconstruction stops with the unmasking of the rhetoric of representation. Lentricchia would have that task followed by the creation of new representations with the power to create a presumably more just or satisfactory social truth. He thus advocates and legitimizes the use of rhetoric as a pragmatic, essential tool for the writer of political texts. Quoting from a paper Burke delivered to the American Writers' Congress of 1935, Lentricchia frankly advocates that revolutionary writers utilize the rhetorical strategies of Madison Avenue and the art of religious eras.[42] To refuse to do so in the name of some kind of illusory "purity" is "to situate oneself on the margin of history, as the possessor of a unique truth disengaged from history's flow" (p. 36).

Lentricchia's willingness to incorporate poststructural and deconstructive insights and techniques into his political mission does not relieve him of what seems to be a fundamental challenge to political writing and teaching: how is the individual to act politically when the notions of the individual subject and of action itself are themselves revealed to be ideological constructs—insights revealed to Lentricchia not only in the writings of deconstruction proper (which he generally opposes) but in the writing of Burke (which he generally admires)? How can one use the critical power of deconstruction without at the same time being rendered politically impotent by what he sees as its overwhelming tendency to induce quietism? Lentricchia thus attempts to work through deconstruction to salvage some basis for power and action. He finds that basis in part by reemphasizing his theme of writing as action. No matter how subverted our sense of power may be, of what we ourselves may be, teaching and writing are actions that will have consequences for the world. They involve confronting a tradition that has been determined, reinterpreting it, and creating a tradition that will be passed along. The identification and preservation of cultural masterworks are not the humble services to enduring masterpieces they purport to be but are creative, political acts.

Tradition-makers—I refer especially to humanist intellectuals as writers and teachers—do not escape the ironic subversions of de Man. But above everything else, tradition-makers of this sort should be keenly aware that they are involved in the dissemination of values; they should understand that they are making choices for contemporaries and for the future; that they are profoundly implicated in the enforcement of a politics of sociocultural conservation and continuity. (p. 140)

Thus, the politics of traditional texts, their "real involvement in human struggle," ignored or repressed by the academy, must be revealed through an active engagement on the part of the teacher-critic. This is a process that involves consciousness, freedom, and responsibility. He argues this freedom not only against deconstruction but also against "a certain Marxism" which views history as teleologically determined. There is in Lentricchia a residual humanism, and not such a small one at that.

[T]he act is in some part irreducibly conscious; we are in some crucial part responsible for what we *are* conscious of. We may never wholly know what we are doing, as de Man argues, but in some part we do, and to that part at least we must hold ourselves to political account. (p. 142)

Lentricchia thus works through deconstruction to identify—at least to his satisfaction—a residual existential humanism which makes action still possible. In attempting to determine the basis of his own politics he similarly falls back on what is, in fact, an existentialist understanding of freedom and responsibility. Lentricchia quotes and discusses an extended allegory of Burke which suggests the relationship between the individual and history. History is presented as an unending conversation taking place in a parlor. The individual arrives after the conversation, a "heated discussion," has been going on for some time, and no one stops to tell the new arrival exactly what has been said. The discussion, in fact, had been going on before any of those present arrived, so no one could give its complete history anyway. The individual listens, gets the gist of what is going on, and then puts in his "oar." An exchange results, some siding with, some against, the newcomer. The discussion never ends. At some point the individual leaves, with it still going on.[43]

We simply choose, freely, how we wish to act, in spite of the fact that we know we are acting on the basis of incomplete information, the fact that there *is* no epistemological certainty, and the fact that we have no certainty regarding the long-term consequences of our actions. Nevertheless, we must act responsible, since the choices we make will affect the future of—in Burke's allegory—the "conversation." Lentricchia's last section sounds distinctly Sartrean, with an emphasis on the role of rhetoric as a mode of action.

Then we act; we just do. We *decide*, with what assurances Burke never says, because there are none to be given. We enter the conversation by putting in our "oar" (our "or"?). It matters not that no one in the room really knows, in the strict epistemological sense of "knowing," what is going on; or that no one who has ever been in the room ever knew. This is a conversation without epistemological "foundation" or "substance." (p. 161)

Lentricchia concludes:

The fate of Marxism will be decided by the active involvement of individuals in the great struggle of persuasion. To say this about the fate of socialism, that it will be decided in rhetorical war, is to say nothing especially specific to its vision. The fate of all visions, or nightmares, as the case may be, of the good life, will be similarly decided. "Decided" is too weak: "chosen." (p. 163)

This is a Sartrean Marxism that is freely chosen, one whose realization is uncertain, dependent on the choices of individuals, as opposed to one that is committed to because it is regarded as a correct description of the determined direction and end of history. The new emphasis here is on the role of rhetoric in revolutionary struggle. Lentricchia is, finally, an existential Marxist humanist with a poststructuralist awareness of the relationship of language, rhetoric, representation, power, ideology, and politics.

Conclusion

A major line of modern thinking, and the major line of postmodern thinking, suggests that the relationship between language, thought, and reality—the "reality" language presents itself as pointing toward—is more complex than previously imagined. Certainly that relationship is not fully understood and, since human understanding is articulated in language, can never be fully understood. No system of representation can contain itself, though the struggle to do so results in interesting literary, dramatic, and visual forms: the fiction of Barth, the plays of Pirandello, and the graphic art of Escher, all of which are examples of art turning in on itself to engage problems of artistic representation itself. Twentieth-century skepticism, with its specifically linguistic emphasis, has resulted in a recent posthumanist cultural phase that not only doubts the capacity of human reason to come to an understanding of reality, but also views the *cogito*, the self itself, as a linguistic construct. This obsession with the role of language and other sign systems in constituting human consciousness, human understanding, and the subject itself has also resulted in a variety of approaches to critical theory—structuralism, semiotics, deconstruction, and poststructuralist Marxism, among others—all of which, in spite of their significant differences, are discourses devoted to analyzing discourse itself.

Nevertheless, the view of language as a merely tautological structure—hermetically isolated from a world separate and inaccessible—and the belief that language always determines the world more than the world determines language are as irrational as a naive realism that assumes that the structures and categories of language mirror exactly the structures and categories of the world. The latter position is certainly simplistic, but the former leads to self-contradiction and an inevitable divorce between one's intellectual existence and one's social, ethical, and political life, where choices must be made and where those choices will inevitably reflect values held as positive, whatever the bases of those values. Skepticism can be an aid to social, ethical, and political analysis, but in and of itself it is as likely to result in conservatism, quietism, or even fascism as in progressive change.

A number of politically engaged writers have attempted, in different ways, to channel the critical power of poststructuralist thought in progressive directions. Eagleton holds to a relatively orthodox faith in Marxist analysis, though he acknowledges the potential of structuralist and poststructuralist analysis as an aid to political criticism. Lentricchia embraces deconstructive-style rhetorical analyses as a mode of uncovering unfounded ideological and ontological suppositions, and he advocates the use of an effective rhetoric as a mode of political action, but in the end he reasserts an ethics and a politics that is fundamentally existential and humanistic. Jameson is perhaps most rigorous in his attempt to reconcile Marxism with poststructuralist insights, describing Marxism as a narrative or a fiction, though one superior to all others, acknowledging the inaccessibility of history except through narrative, yet affirming its existence as an "absent cause." If deconstruction proper has the potential for encouraging quietism and de facto conservatism by presenting our understanding of "reality" as inherently limited by our existence within, by our existence *as,* a Pirandellian hall of mirrors consisting of endless series of signifiers and signifieds that finally lack ontological foundation, then these writers are more connected with the materialism of Brecht, who was politically progressive and whose *verfremdungseffekt* was a kind of nascent theatrical deconstruction, acknowledging the provisional nature of the illusion created in order to create an ethically correct political theatre.

Notes

1. José Ortega y Gassett, *The Dehumanization of Art and Notes on the Novel,* trans. Helene Weyl (Princeton: Princeton University Press, 1948), 3–54.
2. Ihab Hassan, *The Right Promethean Fire, Imagination, Science, and Cultural Change* (Urbana: University of Illinois Press, 1980), xix–xx, 202–204, *et passim.*
3. Jonathan Culler, *The Pursuit of Signs, Semiotics, Literature, Deconstruction* (Ithaca: Cornell University Press, 1981), 32–34.
4. Richard Schechner, *The End of Humanism, Writings on Performance* (New York: Performing Arts Journal Publications, 1982), pp. 96, 106, *et passim.*
5. Jacques Derrida, *Writing and Difference,* trans. Alan Bass (Chicago: University of Chicago Press, 1978), p. 292.
6. Anike Lemaire, *Jacques Lacan,* trans. David Macey (London: Routledge & Kegan Paul, 1981), 6–8.
7. Fredric Jameson, *The Political Unconscious, Narrative as a Socially Symbolic Act* (Ithaca: Cornell University Press, 1981), 52–53, *et passim.* Future citations in parentheses.

8. Friedrich Nietzsche, *The Will to Power*, trans. A. M. Ludovici. *The Complete Works of Friedrich Nietzsche*, general ed. Oscar Levy (New York: Russell & Russell, 1964), sect. 521.

9. Ferdinand de Saussure, *Course in General Linguistics*, ed. Charles Bally and Albert Sechehaye, in collaboration with Albert Riedlinger, trans. Wade Baskin (New York: McGraw-Hill, 1966), p. 112. Future citations in parentheses.

10. See the preface of Jonathan Culler's *On Deconstruction, Theory and Criticism after Structuralism* (Ithaca: Cornell University Press, 1982), 7–13, for a discussion of "theory."

11. Because Saussure anticipates the development of a *"science that studies the life of signs within society,"* which he calls "semiology," under which linguistics would be only one part, he is viewed as one of the founders of semiotics, as well as of structuralism (Saussure, p. 16).

12. Deconstructionists sometimes balk at having their positions "reduced" to or explained by their placement within the context of modern culture. Understandably, they do not want to have their beliefs "explained away" as a response to a cultural milieu. Derrida, for example, begins *Writing and Difference* with an argument that the "question of the sign is itself more or less, or in any event something other, than a sign of the times" (trans. Alan Bass [Chicago: University of Chicago Press, 1978] p. 3). And Christopher Norris, in *Deconstruction, Theory and Practice* (New York: Methuen, 1982), sees Gerald Graff's attempt to historically contextualize deconstruction as reductionist (p. 132). Nevertheless, for the cultural historian this kind of contextual placement is the goal, and Derrida himself goes on to acknowledge that "the structuralist phenomenon will deserve attention by the historian of ideas. For better or for worse" (p. 4). As Culler has noted in *On Deconstruction*, Derrida uses philosophy against history and history against philosophy (p. 129).

13. Pierce discusses his "second trichotomy" of signs in various places, including his "Logic as Semiotic: The Theory of Signs," *Philosophical Writings of Pierce*, ed. and intro. Justus Buchler (New York: Dover, 1955), 102–103.

14. "Linguistics and Grammatology," in Derrida, *Of Grammatology*, trans. Gayatri Chakravorty Spivak (Baltimore: Johns Hopkins University Press, 1976), 27–73. Future citations in parentheses.

15. Christopher Norris, *Deconstruction: Theory and Practice*, p. 22. Future citations in parentheses.

16. Culler, *On Deconstruction, Theory and Criticism after Structuralism*, p. 86. Future citations in parentheses.

17. Since there are clearly different kinds of deconstructionists, this characterization is a generalization. There *are* the more playful deconstructionists who seem to delight in an unabashed interpretative freedom. Norris sees Geoffrey Hartman and J. Hillis Miller as major representatives of this deconstruction "on the wild side" (pp. 92–99). On the other hand, Paul de Man represents, for Norris, a more rigorous and disciplined kind of deconstruction. De Man's writing revolves around identifying various oppositions—rhetoric and reason, metaphor and metonymy, figurative and literal—and challenging traditional prejudices regarding the relative evaluations of the opposed terms (pp. 99–105).

18. Witness for example J. Hillis Miller's response to M. H. Abrams and Wayne Booth's description of deconstruction as "parasitical." Instead of arguing

with his opponents in any traditional fashion, Miller engages in an etymological description of the word "parasite," moves on to do the same with the word "host" (noting its etymological kinship with the word "guest"), and thereby makes Abrams and Booth's metaphor seem much more problematical and ambiguous than it first appeared to be ("The Critic as Host," *Deconstruction and Criticism*, ed. Geoffrey Hartman [New York: Seabury Press, 1979], 217–253). See also the exchange between John Searle and Derrida that appeared in *Glyph*. Searle wrote a reply to Derrida's deconstruction of the speech-act theory of J. L. Austin. Searle's reply is in the vein of a traditional scholarly exchange, taking issue with Derrida's positions on speech and writing and with his understanding of Austin. Derrida refused to respond to Searle in the same manner and, instead, wrote a reply that playfully wreaks havoc with the foundations of scholarly exchange, including the notions of copyright and of authorial identity and control of texts. (Derrida, "Signature Event Context" and Searle, "Reiterating the Differences: A Reply to Derrida," *Glyph, Johns Hopkins Textual Studies*, I [1977], 172–197 and 198–208, and Derrida, "Limited Inc a b c . . . ," *Glyph, Johns Hopkins Textual Studies*, II [1977], 162–254.)

19. John Gardner, *On Moral Fiction* (New York: Basic Books, 1978), p. 69.

20. *Ibid.*, p. 129.

21. Robert Alter, *Partial Magic, The Novel as a Self-Conscious Genre* (Berkeley and Los Angeles: University of California Press, 1975), 221–225.

22. Christopher Butler, *After the Wake, An Essay on the Contemporary Avant-Garde* (Oxford: Oxford University Press, 1980), p. 130.

23. Alan Wilde, *Middle Grounds, Studies in Contemporary American Fiction* (Philadelphia: University of Pennsylvania Press, 1987), p. 51.

24. Gerald Graff, *Literature Against Itself, Literary Ideas in Modern Society* (Chicago: University of Chicago Press, 1979). Future citations in parentheses.

25. See note 12, above.

26. Graff, p. 61. Graff is citing Meisel's "Everything You Always Wanted to Know About Structuralism but Were Afraid to Ask," *National Village Voice* (September 30, 1976), 43–45.

27. True, Derrida's deconstruction of Saussure in *Of Grammatology* may indicate lack of reverence, but it does not amount to a denial of Saussure's skeptical presuppositions. It is instead an attempt to demonstrate that Saussure did not admit the full implications of his own presuppositions relating to the arbitrary nature of the sign and the structural nature of language when he valorized speech above "writing." Thus, deconstruction remains rooted in Saussure—or at least a reading of Saussure—even when it seems to criticize or go beyond him.

28. Of course, even to use the expression "human issue" is itself problematical; in a poststructuralist, posthumanist era the problem is not engaging human beings as traditionally understood, but creating texts that engage texts that exist around and through, texts that themselves constitute that which used to be called human.

29. Terry Eagleton, *Literary Theory, An Introduction* (Minneapolis: University of Minnesota Press, 1983), 143–145. Future citations in parentheses.

30. Frank Lentricchia, *Criticism and Social Change* (Chicago: University of Chicago Press, 1983), p. 51. Future citations in parentheses.

31. Butler, 124–125.

32. Thomas Kuhn, postscript to *The Structure of Scientific Revolutions* (Chicago: University of Chicago Press, 1970), 176–182 *et passim*. Postscript dated 1969, text originally published 1962.

33. Quoted in Gaspare Giudice, *Pirandello, A Biography*. Alastair Hamilton, trans. (London: Oxford University Press, 1975), 147–148.

34. Quoted in Graff, p. 188; Graff cites Henry B. Veatch, *Rational Man: A Modern Interpretation of Aristotelian Ethics* (Bloomington: Indiana University Press, 1964), 41.

35. It is impossible not to mention at this point the recent discovery by Belgian graduate student Ortwin de Graef of the hundred or more articles written by Paul de Man for anti-Semitic, pro-Nazi newspapers, most of them for the collaborationist *Le Soir*, in Belgium during 1941 and 1942. At least two of the articles were themselves anti-Semitic, asking whether Jews "pollute" modern fiction and viewing the strength of Western culture as evidenced by its ability to protect its literature from Jewish influence. Clearly this is bound to provoke a political, if not an intellectual, crisis for deconstruction, the politics of which has already been the subject of impassioned debate. Friends and colleagues, enemies and opponents, may wish to defend or attack de Man, but the important questions to the larger critical community can be answered only when his deconstructive writings are subject to the closest analysis in the context of his earlier articles. To what extent does de Man's deconstruction seem a continuation of or a rejection of the sentiments of these early writings? Does anti-Semitism or authoritarianism somehow reveal itself in his later rhetoric, or does a subversive aspect of his deconstructive criticism work toward equality and democracy? The existence of the early articles was first revealed publically in the *New York Times* ("Yale Scholar Wrote for Pro-Nazi Newspaper," 1 December 1987, B 1 and 6) and has also been discussed by Jon Wiener in *The Nation* ("Deconstructing de Man," 9 January 1988, pp. 22–24). As of this writing serious critical discussion has only just begun with Derrida's "Like the Sound of the Sea Deep within a Shell: Paul de Man's War," trans. Peggy Kamuf (*Critical Inquiry*, 14, no. 3 [spring 1988], 590–652).

36. Sherry Turkle, *Psychoanalytic Politics, Freud's French Revolution* (Cambridge: MIT Press, 1981), p. 74.

37. Edward W. Said, "Opponents, Audiences, Constituencies and Community," *The Anti-Aesthetic, Essays on Postmodern Culture*, ed. Hal Foster (Port Townsend, Washington: Bay Press, 1983), p. 149. Said's article was first published in *Critical Inquiry 9* (September 1982).

38. Jonathan Arac, ed. and intro., *Postmodernism and Politics*. (Minneapolis: University of Minnesota Press, 1986), pp. xxx–xxxi.

39. Paul A. Bove, "The Ineluctability of Difference," *ibid.*, p. 22.

40. Fredric Jameson, *The Political Unconscious*, 34, 52–53, *et passim*. Future citations in parentheses. Commentary on Jameson's difficult text is included in a special issue of *Diacritics* (vol. 12, fall, 1982) and in William C. Dowling's *Jameson, Althusser, Marx: An Introduction to* The Political Unconscious (Ithaca: Cornell University Press, 1984).

41. Jameson accepts, with some qualification, the Althusserian critique of "mechanical causality" (in which "base" or "infrastructure" or economic relations of production are regarded as the "cause" of "superstructure" or the various manifestations of culture and society in a fairly simplistic, "mechanical" fashion)

and "expressive causality" (in which the various aspects of the superstructure are regarded as different expressions of an essential world view unifying a period, which is itself a function of the economy) in favor of "structural causality." Althusser's understanding of a structural "causality" dissolves the distinction between base and superstructure; a social system is regarded as a structure in which relations among the elements are the primary determinants of social reality and the economy takes its place within that system (23–29, 35–41).

42. Kenneth Burke, "Revolutionary Symbolism in America," *American Writers' Congress,* ed. Henry Hart (New York: International Publishers, 1935), p. 87 (cited by Lentricchia).

43. Quoted in Lentricchia, p. 160, from Kenneth Burke, *The Philosophy of Literary Form: Studies in Symbolic Action* (Berkeley and Los Angeles: University of California Press, 1973), 110–111.

Abel, Lionel. *Metatheatre, A New View of Dramatic Form.* New York: Hill and Wang, 1963.
Adams, Robert Martin. "What Was Modernism?" *Hudson Review,* 31, No. 1 (spring 1978), 19–33.
Alberti, Leon Battista. *On Painting,* trans. John R. Spencer. New Haven: Yale University Press, 1966.
Alloway, Lawrence. *American Pop Art.* New York: Macmillan, 1974.
Alter, Robert. *Partial Magic, The Novel as a Self-Conscious Genre.* Berkeley and Los Angeles: University of California Press, 1975.
Arac, Jonathan, ed. and intro. *Postmodernism and Politics.* Minneapolis: University of Minnesota Press, 1986.
Artaud, Antonin. *The Theatre and Its Double,* trans. Mary Caroline Richards. New York: Grove, 1958.
Bann, Stephen, ed. *The Tradition of Constructivism.* New York: Viking, 1974.
Barth, John. *Chimera.* New York: Random House, 1972.
———. *The End of the Road.* Garden City, New York: Doubleday, 1958. Revised edition, Garden City, New York: Doubleday, 1967.
———. *The Floating Opera.* New York: Appleton, Century, Crofts, 1956. Revised edition, Garden City, New York: Doubleday, 1967.
———. *The Friday Book, Essays and Other Nonfiction.* New York: Putnam, 1984.
———. *Giles Goat-Boy.* Garden City, New York: Doubleday, 1966.
———. *LETTERS.* New York: Putnam, 1979.
———. "The Literature of Exhaustion," *The Atlantic,* August 1967, 29–34.
———. "The Literature of Replenishment, Postmodernist Fiction," *The Atlantic,* January 1980, 65–71.
———. *Lost in the Funhouse, Fiction for Print, Tape, Live Voice.* Garden City, New York: Doubleday, 1968.
———. *Sabbatical.* New York: Putnam, 1982.

————. *The Sot-Weed Factor.* Garden City, New York: Doubleday, 1960. Revised edition, Garden City, New York: Doubleday, 1967.

————. *The Tidewater Tales.* New York: Putnam, 1987.

Barthes, Roland. *Writing Degree Zero and Elements of Semiology,* trans. Annette Lavers and Colin Smith. Boston: Beacon Press, 1970.

Beckett, Samuel. *Ends and Odds, Nine Dramatic Pieces by Samuel Beckett.* New York: Grove, 1981.

————. *First Love and Other Shorts.* New York: Grove, 1974.

————. *Krapp's Last Tape and Other Dramatic Pieces.* New York: Grove, 1960.

————. *Rockaby and Other Short Pieces by Samuel Beckett.* New York: Grove, 1981.

————. *Waiting for Godot.* New York: Grove, 1954.

Benjamin, Walter. *Illuminations,* ed. and intro. Hannah Arendt, trans. Harry Zohn. New York: Harcourt, Brace, & World, 1968.

Bergman, Ingmar. *Bergman on Bergman, Interviews with Ingmar Bergman by Stig Bjorkman, Torsten Manns, Jonas Sima,* trans. Paul Britten Austin. New York: Simon and Schuster, 1973.

Bergom-Larsson. *Film in Sweden, Ingmar Bergman and Society,* trans. Barrie Selman. New York: A. S. Barnes & Co., 1978.

Bloom, Harold, Paul de Man, Jacques Derrida, Geoffrey H. Hartman, and J. Hillis Miller. *Deconstruction and Criticism.* New York: Seabury Press, 1979.

Boime, Albert. "Roy Lichtenstein and the Comic Strip." *Art Journal,* 28, No. 2 (Winter 1968–69), 155–159.

Borges, Jorge Luis. *Labyrinths, Selected Stories & Other Writings,* ed. Donald A. Yates and James E. Irby. New York: New Directions, 1964.

Bove, Paul A. "The Ineluctability of Difference," *Postmodernism and Politics,* ed. and intro. Jonathan Arac. Minneapolis: Univ. of Minnesota Press, 1986, 3–25.

Brecht, Bertolt. *Brecht on Theatre, The Development of an Aesthetic,* ed. and intro. John Willett. New York: Hill and Wang, 1964.

————. *Mother Courage and Her Children, A Chronicle of the Thirty Years' War,* English version by Eric Bentley. New York: Grove, 1963.

Burnham, Jack. *The Structure of Art,* revised edition. New York: Braziller, 1973.

Butler, Christopher. *After the Wake, An Essay on the Contemporary Avant-Garde.* Oxford: Clarendon Press, 1980.

Christensen, Inger. *The Meaning of Metafiction, A Critical Study of Selected Novels by Sterne, Nabokov, Barth and Beckett.* Bergen: Universitetsforlaget, 1981.

Clarke, Garry E. *Essays on American Music.* Westport, Connecticut: Greenwood Press, 1977.

Coover, Robert. *Pricksongs and Descants.* New York: Dutton, 1969.

Coplans, John, with contributions by Jonas Mekas and Calvin Tomkins. *Andy Warhol.* New York: Graphic Society Ltd., printed in England by Curwen Press, 1970.

Corbusier. *The Modulor I and II.* Cambridge: Harvard University Press, 1980.

————. *Towards a New Architecture,* trans. Frederick Etchells. New York: Praeger, 1972.

Cortazar, Julio. *End of the Game and Other Stories,* trans. Paul Blackburn. New York: Random House, 1967.

Croyden, Margaret. *Lunatics, Lovers, and Poets, The Contemporary Experimental Theatre.* New York: Delta, 1974.

Culler, Jonathan. *On Deconstruction, Theory and Criticism after Structuralism.* Ithaca: Cornell University Press, 1982.
———. *The Pursuit of Signs, Semiotics, Literature, Deconstruction.* Ithaca: Cornell University Press, 1981.
Curtis, David. *Experimental Cinema.* New York: Dell, 1971.
Derrida, Jacques. "Like the Sound of the Sea Deep within a Shell: Paul de Man's War," *Critical Inquiry,* 14 No. 3 (Spring 1988), 590–652.
———. "Limited Inc a b c . . . ," *Glyph, Johns Hopkins Textual Studies,* 2 (1977), 162–254.
———. *Of Grammatology,* trans. Gayatri Chakravorty Spivak. Baltimore: Johns Hopkins University Press, 1976.
———. "Signature Event Context," *Glyph, Johns Hopkins Textual Studies,* 1 (1977), 172–197.
———. *Writing and Difference,* trans. Alan Bass. Chicago: University of Chicago Press, 1978.
Diacritics. 12 (fall 1982). Special issue on Jameson's *The Political Unconscious.*
Dowling, William C. *Jameson, Althusser, Marx, An Introduction to* The Political Unconscious. Ithaca: Cornell University Press, 1984.
Dreyfus, Hubert L., and Paul Rabinow. *Michel Foucault, Beyond Structuralism and Hermeneutics,* second edition with an afterword by and an interview with Michel Foucault. Chicago: University of Chicago Press, 1983.
Dukore, Bernard F., and Daniel C. Gerould, eds. *Avant-Garde Drama: Major Plays and Documents Post World War I.* New York: Bantam, 1969.
Eagleton, Terry. *Literary Theory, An Introduction.* Minneapolis: University of Minnesota Press, 1983.
———. *Marxism and Literary Criticism.* Berkeley and Los Angeles: University of California Press, 1976.
Esslin, Martin. *Brecht, the Man and his Work,* new revised edition. Garden City, New York: Doubleday, 1971.
———. *The Theatre of the Absurd.* Garden City, New York: Doubleday, 1969.
Foucault, Michel. *The Order of Things, An Archaeology of the Human Sciences,* a translation of *Les Mots et les choses.* New York: Vintage, 1973.
Fowles, John. *The Aristos: A Self-Portrait in Ideas.* Boston: Little, Brown, 1964.
———. *The Collector.* Boston: Little, Brown, 1963.
———. *Daniel Martin.* Boston: Little, Brown, 1977.
———. *The Ebony Tower.* Boston: Little, Brown, 1974.
———. *The French Lieutenant's Woman.* Boston: Little, Brown, 1969.
———. *A Maggot.* Boston: Little, Brown, 1985.
———. *The Magus.* Boston: Little, Brown, 1965. Revised version, Boston: Little, Brown, 1978.
———. *Mantissa.* Boston: Little, Brown, 1982.
———. "Seeing Nature Whole," *Harpers* (November 1979), 49–68.
Fowles, John (text), and Frank Horvat (photographs). *The Tree.* Boston: Little, Brown, 1979.
Gamow, George. *Thirty Years that Shook Physics.* Garden City, New York: Doubleday, 1966.
García Márquez, Gabriel. *One Hundred Years of Solitude,* trans. Gregory Rabassa. New York: Harper & Row, 1970.

Gardner, John. *On Moral Fiction.* New York: Basic Books. 1978.

Genet, Jean. *The Balcony,* trans. Bernard Frechtman. New York: Grove, 1966.

―――. *The Blacks: A Clown Show,* trans. Bernard Frechtman. New York: Grove, 1960.

―――. *The Maids and Deathwatch, Two Plays by Jean Genet,* trans. Bernard Frechtman, intro. Jean-Paul Sartre. New York: Grove, 1978.

Giudice, Gaspare. *Pirandello, A Biography,* trans. Alastair Hamilton. London: Oxford University Press, 1975.

Goldberg, RoseLee. *Performance, Live Art 1909 to the Present.* New York: Abrams, 1979.

Gottlieb, Carla. *Beyond Modern Art.* New York: Dutton, 1976.

Graff, Gerald. *Literature Against Itself, Literary Ideas in Modern Society.* Chicago: University of Chicago Press, 1979.

―――. "Under Our Belt and Off Our Back: Barth's *LETTERS* and Postmodern Fiction," *TriQuarterly,* 52 (fall 1981), 150–164.

Grotowski, Jerzy. *Towards a Poor Theatre.* New York: Simon and Schuster, 1968.

Guzzetti, Alfred. *Two or Three Things I Know about Her, Analysis of a Film by Godard.* Cambridge: Harvard University Press, 1981.

Harari, Josue V., ed. *Textual Strategies, Perspectives in Post-Structuralist Criticism.* Ithaca: Cornell University Press, 1979.

Hassan, Ihab. *The Dismemberment of Orpheus, Toward a Postmodern Literature,* second edition. Madison: University of Wisconsin Press, 1982.

―――. "The Question of Postmodernism," *Performing Arts Journal 16,* 6, No. 1 (1981), 30–37.

―――. *The Right Promethian Fire, Imagination, Science, and Cultural Change.* Urbana: University of Illinois Press, 1980.

Hawkes, Terence. *Structuralism and Semiotics.* Berkeley and Los Angeles: University of California Press, 1977.

Hayman, Ronald. *Theatre and Anti-Theatre.* London: Secher & Warburg, 1979.

Heisenberg, Werner. *Physics and Philosophy, The Revolution in Modern Science.* New York: Harper & Row, 1962.

Henri, Adrian. *Total Art: Environments, Happenings, and Performance.* New York: Praeger, 1974.

Hofstadter, Douglas R. *Godel, Escher, Bach, An Eternal Golden Braid.* New York: Basic Books, 1979.

Huffaker, Robert. *John Fowles.* Boston: Twayne, 1980.

Hutcheon, Linda. *Narcissistic Narrative, The Metafictional Paradox.* New York: Methuen, 1984.

―――. *A Theory of Parody, The Teachings of Twentieth-Century Art Forms.* New York: Methuen, 1985.

Jameson, Fredric. *The Political Unconscious, Narrative as a Socially Symbolic Act.* Ithaca: Cornell University Press, 1981.

―――. *The Prison-House of Language, A Critical Account of Structuralism and Russian Formalism.* Princeton: Princeton University Press, 1974.

Jencks, Charles A. *The Language of Post-Modern Architecture.* New York: Rizzoli, 1977.

Kandinsky, Wassily. *Concerning the Spiritual in Art,* Documents of Modern Art, Vol. 5, trans. Michael Sadleir, Francis Golffing, Michael Harrison, and Ferdinand Ostertag. New York: George Wittenborn, 1972.

Kaprow, Allan. " 'Happenings' in the New York Scene," *Art News*, 60, No. 3 (May 1961), 36–39, 58–62.

Kawin, Bruce F. *Mindscreen: Bergman, Godard and First-Person Film*. Princeton: Princeton University Press, 1978.

Kirby, Michael, et al. *Happenings, An Illustrated Anthology*. New York: Dutton, 1965.

Koch, Stephen. *Stargazer, Andy Warhol's Films and His Work*. New York: Praeger, 1973.

Kreidl, John. *Jean-Luc Godard*. Boston: Twayne, 1980.

Kubler, George. "The 'Mirror' in *Las Meninas*," *The Art Bulletin*, 67, No. 2 (June 1985), 316.

Kuhn, Thomas S. *The Structure of Scientific Revolutions*. Chicago: University of Chicago Press, 1970.

LeClair, Thomas. "Avant-Garde Mastery," *TriQuarterly*, No. 53 (winter 1982), 259–267.

———. "A Pair of Jacks, John Barth & John Hawkes Gamble with New Fiction," *Horizon*, 22 (1979), 64–71.

Le Grice, Malcolm. *Abstract Film and Beyond*. Cambridge: MIT Press, 1977.

Lemaire, Anika. *Jacques Lacan*, trans. David Macey. London: Routledge & Kegan Paul, 1981.

Lentricchia, Frank. *Criticism and Social Change*. Chicago: University of Chicago Press, 1983.

Levin, Harry. *Refractions: Essays in Comparative Literature*. New York: Oxford University Press, 1966.

Lichtenstein, Roy. *Roy Lichtenstein: Graphics, Relief, & Sculpture*, catalogue for exhibition at University of California, Irvine, October 27 to December 6, 1970. Los Angeles: Gemini G. E. L., 1970.

Lipman, Jean, and Richard Marshall, intro. Leo Steinberg. *Art About Art*, catalogue of exhibition at Whitney Museum of American Art, July 19 to September 24, 1978. New York: Dutton, in association with Whitney Museum, 1978.

Lippard, Lucy R., ed. *Dadas on Art*. Englewood Cliffs, New Jersey: Prentice Hall, 1971.

Lippard, Lucy R., et al. *Pop Art*. New York: Oxford University Press, 1966.

MacCabe, Colin, with Mick Eaton and Laura Mulvey. *Godard: Images, Sounds, Politics*. Bloomington: Indiana University Press, 1980.

Marck, Jan van der. *George Segal*. New York: Abrams, 1975.

Mitchell, W. J. T., ed. *The Language of Images*. Chicago: University of Chicago Press, 1980.

Monaco, James. *The New Wave, Truffaut, Godard, Chabrol, Rohmer, Rivette*. New York: Oxford University Press, 1976.

Morrell, David. *John Barth, An Introduction*. University Park: Pennsylvania State University Press, 1976.

Morris, Christopher D. "Barth and Lacan: The World of the Moebius Strip," *Critique*, 17, No. 1 (1975), 69–77.

Motherwell, Robert, ed. *The Dada Painters and Poets: An Anthology*. Boston: G. K. Hall, 1981.

Museum of Modern Art, New York. *Three Generations of Twentieth-Century Art, The Sidney and Harriet Janis Collection of the Museum of Modern Art*, foreword Alfred H. Barr, Jr., intro. William Rubin. New York: Museum of Modern Art, 1972.

New York Times. "Yale Scholar Wrote for Pro-Nazi Newspaper." 1 December, 1987, B 1 and 6.

Nichols, Bill, ed. *Movies and Methods, An Anthology.* Berkeley and Los Angeles: University of California Press, 1976.

Nietzsche, Friedrich. *The Will to Power,* trans. A. M. Ludovici, in *The Complete Works of Friedrich Nietzsche,* general ed. Oscar Levy. New York: Russell & Russell, 1964.

Norris, Christopher. *Deconstruction, Theory and Practice.* New York: Methuen, 1982.

Olschen, Barry N. *John Fowles.* New York: Ungar, 1978.

Ortega y Gassett, José. *The Dehumanization of Art and Notes on the Novel,* trans. Helen Weyl. Princeton: Princeton University Press, 1948.

Pierce, Charles Sanders. "Logic as Semiotic: The Theory of Signs," *Philosophical Writings of Pierce,* ed. and intro. Justus Buchler. New York: Dover, 1955.

Pirandello, Luigi. *Maschere Nude,* I. Verona: Mondadori, 1958.

———. *Naked Masks,* ed. Eric Bentley. New York: Dutton, 1952.

Pynchon, Thomas. *The Crying of Lot 49.* Philadelphia: Lippincott, 1966.

Robbe-Grillet, Alain. *Project for a Revolution in New York,* trans. Richard Howard. New York: Grove, 1972.

Roud, Richard. *Jean-Luc Godard.* Bloomington: Indiana University Press, 1970.

Russell, John, and Suzi Gablik. *Pop Art Redefined.* New York: Praeger, 1970.

Said, Edward W. "Opponents, Audiences, Constituencies and Community," *The Anti-Aesthetic, Essays on Postmodern Culture,* ed. Hal Foster, Port Townsend, Washington: Bay Press, 1983, pp. 135–159.

Samuels, Charles Thomas. *Encountering Directors.* New York: Putnam, 1972.

Saussure, Ferdinand de. *Course in General Linguistics,* ed. Charles Bally and Albert Sechehaye, in collaboration with Albert Riedlinger, trans. Wade Baskin. New York: McGraw-Hill, 1966.

Schechner, Richard. *The End of Humanism, Writings on Performance.* New York: Performing Arts Journal Publications, 1982.

Scholes, Robert. *Fabulation and Metafiction.* Urbana: University of Illinois Press, 1979.

Searle, John. "Reiterating the Differences," *Glyph, Johns Hopkins Textual Studies,* 1 (1977), 198–208.

Shank, Theodore. *American Alternative Theatre.* New York: Grove, 1982.

Simon, John. *Ingmar Bergman Directs.* New York: Harcourt Brace Jovanovich, 1972.

Sontag, Susan. *Styles of Radical Will.* New York: Farrar, Straus and Giroux, 1969.

Steiner, Wendy. "Collage or Miracle: Historicism in a Deconstructed World," *Reconstructing American Literary History,* ed. Sacvan Bercovitch. Cambridge: Harvard University Press, 1986.

Swenson, G. R. "What is Pop Art: Answers from 8 Painters, Part I," *Art News,* 62, No. 7 (November 1963), 24–27, 60–64.

———. "What is Pop Art? Part II," *Art News,* 62, No. 10 (February 1964), 40–43, 62–67.

Sypher, Wylie. *Four Stages of Renaissance Style, Transformations in Art and Literature, 1400–1700.* Garden City, New York: Doubleday, 1955.

———. *Loss of the Self in Modern Literature and Art.* New York: Random House, 1962.

Tharpe, Jac. *John Barth, The Comic Sublimity of Paradox.* Carbondale: Southern Illinois University Press, 1974.

Tomkins, Calvin. *The Bride and the Bachelors, Five Masters of the Avant Garde.* New York: Viking, 1968.

———. *Off the Wall, Robert Rauschenberg and the Art World of Our Time.* New York: Penguin, 1981.

Trachtenberg, Stanley, ed. and intro. *The Postmodern Moment, A Handbook of Contemporary Innovation in the Arts.* Westport, Connecticut: Greenwood Press, 1985.

Tuchman, Phyllis. "Pop! Interviews with George Segal, Andy Warhol, Roy Lichtenstein, James Rosenquist, and Robert Indiana." *Art News,* 73, No. 5 (May 1974), 24–29.

Turkle, Sherry. *Psychoanalytic Politics, Freud's French Revolution.* Cambridge: MIT Press, 1981.

Vargas Llosa, Mario. *Aunt Julia and the Scriptwriter,* trans. Helen R. Lane. New York: Farrar, Straus and Giroux, 1982.

Venturi, Robert. *Complexity and Contradiction in Architecture.* New York: Museum of Modern Art, 1966.

Venturi, Robert, Denise Scott Brown, and Steven Izenour. *Learning From Las Vegas.* Cambridge: MIT Press, 1972

Walsh, Martin. *The Brechtian Aspect of Radical Cinema,* ed. Keith M. Griffiths. London: British Film Institute, 1981.

Warhol, Andy. *Andy Warhol,* published on the occasion of the Andy Warhol exhibition at Moderna Museet in Stockholm, February–March 1968. Boston: Boston Book and Art, 1970.

Waugh, Patricia. *Metafiction, The Theory and Practice of Self-Conscious Fiction.* New York: Methuen, 1984.

Wiener, Jon. "Deconstructing de Man," *The Nation,* 9 January 1988, pp. 22–24.

Wilde, Alan. *Middle Grounds, Studies in Contemporary American Fiction.* Philadelphia: University of Pennsylvania Press, 1987.

Wilson, Simon. *Pop.* Woodbury, New York: Barron's, 1978.

Wood, Robin. *Ingmar Bergman.* New York: Praeger, 1970.

INDEX